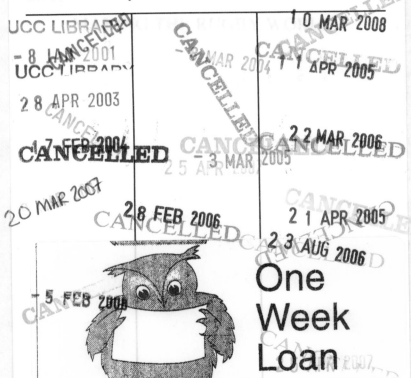

SPORT IN THE GLOBAL SOCIETY
General Editor: J.A. Mangan
ISSN 1368-9789

The interest in sports studies around the world is growing and will continue to do so. This unique series combines aspects of the expanding study of *sport in the global society*, providing comprehensiveness and comparison under one editorial umbrella. It is particularly timely, with studies in the political, cultural, social, economic, geographical and aesthetic elements of sport proliferating in institutions of higher education.

Eric Hobsbawm once called sport one of the most significant practices of the late nineteenth century. Its significance is even more marked in the late twentieth century and will continue to grow in importance into the next millennium as the world develops into a 'global village' sharing the English language, technology and sport.

Other Titles in the Series

Making Men
Rugby and Masculine Identity
Edited by John Nauright and Timothy J.L. Chandler

Footbinding, Feminism and Freedom
The Liberation of Women's Bodies in Modern China
Fan Hong

The Games Ethic and Imperialism: Aspects of the Diffusion of an Ideal
J.A. Mangan

The Nordic World: Sport in Society
Edited by Henrik Meinander and J.A. Mangan

The Race Game: Sport and Politics in South Africa
Douglas Booth

Rugby's Great Split: Class, Culture and the Origins of Rugby League Football
Tony Collins

Sporting Nationalisms: Identity, Ethnicity, Immigration and Assimilation
Edited by Mike Cronin and David Mayall

France and the 1998 World Cup: The National Impact of a World Sporting Event
Edited by Hugh Dauncey and Geoff Hare

Cricket and England: A Cultural and Social History of the Inter-war Years
Jack Williams

Scoring for Britain: International Football and International Politics, 1900–1939
Peter J. Beck

The First Black Footballer: Arthur Wharton 1865–1930: An Absence of Memory
Phil Vasili

MAKING THE RUGBY WORLD

Race, Gender, Commerce

Editors

TIMOTHY J.L. CHANDLER
Kent State University

and

JOHN NAURIGHT
University of Queensland

FRANK CASS
LONDON • PORTLAND, OR

First published in 1999 in Great Britain by
FRANK CASS PUBLISHERS
Newbury House, 900 Eastern Avenue
London, IG2 7HH

and in the United States of America by
FRANK CASS PUBLISHERS
c/o ISBS, 5804 N.E. Hassalo Street
Portland, Oregon 97213-3644

Website: www.frankcass.com

British Library Cataloguing in Publication Data

Making the rugby world : race, gender, commerce. – (Sport
  in the global society ; no. 10)
  1. Rugby Union football – Psychological aspects
  2. Masculinity 3. Rugby Union football – Social aspects
  I. Chandler, Timothy John Lindsay II. Nauright, John, 1962–
  796.3 33 019

          ISBN 0-7146-4853-1 (cloth)
          ISBN 0-7146-4411-0 (paper)
          ISSN 1368-9789

Library of Congress Cataloging-in-Publication Data

A catalog record of this book is available from the Library of Congress.

Printed in Great Britain by
Bookcraft (Bath) Ltd, Midsomer Norton, Somerset

To Margie and Tara

Contents

Preface and Acknowledgements

In 1996 we published a collection of essays entitled *Making Men: Rugby and Masculine Identity* where we examined masculine codes surrounding rugby cultures in the British Isles and the settler societies of South Africa, New Zealand and Australia. While we are pleased with the success that volume has achieved, we recognized there, as have some reviewers, that much more remained to be told about rugby union and the places and cultures in which it has been played. In this volume we seek to expand on the start we made in *Making Men* to examine what has happened to rugby union and its attendant social and cultural practices as it has moved from its core in British public and Empire private schools. Again, it has not been possible to be all-encompassing here as we still have not explored significant rugby playing areas such as Samoa, Fiji and Tonga in the South Pacific, or Argentina or Romania. What we hope to have achieved here is a book that both complements and moves beyond *Making Men* as we examine rugby among the Maori and mixed-race or 'Coloured' South Africans, rugby in France, Italy, the USA and Japan, women's rugby and the commodification and professionalization of rugby union in the late twentieth century. In all of these cases, rugby has not merely reproduced itself but has been shaped by local cultural differences, gender and finally by global sporting markets.

The preparation of such a volume is never easy even in this age of global telecommunications. Fortunately, the editors were able to meet in England in late 1998 to complete much of the task of putting the volume together. We would like to thank Professor Trevor Slack, head of the School of Physical Education, Sport and Leisure at De Montfort University in Bedford for providing us with office space and encouragement. We would also like to thank Tim's family for indulging us in an intense few days of work in the fairly tight quarters of their St John's Wood flat in London as we struggled with all that we had before us. John Nauright would like to thank the Australian Research Council, the University of Queensland's New Staff Research Grant program and the Division of Sciences at the University of Otago for funding that has made his research on South Africa possible while being based in Australia and New Zealand. Thanks also go to the Football Studies Group and Kent State University who helped fund a trip by Tim Chandler to the inaugural Football Studies Group Conference on 'Football and Identities' in Australia in February 1997, where the editors and many of the authors were able to discuss the shape that the book would take. Several of the chapters were originally presented at one of the first two Football Studies Group conferences in 1997 and 1998. Versions of the chapters by Booth and by Carle and Nauright appear in *Football Studies*. Thanks too to the journal editor and the Football Studies Group for permission to publish the versions that appear here.

We would like to thank Jonathan Manley at Frank Cass Publishers for his encouragement and patience as we first endeavoured to revise *Making Men* and then produce this volume in time for the 1999 Rugby World Cup. Once again Dr Tara Magdalinski has been an invaluable source of help with her efficient system for rapidly producing an excellent index. While a number of chapters were produced by members of the Rugby Research Group at the University of Queensland (Alison Carle, Brett Hutchins, Richard Light, Malcolm MacLean and John Nauright), this has been a truly international collaborative effort. We thank all the contributors for their efforts and hope that we have done their work justice in our introduction and conclusion. Richard Light, Alison Carle, John Nauright and David Howe would like to thank the clubs, schools and associations they worked with in their ethnographic and oral history studies, though none of this book was produced in conjunction with, or with the direct support of, any rugby organization. As with any work, we hope that what we have provided here is a useful guide for people interested in gaining a better understanding of rugby union as we move into a new millennium. As we finished the book in late 1998 and early 1999 some results showed that rugby can throw up its share of surprises, for England defeated South Africa and Wales won in France for the first time since the 1960s.

JN, Brisbane, Queensland
TJLC, St John's Wood, London

July 1999

Series Editor's Foreword

This volume deserves a double helping of praise. It not only takes up its editors' own challenge to themselves thrown down in the recently published volume in this Series, but it simultaneously accepts the similar and earlier challenge, I am more than pleased to note, issued by myself in *The Cultural Bond: Sport, Empire, Society* in 1992, to all historians interested in sport in society, namely 'to explore ... the subtleties of the relationship between imperial proselytizer and proselytized ... to investigate ... the complexities of this relationship, and to explore modifications to, re-interpretations of, resistance to and rejection of ... the culture of *homo ludens imperiosus*', and in both the imperial setting and beyond, to be prepared 'to confront fully the possible disparities between ideological assertion, intention, and realization' – in short, to attempt 'analytical subtlety in response to cultural complexities' (p.7).

The resulting response to this challenge in *Making the Rugby World* is an eclectic enquiry into the means and the manner by which one modern sport, rugby union football, has been disseminated, assimilated, accommodated, utilized and, it should be added, 'translated' in a variety of cultural locations.

The volume, as all subtle studies should, operates at several analytical levels: it is an investigation of initial cultural diffusion, of eventual indigenous cultural response and of eventual independent cultural evolution. It is also an enquiry into the making of modern masculinity – its global similarities and dissimilarities – and in turn, although more surely should have been made of this, of the early moments of a pre-, and without any doubt, post-millennium androgynous international culture – the certain inheritance of the twenty-first century.

In fact, the volume contains rather more. It is also a shrewd inspection of self-constructed cultural myopia in the interest of ethnocentric prejudice, a cautionary reflection on the relationship between politics, sport and authoritarianism and a useful contribution to a growing realization of the role of class, and by extension the extensive but far from exclusive part that the middle classes have played in the shaping of the sports of 'the global village'.

It is also a perceptive contribution to the now significant literature dealing with sport as a moral medium and militaristic 'rite of passage'.

Making the Rugby World is also a timely discussion of the commercial culture of modern professional rugby union and the consequent and associated advantages and disadvantages including the actual and potential shifts in administrative power, the increasing domination by the entertainments industry and last but far from least, the continuation of preferential access by the plutocratic privileged!

All in all, there is something almost for everyone in the volume – those who like their menu 'à la carte' and those who prefer it 'table d'hôte'. *Bon appétit.*

J. A. MANGAN
International Research Centre for Sport, Socialisation, Society
University of Strathclyde

July 1999

Introduction: More than the Making of Men, the World(s) of Rugby

John Nauright and Timothy J.L. Chandler

In selecting and editing the contributions to this volume we took as our task the production of both a supplementary and a complementary sequel to our previous volume on rugby, *Making Men: Rugby and Masculine Identity* in which we sought to develop an understanding of the links between the sport of rugby union and masculine identity as practised in Britain and the settler colonies of the British Empire.[1] In exploring the relationship between rugby and masculine identity we chose to focus on a specific set of contexts whereby rugby moved out from its originating core of the English public schools to other parts of Britain and through the private schools to the settler communities of South Africa, New Zealand and Australia. Constraints of space and limited expertise made such a choice necessary. Rugby union, however, has not remained confined to these areas but is now played on all continents and by women as well as men.

Our aim in *Making the Rugby World* is to continue the pattern of analysis we began in *Making Men* but to cover some of the important areas left largely unexplored in that volume. Specifically, we seek to understand what has happened to the sport of rugby union as it has moved progressively from the private realm of the playing field of the English public school to the global, public realm which is increasingly dominated by Rupert Murdoch and other entrepreneurs with multi-national media interests. Along the way, rugby has been a source of class, gendered, racial and national identities that have not been immutable constructs but have been actively shaped and reshaped over the past century and more. Furthermore, new developments in rugby union since 1995 have altered the game forever. The twin thrusts of professionalization and commodification have had an enormous impact on the game. In addition, rugby is no longer the preserve of a homophobic, white, upper-class masculinity, even though it remains entrenched in a global, white-dominated, old-boys' world order, as a number of our contributors imply. In exploring further the development of rugby union within the context of modern sport, we go well beyond the confines of *Making Men* to explore rugby and issues of race in the Empire/Commonwealth, rugby in non-British societies, women's rugby, and nationalism and rugby before turning to the massive impact of globalization, professionalization and commercialization on rugby. Although our coverage is in no way comprehensive, the themes addressed by the contributors provide a starting point for the analysis of the myriad of changes that have taken place in rugby union during its globalization process. Many of the chapters highlight the importance of the development of world-wide competition in the form of the World Cup, as well as the influence of sponsorship, television coverage and the payment of players from the international down to the club level. These facets are indicative of the new ground rules that make rugby a commodity, and its players raw materials in the production process. Nevertheless, while these forces are currently the overriding influences in the game and loom large in all discussions of rugby and its future, in the past other equally significant factors have had an impact on the development of the game in each of the countries and cultures we examine. As such, we have found it necessary to remind ourselves and our contributors not to let the present diminish the past by looming too large. For to understand the current processes of change in rugby union at the local, the national and the international level it is imperative that we see the development of the game as a much longer historical process. While we demonstrate a rapidly changing and almost revolutionary present in contrast to an evolutionary past, we aim to present a balanced picture that takes account of both the *longue durée* and the rapidly commercializing rugby world that has emerged in the World Cup era. We also present rugby's transformation less as the funeral of the past and more as a slow erosion of the old amateur, old-boy world order. We reject a simple description that sees professionalized, global rugby as something entirely different from the rugby of the past, but rather argue that we must carefully contextualize complex processes of change and ground rugby in its varying sites if we are to understand such matters as the emergence of rugby as commodity, the forms of masculinity that surround rugby, the impact of the development of women's rugby on the game around the world, and the impact of race and nation on the world of rugby.

One example of the need to connect the past with the present may be seen in the commodification of rugby. This process has been present in rugby union and contested for at least the past century. Failure to agree on the way in which professionalism and commercialism would be practised in rugby led to the splits of 1895 in England and 1908 in Australia, whereby a separate professional code of rugby league emerged. In addition, differing practices within an elusive ideology of amateurism led to strains between rugby playing nations. In Wales, the under-the-table payment of players was quite common and Scotland refused to play New Zealand in 1924 owing to a dispute about gate-money originating in 1905. More dramatic was the exclusion of France from the Five-Nations' championship between 1930 and 1946, and the controversies caused by the payments made to induce (rebel) New Zealanders, Welsh players and others to play rugby in apartheid South Africa in the 1970s and the 1980s. Many leading southern hemisphere players also began to play in Italy for significant financial rewards at this time. Finally, moves towards professionalism and ultimately the threat of an international player breakaway in the southern hemisphere nations of New Zealand, South Africa and Australia pushed the issue of professionalizing the sport almost to breaking point. Northern hemisphere administrators were unable to resist this last assault and sanctioned full and open professionalism in late 1995 following the Rugby World Cup. It is with such an approach in mind that we have structured this volume.

The book is set out in four broad sections. The first two chapters deal with the hitherto unexplored role of race in the development of rugby in the Empire. The chapters by MacLean and Nauright demonstrate that there was no uniform policy of racial exclusion when it came to rugby in the settler societies of New Zealand and South Africa. In New Zealand, Maori men played rugby from its beginnings in the 1870s. In South Africa, mixed race or Coloured men and African men began playing rugby soon after whites did in the 1880s. However, Maori were never completely excluded from official New Zealand rugby competitions. In fact, by the 1920s Maori players such as the great George Nepia were visible members of the national All Black rugby side, except when New Zealand played South Africa. On those occasions New Zealand rugby officials for decades went along with the South African practice of racial exclusivity in sporting clubs and representative teams by not selecting Maori players for tours of South Africa. By contrast, the first mixed-race or Coloured player to represent South Africa did not appear until 1980, and then only to prevent a full-scale rugby boycott. By the beginning of 1999 no fully African-descended player had appeared in a test match for the Springboks, though changes at the Super 12 international provincial competition level have made it more likely that a black African man may wear the national rugby jersey in the near future.

Despite the appearance of Maori in All Black teams, it is clear, as MacLean demonstrates, that Maori were not included on an equal basis and the cultural appropriation of Maori symbols was used in establishing New Zealand as different (exotic, even Other) from the 'Mother Country' (England) and distinctive from other settler dominions. The arrival of an All Black team on the rugby field is signalled in the performance of the haka. Yet, as MacLean explains, it is not *the* haka, but rather *a* haka that is perfomed, the *ka mate* haka, one of a number of hakas and one that, for many Maori, has been heartily maligned. Indeed, when it was proposed that the crowd perform the haka *en masse* at a test match between Australia and the All Blacks at Dunedin in 1994, South Island Maori protested as the *ka mate* was a haka that had been used by invading Maori from the North Island before massacring many of their people. Indeed, the *ka mate* has not been the only haka used by the All Blacks. In their triumphant tour of the British Isles and France in 1924 a haka was composed by George Nepia and other Maori players with specific reference to rugby. Nepia's haka was soon discarded and the *ka mate,* used originally by the 1905 All Blacks, became the standard All Black haka, even though it has nothing to do with rugby and is textually dubious in its masculinity.

As Nauright shows in his case study of Coloured rugby in Cape Town, black rugby players in South Africa were confined to racially-segregated rugby structures from the outset. No South African government ever legislated against racially-mixed sport; white sportsmen and women accomplished this all on their own, as did some black sportspeople. One rugby organization for Coloureds in Cape Town excluded Muslims from their competition until the early 1960s, while another allowed both Muslims and Christians (practising and nominal) to play. As a result of their exclusion from white competitions, blacks were left to develop their own organizations, competitions and cultural practices in sport, and rugby was no exception. Thus, from an early stage, black rugby both on and off the field developed distinctive practices that emerged from spatial, social and cultural segregation. Though most New Zealand Maori lived apart from Pakeha or white New Zealanders until quite recently, on the rugby field Maori and Maori culture were assimilated into what became a New Zealand-wide, male cultural practice dominated by white cultural norms, but inclusive of some elements of Maori culture. The assimilation of Maori into the New Zealand culture was such that by the time of the first All Black tour of Britain in 1905, the imperial press often referred to New Zealand and its people as Maoriland and

Maorilanders.[2] Rugby at this time became one of the leading imperial sports linking Britain with settlers in the dominions.

It was not to the settler empire alone that rugby was transported. British men who had been trained in the game took it with them in their travels, persuading elite young men from other countries (many of whom were university students) of the value of this British upper- and middle-class, masculine activity. By World War I rugby was being played in France, Italy and Romania, Argentina and Uruguay, Canada and the United States, and Japan. Although taken initially to the white settler colonies, rugby also spread throughout British spheres of influence in the south Pacific. The first recorded rugby match in Fiji took place as early as 1884 and Australian teachers took rugby to Tonga in 1900, though rugby did not appear in Western Samoa until the 1920s after New Zealand took over the administration of the former German colony. While the development of rugby in each of these settings is worthy of close investigation, it is not possible to include them all here. Therefore we have selected four case studies of the expansion of rugby into non-British imperial settings to form the second section of the book. These relate to the United States, France, Italy and Japan.

In the case of the United States, Chandler shows that rugby played at McGill University in Canada heavily influenced the early development of football in America. Shortly after McGill played Harvard University in two matches in 1874, Harvard adopted most of the rugby rules used by McGill. Other American 'Ivy League' colleges soon followed Harvard's lead and embraced rugby, turning away from the soccer-style rules that had been in use. By the latter part of the nineteenth century, however, rule changes led to a distinctly American game that was significantly different from rugby union. These changes coincided with a heightened American nationalism that emerged from the 1876 centenary celebrations of independence where unique American cultural and sporting practices were valued, often at the expense of English ones. American masculinity became centred on strenuous physical activity, embodied at the turn of the century in President Theodore Roosevelt, and football was elevated to a leading position within this strenuous masculinity.[3]

Rugby was not dead in America, however, as many officials and observers became highly concerned about the violence in football that the new rules had unleashed. By 1905 there was public outcry over deaths in football largely due to the widespread use of the flying wedge. The state of Georgia even temporarily banned the playing of football while, as Chandler shows, the leading West Coast universities switched from American football to rugby union. Rule changes allowing the forward pass and banning the flying wedge further altered American football and thus made it even more distinct from rugby. As a result of these the attack on football was relatively short-lived nationally. Rugby retained a stronghold on the American West Coast, however, helped in no small part by important international contacts. Contacts with Antipodean teams have been especially significant from the time of the 1905 All Blacks tour, which began a trend for New Zealand and Australian teams stopping off on their way to Britain. Later, club teams began touring the West Coast of the United States, often combining this with visits to play Canadian West Coast teams in and around British Columbia. All these contacts helped rugby to maintain a foothold and a following in the United States, but it remained very much a minority sport.

There were few significant changes in American rugby until the 1960s when the game became part of resistance to traditional American mainstream masculinity. As the major site of resistance the American college campus, long the home of rugby in the country, became the focus of rugby's resurgence. Chandler shows the importance of sociability and conviviality, focused around heavy beer drinking, as central elements of this new rugby culture that then moved from the campuses to the hundreds of rugby clubs springing up nationwide. Because of rugby's association with drinking, the United States Rugby Football Union sought to try to improve the game's image. This came at a time when rugby was ever expanding and a market for it emerged with the potential to attract commercial sponsorship and media attention. Indeed, in the 1990s Rupert Murdoch's Fox Sports Channel rapidly expanded its coverage of international rugby, and in 1998 an American team competition to be shown on Fox was planned for the new millennium, suggesting that the game had finally expanded beyond its university base.

Thierry Terret shows that in France university students also played a key role in the early development of rugby. As in the USA, when rugby went to France it was not constrained by ties to imperial ideologies. In the late nineteenth century many French elites, however, shared the view of Baron Pierre de Coubertin that English sporting practices were superior ones that would reinvigorate the manhood of the French nation, seen to have been humiliated by the Prussians in 1870. As Terret argues, in France, and particularly in the south-west regions in and around the cities of Bordeaux and Toulouse, rugby rapidly departed from its English origins. Attempts by anglophile Parisians such as de Coubertin and Paschal Grousset were unsuccessful in transplanting English rugby practices to France. Rather, a distinctive playing style emerged centred on French concepts of masculinity and resistance to central authority. This manifested itself clearly in the rise of the game in the south-west where anti-Parisian sentiments were literally played out on the rugby field. Terret demonstrates that this divide had long historical roots going back to the Revolution and the differing traditions of the Jacobins and the Girondists. As *Le Journal des Sports* argued in 1909, 'Bordeaux and Toulouse will avenge ... all the provinces for the great injustices they have too long endured and for the unjustified humiliations that Paris believes it can inflict'.[4] Rugby rapidly then became part of regional resistance to central authority, a cultural practice that symbolically played out long political and cultural differences. Indeed, as in the north of England, south-western French clubs soon outstripped their elitist rivals in performance. From 1904 when Bordeaux defeated Stade Francais in the French championship, southern clubs dominated. Indeed, again, as in the north of England, it is in the south-west that rugby league, known in France as *rugby treize* (or the 'game of thirteen'), eventually emerged.[5]

Rugby playing styles initially fused with concepts of class-based masculinity of the *belle epoque* that stressed elegance over strength in the performance of the game. When rugby went to the south of France it was infused with different concepts of masculinity that centred on regional and cultural resistance and the increasing participation of farm labourers who were then able to use their 'physical capital' from their work in taming the men of the urban middle classes. This parallels the situation in England where one of the driving forces behind the entrenchment of amateurism was that the working classes gained an unfair advantage over the more sedentary middle and upper classes because of their more physically demanding occupations.[6] As Terret argues for France, 'The symbolic battles taking place on the playing fields at the beginning of the century only intensified the conflict between the southern ideal of the strong man and the northern ideal of the urban intellectual.' A new playing style emerged based on muscularity and forward play that diverged from earlier stylistic back play. This was reinforced in the media which positively described scrums and rolling mauls as the more valued style of manly rugby and stressed the off-field exploits of local players, linking both elements to conceptions of regional popular culture. Thus rugby and rugby culture were linked into the south-western symbol of the *castagne*, a Gascon noun meaning 'fight'.

It was Italian students who studied in France who took the game

back with them to Italy in 1909. Rugby first became organized in the
northern cities of Milan and Turin, with strong early links to France. In
Italy, as Bonini shows, rugby has 'long been appreciated for its
pedagogical value as a "maker of men"'. Unlike France, in Italy rugby
remained an elite game tied to class-based concepts of masculinity.
Rugby expanded further in the Fascist era as a propaganda tool for
conditioning the masses to Fascist aims. Such conditioning combined
the physical with the ideological in the making of men to serve the
state and its aims. Bonini, in citing Aldo Cerchiari's 1928 translation
of a French introductory rugby text, states that for the Fascists rugby
was 'the game that proves the athletic and moral potential of the
individual'. Furthermore, rugby was 'the most complete and rational
team game, a game that "makes men"'. The Fascists initially liked
rugby because it was a physical game that allowed players to use their
whole bodies and developed a sense of co-operation, self-discipline
and the subjugation of the individual to the needs of the group. Indeed,
these factors would combine to resurrect the ancient traditions thought
to have existed in imperial Rome and that such a resurrection would
help Italy emerge as a leading world power. As with football in the
USA, a new Italian game called *volata* appeared that, in drawing on
local traditions, could be cast as a uniquely Italian sport. Rugby thus
lost favour with the Fascists by 1929 as it was thought to be too British
and not Italian.

By 1932, however, rugby had regained favour as a better game than
other football codes for the development of military preparedness. In
that year a university rugby competition began and a new national
federation was formed. The return of Fascist favour helped rugby grow
to 106 official clubs affiliated to the national union and nearly 7,000
non-affiliated clubs by the outbreak of World War II in 1939. After the
war rugby's previous links to Fascism limited its growth and rugby
suffered in comparison with other sports, including those introduced
by American troops stationed in the country during the latter part of the
war and after. Rugby retained its foothold in the universities, however,
and expanded to smaller towns in the north and the east during the
1950s. Some towns developed reputations as rugby towns and became
known more widely for the success of their local teams. In L'Aquila,
for example, Bonini argues that everyone is involved in rugby at some
level. Rugby has become a symbol of the town's success such that
there, as Bonini says, 'rugby is life'. Problems occurred in Italian
rugby in the 1960s and the 1970s when leading clubs began to lure
talented players away from the smaller ones. To protest against
Fiamme Oro of Padua's loading up on top players and winning four

consecutive national championships between 1958 and 1961, some clubs left rugby union to form a rugby league competition. In response, the Italian Rugby Federation in 1971 allowed clubs to engage the services of foreign players in efforts to lift the profile of rugby union within the Italian sporting scene. Many of these players were *oriundi*, men from France and Argentina whose family origins were in Italy. The influx of these players, however, threatened the development of local talent according to the smaller clubs. They sought a reduction in the number of foreign players and in 1980 teams were restricted to one foreign player each. As the clubs brought in these players and lifted the level of rugby, sponsorship interest grew, with companies becoming involved directly in clubs. Most significantly, these companies brought leading foreign players such as David Campese and Naas Botha, from Australia and South Africa, respectively, to Italy to play for clubs in which they had an interest thereby challenging older amateur traditions in the Italian game.

Even more than in Italy, competitive rugby at the elite level in Japan is organized by corporations such as Kobe Steel which field their own teams. Leading foreign players such as John Kirwin have also been engaged to play in these teams. Company teams, however, draw their base of players from the universities and high schools. It is the latter arena that Richard Light explores in some detail. As was the case in France and Italy, rugby in Japan fused with local masculine cultural practices such as *seishin*. *Seishin* is an opaque term that comes from the samurai and refers to 'the inner being, spiritual fortitude and self-discipline developed through particular physical training', stressing unity of mind, body and soul and differs dramatically from Western Cartesian dualism. As with the Fascist regime in Italy in the 1920s and the 1930s, in Japan *seishin* was promoted by the military to enable the Japanese to counter the greater American material power in the years before the Pacific war. Western occupation forces identified *seishin* as being too closely linked with Japanese militarism and worked to eradicate it from the school curriculum. As a result, *seishin* re-emerged in university and school sporting clubs that operated outside the formal curriculum, with rugby clubs practising the more severe form. Thus, although rugby in Japan operates similarly to the rugby of Victorian England, it also displays distinctive Japanese concepts of manliness brought forward from the feudal *samurai* classes. Honour and gentlemanly behaviour go even further in Japan where fighting on the field is seen as a sign of personal weakness both in physical and emotional terms. In addition, individualism must not encroach on an arena centred on group spirit and sacrifice, commitment and aggression that serve the greater good of the whole.

Similar notions of the virtues of commitment to the team and the sacrificing of the body to save a teammate under attack are clear in the case of women's rugby explored by Carle and Nauright. In their chapter we move beyond our analyses begun in *Making Men* and continue here by examining gender and rugby from outside the confines of the traditional masculine cultures that have surrounded it; this forms the book's third section. In this process we see that Australian women who play rugby draw on many of the heretofore masculine-only codes that have conditioned how rugby is played and interpreted. Australian women players stress the power of teamwork and their willingness to put their bodies 'on the line', knowing that their teammates will throw themselves into the fray to protect them. Differing from many other sports, in rugby a good player cannot succeed or indeed survive without the support of the team, and players refer to their 'desperation' to get to any teammate who has been tackled to protect her from physical damage. Light argues that in Japan the 'ideals of courage, personal sacrifice and "putting your body on the line" for the team can be linked with Victorian ideals of manliness' as well as to a uniquely Japanese masculinity. Yet as the Australian women show, such concepts of bodily self-sacrifice are not limited to men who play rugby. Carle and Nauright argue that it is possible that 'the rough nature and teamwork of the game is rugby's biggest attraction, not because of physical contact itself, but rather the emotional bonds it facilitates between teammates'. Yet for both Japanese men and Australian women, rugby goes beyond Victorian ideals of self-sacrifice for the greater good in stressing the emotional, which Victorians thought should be sublimated in favour of mental control over physical expression. The discourses of masculinity which dominated the rugby playing world which we reviewed in *Making Men* have been adapted and manipulated and yet are still visible in a variety of non-male and non-imperial contexts around the world.

Byrnes argues that there is an active process of constructing leading New Zealand women rugby players as tough, hard-hitting and aggressive with 'a touch of intimidating brutality'.[7] That the construction of New Zealand women who enter the masculine world of rugby is actively portrayed in the media is just that – a construction, and is borne out in Carle and Nauright's work and in the ethnographic study of Farah Palmer on women's rugby in New Zealand. Palmer has suggested that women are tolerated as acceptable members of rugby clubs only as long as they do not become overly masculinized and thus cross the line between femininity and masculinity.[8] In Italy, as Bonini shows, women rugby players in the 1980s were initially completely ostracized, with sanctions placed on any male official who showed support or refereed women's matches. By 1991, however, the Italian Rugby Federation affirmed women's right to play, though this was by no means a unanimous decision. Women's role in rugby is still thought to be primarily one of providing the domestic servicing of the game. And, as Carle and Nauright show in Australia, it is often other women who ostracize women rugby players. We can, therefore, see different approaches to women entering the masculinist world of rugby that all work to defend the boundaries of masculinity whether they incorporate women within masculine conceptions, as in the internationally successful New Zealand national team, they try to exclude women altogether, or women rugby players themselves are publicly condemned for transgressing the gender boundary. Women who dare to 'cross the line' and play 'a man's game' face tremendous obstacles.

Rugby was one of the last sporting forms, particularly among those that have been linked inextricably to hegemonic masculinities internationally, to become fully commodified and professionalized. What this has meant in terms of traditional masculinist rugby cultures is both complex and rapidly changing. In the final section of the book we turn to the impact of commodifying processes on both the nature and the structure of rugby union.

Hutchins and Phillips argue persuasively that the changes brought on by moves towards international rugby as a commodified form, most particularly situated in the Rugby World Cup held every four years since 1987, have dramatically and profoundly effected the game down to its lower levels. While they are unable to conclude what the longer term impact of these changes will be, the authors nevertheless argue that rugby has moved decisively from being a cultural practice centred on play to one focused on display that began with international rugby and the World Cup, but which now affects rugby at the national, the regional and even the local or the club level. The chapter by Douglas Booth illustrates this process further in his case study of the 1995 World Cup and its impact on the process of forging a new South Africa. In keeping with the finer-grained analysis of rugby provided by the cases reviewed by Light, and by Carle and Nauright, David Howe examines the impact of commercial changes on one of the leading Welsh rugby clubs, Pontypridd.

Rugby clubs the world over have had to begin to adapt to the dictates of professionalized rugby, particularly in countries where the game is highly commodified such as the British Isles, France, Italy, Australia, New Zealand and South Africa. In other places the drain of leading players to clubs offering financial pay for play has caused

concerns about the future prospects of national sides. Howe asks more
specifically in what ways the impact of professionalism has manifested
itself in a club such as Pontypridd with a long tradition of success in
amateur club rugby. Using an ethnographic approach, he is able to
observe how both professionalism and commercialism have
manifested themselves in a particular habitus/context. From Howe's
point of view professionalism has not just affected the manner in
which players are expected to train and perform, but has just as
critically affected the attitudes of club officials who have been
responsible for the well-being and day-to-day running of the club,
hitherto in an unpaid capacity. Likewise, the impacts of
commercialization have transformed club habitus such that shifts in
attitude have led to changed interpersonal relations between players
and supporters. He argues that in the Pontypridd case the major
impacts of commercialization and professionalization have been to
transform the club from a co-operative organization to a commercial
enterprise. Likewise, in their work on Bedford rugby club in England,
Daniel O'Brien and Trevor Slack argue that professionalism and
commodification have forced some significant changes in
organizational structure and culture.[9] Indeed, it is easy to find many
rugby supporters and former officials who argue that the game is
simply not what it used to be and that professional rugby has changed
the rugby culture dramatically. Howe goes on to suggest that the
change of culture that now surrounds the club has meant that spectator
roles have also been transformed from observer-participants –
observers of, and participants in, the game – to being spectating-
consumers who are paying for a product. In this commodification
process markets for local businesses have increased as companies seek
to link their products with the club's rugby product and, it is hoped, the
club's success. Although the processes unleashed by professional
commodified rugby have altered the structures and cultures of rugby
clubs, it is clear that these processes are not uniform and vary
particularly between countries. The conflicts within the rugby unions
of Wales and England and between the unions and the enterprises that
are driving commercialization have manifested themselves somewhat
differently. Nevertheless, the power struggles have been between the
'old boy' administrator/guardians of the game (the blazers) and the
new entrepreneurs who seek to profit from it or control it for their own
ends (the suits). Howe suggests that over the long term rugby has
changed at Pontypridd from being 'an organization that allowed for the
playing of structured games... into an institution that drew the
attention of spectators and by doing so became a spectacle. This

spectacle has become one of the symbols of Pontypridd... .' We can see therefore that rugby as organized in the club has gone from its origins in organized play, to structured dis-play, and finally is emerging as commodified spectacular entertainment. Howe's ethnographic approach needs to be repeated in a number of settings before we can assess, with any degree of certainty, the extent of such changes throughout first-class rugby, but his chapter certainly suggests a number of potential sites of conflict and resistance as clubs have to face up to the impact of increased commercialization and professionalization and as top-level players become increasingly distant from long-time club supporters.

In South Africa, as Booth and Black and Nauright among others have argued, rugby has been intimately linked with contests about identity both in the old and the new South Africa. As a sport, rugby has been historically linked to public white culture and expressions of identity. This linkage has now been transformed into a commodified form whereby the national Springbok team is repositioned as a symbol for the new nation. The identity struggle is on-going and is a complex process. For as Booth argues, rugby is tied to the power of a white oligarchy in the country. Indeed, a repositioning of the Springboks was made possible only through President Mandela's support of the 1995 Rugby World Cup. Though the Springboks, at least into 1999, remained a nearly (and sometimes) all-white team, the media hype of rugby's centrality to South Africanness continues and commercial forces continue to do battle for control of this important symbol of nationhood. As Black and Nauright have suggested, the business of rugby is now a part of South Africa's economic development programme,[10] meaning that the commodification of rugby is crucial to the reinvention of rugby as symbol in the new South Africa. Following Etienne Balibar, Booth asks the crucial question of how states nationalize their populations in attempts to generate identification with and a belonging to the new social formation. Bonini has given us some insights into this process in Fascist Italy and beyond, as has Light for the period after World War II in Japan. In demonstrating the complex nature of this process in the former East Germany after the war Tara Magdalinski has shown that the state became an active agent in using preferred and particular forms of sporting history as a part of this process in overcoming the difficulties in identifying with a German whole that included the problemmatic history of the Nazi era.[11] Likewise, in South Africa links to the apartheid era must be overcome if true transformation is to take place. Yet, as Booth demonstrates, the ruling African National Congress has sought not to wipe away the entire past but to recast former racially-based traditions into ones that can be felt by all South Africans. As Paul Connerton shows in his work on social memory, all newly formed societies must form links with the past and with memories and traditions with which living people identify, but these can be reshaped into new traditions within new political and social formations.[12] In the case of South Africa and rugby, while many white administrators from the old racist structures resisted or simply did not care about transformation, it was clear to many inside and outside the game that changes had to take place. By 1995 it was evident that rugby lagged well behind other formerly white-dominated sports and especially cricket. Rugby ran the risk of being left behind as the sport of the recalcitrant and racist rump of white South Africa. Although the Springboks repositioned themselves through the learning of the words to the new co-national anthem *Nkosi Sikelel' iAfrika* and rugby administrators agreed in principle with Mandela's assertion that the 1995 team would be the last 'lily-white' team to represent the country at a World Cup, the process of change has been difficult as throughout 1996 and 1997 problems continued to arise that had been lurking just below the surface.

In addition to playing an important role in the politics of reconciliation in the new South Africa, rugby has also become a prized commodity sought by local and international capital as they seek to further penetrate the South African market now opened up for conscience-free investment. The Springboks are perhaps the highest valued commodity on the international rugby scene as they have been either nominal or actual world champions for much of the century, only challenged regularly by New Zealand or on occasion by the combined power of the home nations collected in the form of the British Lions. Indeed, Rupert Murdoch did not even wait for the end of the 1995 World Cup to offer a massive sum to corner the market on elite southern hemisphere rugby and the Springboks signed major marketing contracts with Nike and Reebok. Before that, the logo and the team itself were registered as trademarks, symbols of nation, perhaps, but certainly symbols in a newly commodified, global, rugby marketplace. While the South African case provides us with examples of the problems which surround racial, gendered, commercialized and professionalized rugby in the 1990s, it is equally clear that the game is undergoing transformation in all the countries in which it is played.

In the chapters that follow we explore in some detail many of the changes that have occurred in rugby union over the past century that will give context to the present situation. The story is necessarily partial, yet we believe that a greater understanding of the intersections between race, gender, class and capitalist development in modern society may be best examined in sport through our confining our efforts to a reading of these changes within one specific sport rather than further partializing the story through the examining of these issues across several sports. Indeed, we argue that rugby union is different from many other sports in its long adherence to amateurism, its class, race and gendered focus on developing specific masculine behaviours and in its focus for much of its history on a complex web of interactions between players, supporters and administrators. While rugby union in the post-1995 world may be in the process of becoming more like other professionalized sporting codes, its historical development and cultural practices remain an indelible part of a game that those within it refer to, and believe is, 'the game they play in heaven'.

NOTES

1. John Nauright and Timothy J.L. Chandler (eds), *Making Men: Rugby and Masculine Identity* (London, 1996; revised reprint, 1999).
2. For a full discussion of this tour and the British press coverage of it, see John Nauright, 'Colonial Manhood and Imperial Race Virility: British Responses to Post-Boer War Colonial Rugby Tours', in Nauright and Chandler, *Making Men*, pp. 121–39; ibid., 'Sport, Manhood and Empire: British Responses to the New Zealand Rugby Tour of 1905', *International Journal of the History of Sport*, Vol.8, No.2 (September 1991), pp. 239–55.
3. See S.W. Pope, *Patriotic Games: Sporting Traditions in the American Imagination 1876-1926* (New York, 1997).
4. *Le Journal des Sports*, 10 April 1909.
5. For a detailed analysis of the process of differentiation in the north of England, see Tony Collins, *Rugby's Great Split: Class, Culture and the Origins of Rugby League Football* (London, 1998); and James Martens, 'Rugby, Class, Amateurism and Manliness: the Case of Rugby in Northern England, 1871–1895', in Nauright and Chandler, *Making Men*, pp. 32–49.
6. See Richard Holt, *Sport and the British* (Oxford, 1989), especially Ch.2.
7. Kiri Byrnes, 'A Season to Savour', *Mana*, December/January 1996–97, p. 56.
8. Farah Palmer, 'An Ethnographical Study of the Women's Rugby Subculture in New Zealand: Challenging and Contributing to Societal Norms of Femininity', BPhed Honours Thesis, University of Otago, 1995.
9. Daniel O'Brien and Trevor Slack, 'Deinstitutionalizing the Amateur Ethic: an empirical Examination of Change in a Rugby Union Football Club', *Sport Management Review* (forthcoming).
10. David Black and John Nauright, *Rugby and the South African Nation* (Manchester, 1998).
11. Tara Magdalinski, '*Traditionspflege* and the Constuction of Identity in the German Democratic Republic, 1970–1979, *Occasional Papers in German Studies*, No.14 (1997), pp. 1–48; 'Organized Remembering: the Construction of Sporting Traditions in the German Democratic Republic, *European Review of Sports History*, Vol.1 (1998), pp. 144–63.
12. Paul Connerton, *How Societies Remember* (Cambridge, 1989).

Of Warriors and Blokes: The Problem of Maori Rugby for Pakeha Masculinity in New Zealand

Malcolm MacLean

In 1982 the doyen of New Zealand rugby journalists, T.P. (Terry) McLean, asked, 'Who were the really great among Maori players? Who stood out? Who would be fit to rank among the elect of players produced by the race?'[1] The article itself is in the reminiscence style of so much rugby writing. It is not the content that is of relevance though – it is just another list and justification for a particular group of 15 being the greatest. McLean's status in New Zealand sports journalism does give the list some additional noteworthiness, but little else. The real significance of the piece lies in the title. McLean sees the great Maori rugby players as *warriors* and has, as a result, exposed the dominant discursive frame surrounding views of and attitudes towards Maori rugby.

Maori have been significant actors in and users of rugby almost since its introduction to New Zealand in 1870. At the same time, rugby has been a key element in the construction of a legitimate masculinity in New Zealand. This masculinity is characteristically Pakeha[2] cementing the elite status of men in the colonizing group. Class power is maintained by accentuating a supposed egalitarianism, centred on the notion of the hard man, the 'real' bloke, denying the social divisions of power and wealth. Through this dynamic an image of New Zealand men derived from a supposed glorious pioneer past has held sway in an almost unchallenged manner for the first 70 or so years of this century.

J.O.C. Phillips has revealed the development of this man in his work.[3] In doing so, and restricting his study to Pakeha men, Phillips consequently undermines the usefulness of the model when we consider New Zealand's colonial form. He is unable to expose the contradictory position of Maori within many of the iconic sites of Pakeha masculinity and, as a result, a hegemonic national imaginary. Phillips stresses the significance of both war and sport, particularly rugby, as factors in this invention. These factors mean that Pakeha, and colonial, masculinity is situated in a homosocial environment. This homosociality is both gendered and ethnicized. The kiwi bloke is a Pakeha working man, at home on the football field, in the sands of North Africa, at the pub (but in the public bar). He is a loner, hard, resolute, tall, strong but comradely and supports other men in their toils. These characteristics of Pakeha masculinity are widely touted and legitimated through a range of acceptable cultural institutions. In the Frank Sargeson story 'The Hole that Jack Dug', Jack, unable to cope with having to spend time with his wife during the weekend, spends his days digging a large hole in the backyard for no purpose other than to be in a masculine world.[4] His mate Tom finds all this a bit odd, but entirely understandable. Jack, of course, links this to a wider masculine world, explaining to his wife that:

> some people say they don't like to work, but what would we ever have if we didn't work? And now the war's on we've all got to do our share. Think of the soldier-boys. Fighting's hard work, and Tom and me want to do our bit as well.[5]

Ultimately Jack's hole is nothing but his chance to spend time away from his wife and with Tom. In the end, Jack fills the hole in again – it had served its purpose. Teamwork is a crucial part of this masculine world. Writing in 1906, E.W. Taylor argued that the reason the All Blacks were so successful during their tour of Britain the previous year was because of 'the unselfish manner in which they play to each other'.[6] Phillips argues that this appeal to teamwork is a crucial element of the homosocial mythology of Pakeha masculinity.

Despite the early role that Maori played in New Zealand rugby, to the extent that Dave Gage as captain of the first representative team to tour overseas (to Australia in 1883) was Maori, the hegemonic image of the New Zealand man excludes Maori. Maori have been active participants in all the key moments defining the masculinity that Pakeha men have appropriated. The New Zealand Wars could not have happened without them, Maori soldiers served in both World War I and World War II, they were key players in early rugby success, and shared in the hard work of colonial development. They are excluded from the hegemonic group, however, because they disrupt the homosociality. The problem is that Maori men proved their right to be admitted to the Pakeha masculinist elite. The discourses of colonization privilege the masculine, the colonizer and the cultured over the feminine, the colonized and nature. The invocation of this discursive frame means that the colonized were gendered female by the discourse of British high colonialism.

The objective here is to expose this contradiction between Maori men as gendered female by colonialist discourses while they play a key part in the maintenance of the tools of dominant masculinities. The objective is not to propose characteristics of a range of Maori masculinities in opposition to legitimate Pakeha masculinity, but to show the uncomfortable relationship between this masculinity and the social conditions of a colonial state. Attention will be paid to the ways in which Maori are admitted to the sporting element (and therefore the martial component) of the foundations of New Zealand masculinity and the contradictory images that result. In considering Maori relationships with rugby there are three significant aspects. In the first section attention will be turned towards the use of rugby in Maori contexts. The two subsequent sections will consider, first, the question of Maori rugby in colonial(ist) discourses through issues such as the legitimacy of warrior rugby, the suggestion that the adoption of rugby by Maori is a sign of their civilization, that it leads to the removal of a lack thereby enhancing the contemporary hegemonic norm as naturalized, that assimilationist policies work, and as a factor in giving New Zealand the 'best race relations in the world'. In particular, this discussion will consider attitudes to Maori rugby in popular discourses through sports journalism and the first New Zealand rugby tour to the United Kingdom in 1888–89.

Discourses of Colonialism

Two recent, and quite different, analyses of colonialism are particularly useful to discussions of images of Maori in New Zealand and their relations to dominant masculinities.[7] Nicholas Thomas makes an appeal for particularist analyses that develop theoretical positions clearly relevant to the context of study. In an overview of post-colonial writing, he suggests that:

> the field, however, seems less inclined to localise or historicise analysis, than to put Fanon and Lacan (or Derrida) into a blender and take the result to be equally appetising for premodern and modern; for Asian, African and American; for metropolitan, settler, indigenous and diasporic subjects.[8]

This is a particular challenge for New Zealand. It is a former colony of settlement where the settlers significantly outnumber the indigenous population, but specifically invoke the characteristics of the indigenes for cultural and state purposes. There is little in post-colonial analysis that is clearly applicable to this sort of setting. The terms of the discussion of colonial relations in New Zealand are, as a result, overwhelmingly primordialist in tenor. As a result, the bases of ethnic relations are depicted as permanent and unchanging – in other words, as ahistorical.

Thomas has argued that colonialism should not be best understood as a simple process of economic or political domination legitimized by ideologies of racism but as a cultural process that does not simply mask relations but expresses and constitutes them. Under this framework, he depicts splits in colonizing projects between assimilationist and segregationist approaches. Further ruptures are caused by the tendency to define new lands as vacant for European use and to define, collect and map cultures already present. This tendency problematizes colonizers' identities which seek reconciliation between metropolitan values as civilized and the rawness of sites of settlement as a sign of a breach with the flaws and weaknesses of the old world. The smoothness of the process of colonization is therefore confronted by two sets of influential factors: colonialism's internal contradictions and the intransigence and resistance of the colonized.

In New Zealand these factors are conflated. The intransigence and resistance of the colonized accentuated and played out the contradictions of colonialism. Although this resistance has been most clearly understood in terms of war, Maori cultural resistance was also profound. Despite repeated claims to the contrary, imperial and colonial troops were overwhelmingly unsuccessful in their attempts to subdue Maori militarily. James Belich, the leading historian of New Zealand's colonial wars, has argued that Maori won the majority of military conflicts with the British between the 1840s and the 1870s. Despite this, they lost the wars because they were engaged in a different style of conflict – one constrained by community needs for farmers and agriculturalists facing a standing army.[9] Maori cultural resistance was also great.[10] The *whanau* and *hapu*[11] as the basis of social life have survived and prospered. Maori continue their attempts at independent political organization. The language survived, just, although for many until well into the twentieth century it was the vernacular. This is not to suggest that Maori retained their former position. The impact of colonization was horrific in many cases. Maori were deprived of their land, fisheries and other *taonga* (treasures). Poverty rates were, and in many areas remain, very high.

This was a predicament few Pakeha ever saw. They remained isolated from Maori communities and few had any direct contact with individual Maori until the great Maori urban migration of the late 1950s and the 1960s. Indeed, as late as the beginning of 1997 two of the most influential leaders in Maoridom, Sir Hepi Te Heu Heu and Dame Te Atairangikaahu, remained largely unknown to most Pakeha. Most seem to have heard of Sir Hepi only after his death in August 1997 while most could not name Dame Te Ata as the Maori Queen. Yet New Zealand prides itself on its good 'race relations', Maori imagery is widely invoked in depictions of the nation – from the corporate logo of Air New Zealand to the opening of the 1990 Commonwealth Games. Thomas points to this tendency in colonies of settlement to cherish indigenous cultures where they are identified with the mythological, spirituality, caring for the land; with the primordial, metaphysical and natural. For many Australians, he suggests, 'Being Aboriginal is about not being greedy; it is about things that are elemental and ancestral; forces of the landscape and nature rather than artifices of the city and the self'.[12] When the New Zealand views that parallel this vision are conflated with Maori as New Zealand-specific markers it is clear that there are strong parallels between many sympathetic representations of the natives in the present and the primitivist discourses of earlier times. Hegemonic icons of national identity are firmly placed in the on-going appropriation of 'Maoriness'.

Phillips exposes a countervailing tendency in national imaginary with his case that Pakeha masculinity is an underground tendency producing an unofficial identity. It is rough and beyond the pale of acceptability. While this may be true, it does not suggest that colonial relations were ideologically genderless. Sara Mills has argued that 'representations of women [were] central to the process of constructing a male national identity in the colonial period, but that paradoxically has been based on an excising of women's involvement in colonialism'.[13] This process required that women in the colonial exercise remained 'signifiers, but not ... producers of signification'.[14] Associated with the exclusion of women from the process of colonization was the development, for the purposes of exclusion, of the notion of the country being colonized as female, and weaker. The vocabulary of sexuality was, and still is, widely exploited in colonialist texts. There are repeated discussions of the penetration inland and the country is often explicitly labelled female – 'she'. Among those labelled female by New Zealand colonialist discourse are those very same Maori men who so often defeated the imperial and colonial armies in battle.

Within colonialist discourses the tendency to depict (male) natives as violent shifts the focus from the Europeans' violent role and acts in colonizing. This displacement of aggression is impelled by the Europeans' God-given right to colonize and civilize, coupled with a eugenicist-inspired fear that if the English (or other northern Europeans) did not spread out to fill the world then the 'savages' would. This violence of the male native was balanced by a process where women were sexualized. In the Pacific this sexualization was restricted to Polynesian women (dusky maidens) while some men (again, especially Polynesian) were classicized and made noble. There were few natives made nobler than the Maori, although this nobility was balanced by a dissoluteness that was held to explain Maori poverty. The point is that as colonialist discourses are not *necessarily* pejorative, Maori were admitted to an upper echelon as easily civilizable. Maori could, therefore, become 'almost the same, *but not quite ... Almost the same but not white ...* to be Anglicized is *emphatically* not to be English'.[15] Bhabha's point, as echoed by Thomas, is that the 'almost but not quite' status accorded these noble savages inadvertently produced a hybridity to threaten and subvert colonial hegemony. In the same way that colonial artefacts are appropriated or redefined, colonial discourses are also reformed and refashioned in the light of indigenous formations such that 'they are projected back at Europeans with a variety of serious and parodic intentions, and enter into discourses of tribal, customary and national identities'.[16] This is precisely the challenge posed to dominant masculinity by Maori rugby (and other martial) success.

Rugby union is a fundamental tool of colonialist legitimation and a vital weapon in legitimate masculinity's war of position with other masculinities and challenge(r)s. Phillips is not the first to consider the place of sport and war in the construction of New Zealand's national identity. Keith Sinclair has argued that New Zealand's identity is deeply masculine, claiming that the:

New Zealander's national self-image has been extremely physical, emphasizing hard work, athletic prowess. There has been a constant demand for fitness, not only for sport and war, but in education; an affirmation of health and efficiency. Sometimes this was accompanied by some contempt for intellectual achievements. Themes related to fitness arise constantly in any consideration of New Zealand nationalism. Associated with fitness was a strong emphasis upon military training.[17]

This attempt by Sinclair to essay the nature and sources of New

Zealand national identity is one of the first to give significant regard to sport. In arguing that 'Peace hath its Victories', Sinclair sees sport as a crucial element in the analysis of New Zealand and Australian nationalism. Devoting most of his attention to rugby, he points to the emergence of national sport as a factor of self-identity relating to the emergence of nation from around 1890 onwards.[18]

Sinclair claims that rugby was the chief sport of New Zealand men by end of the nineteenth century. It was seen as a masculinizing pastime, as a soldier-making game, and it was clearly associated with war and service, especially during World War I. He points to New Zealand's considerable success in early tours during the 1890s, mainly to Australia, and to the high praise bestowed on touring teams by politicians. Despite success in the Australasian competitions, he argues that doubts about the ability to defeat the British persisted, only to be dispelled in 1905 (though a New Zealand team defeated the British team that toured New Zealand in 1904). He is able to elevate the status of the 1905 tour by arguing that the earlier 1888–89 tour of Britain was not fully representative because it was primarily a Maori team, although four Pakeha were included.[19] Assessments of the 1888–89 tour such as this are flawed. Greg Ryan shows that the tour had a high profile in the English and the New Zealand popular media, and that the team faced stronger opposition because they toured before the 1895 split and the formation of the Northern Union, the precursor to rugby league.[20]

The connection between sport and war is further accentuated by Sinclair's argument that the 1905 loss to Wales after a disputed try is New Zealand sport's equivalent of Gallipoli. The invasion of the Gallipoli Peninsula in 1915 is widely seen as the initial defining moment of a fully-matured New Zealand taking an independent place on the world stage.[21] The national standing of New Zealand is stressed in this case through the argument that the assertion of the country's physical prowess fed into the crisis of British national efficiency and health. That rugby began to assume national significance is also seen in the welcoming home of the 1905 and the 1924 team as public rituals and celebrations of nation and national pride.

Sinclair's approach is highly problematic. He clearly identifies the position of rugby in shaping the hegemonic national identity: the masculine, colonial self-image. In doing so he denies the existence of alternative voices. His separate discussions of Maori and women (along with children, he labels these groups the 'peripheral majority') do little more than present them as an adjunct to this dominant imagining. Indeed, a greater portion of the argument is spent specifically discussing 'the world of men' than is devoted to this majority. Sinclair's vision is of an outdated, almost unitary nationalism. His focus on the centre means that the lived experiences of non-hegemonic groups are not factors in the invention of the New Zealand nation. It is not sufficient to problematize the hegemonic nation Sinclair traces when Maori, women and the young are seen as merely auxiliaries to the main struggle for identity.[22]

Any analysis of the relationship between Maori and hegemonic identities, be they colonial or masculine, as mediated by rugby, needs to address a range of questions. In particular, this analysis needs to investigate relations of power in analyses of sport.[23] These questions include assessments of who attempts to control how a sport is played and by whom, how the sport is represented, and how the sport is to be interpreted. Within this approach there are a series of social functions that sport performs in identity formation and assertion. In particular, it works to define existing boundaries of social and moral communities, assist in the creation of new social identities, provide physical expression of certain values and reflect on those values as contested space for opposing groups. These issues are problematized when marginalized groups such as Maori are full participants in such a central iconographic site.

Rugby and the Maori World

In granting and permitting the colonized agency, hegemony theory allows a far greater range of factors to be analysed within understandings of colonization. The ways in which sport is used by colonized peoples may therefore become as legitimate and important an area of analysis as the role of sport, or any other cultural institution, in interpretations of colonization and the role of these institutions in the colonial mission of the metropole. A recurring debate in New Zealand history, one that has shaped understandings of colonial relations, has centred on the extent to which Maori adopted or adapted European institutions. One of the key subjects of this debate has been the question of Christianity.[24] At the heart of this has been the 'fatal impact' question. This issue turns on the degree of fragility exhibited by Maori social organizational forms and, as a result, the ability of Maori to adopt to new social conditions. Fatal impact ideology is pervasive through historical writing dealing with issues of colonization and assumes that Maori, and other colonized peoples, adopt European institutions out of a realization that indigenous forms are unable to manage the new world. Often this approach is subtle, but is nevertheless premised on the assumed potency of colonizers' institutions and the frailty of the colonized.

These attitudes are revealed in elements of the mimetic analysis of colonial sports. There are clear signs of adaptation and appropriation of sports to indigenous ends in many settings. In these contexts sport is naturalized to its new setting and used for explicitly indigenous ends. Trobriand cricket is perhaps the best known example of this in the anthropological literature. In this instance cricket was adapted to local mores and used to play out village rivalries in much the same way that warfare once did.[25] In the Trobriand Islands cricket shows clear evidence of colonial(ist) and corporate appropriation – one village team are the PKs, after the Wrigley's chewing gum, because their hands are so sticky that they never drop the ball. The cricket is not played by the standard rules, but by Trobriand rules.

There is no evidence of the same development in Maori rugby, but there is clear sign of Maori using rugby for a range of different social ends. Rugby success was an instrumental factor in the recognition, in the late 1950s, of Ngati Ruahine as an *iwi* in its own right rather than a *hapu* of Ngati Ruanui.[26] Also, in Taranaki rugby is a key factor in community identification among the overwhelmingly Maori communities around the coast between New Plymouth and Parihaka. For many Maori communities in this area 'coastal rugby' is the core of being from Taranaki.[27] This use of Pakeha institutions to assert particularly Maori characteristics is nothing new. Parsonson has argued that through much of the nineteenth century Maori used Pakeha institutions to assert their *mana*.[28] Mana is a complex institution that is a measure of social standing or authority. It may be held individually or collectively, and all people or groups have mana, although some have more than others. Among Ngati Ruahine and the Taranaki *iwi*, here is clear sign of rugby as a cultural symbol being adopted and adapted to Maori needs and ends.

Other Maori institutions have adapted Pakeha sports to indigenous ends. A key institution-building tool within the Ratana church was a series of sports tournaments. The church was formed in the 1920s by T.W. Ratana, a farmer, who, after a series of visions, became recognized by many as a *mangai*, a mouthpiece of God or prophet. His flock was drawn from among the increasingly dispossessed Maori who had drifted from their tribal roots and communities. He identified tribalism as a major barrier to Maori advance or success and developed a series of strategies to build a pan-Maori church. There are significant Christian elements in it, but these have been adapted to Maori frames of reference. A key element in building a non- or pan-tribal Maori identification was a regular sports tournament, rugby for the men and tennis or netball for the women. More significantly, the Church

organized competitions in a range of sports including rugby and netball
where the main purpose was the stimulation of sport among the
young.[29] These were organized and managed by the Church, which ran
itself on a non-tribal basis. Ratana's vision remained one where Maori
participated in a Pakeha world without reference to tribal or other
social similar forms.

In other settings rugby clubs take on specifically Maori
characteristics. The Young Maori Party rugby club has a long record of
success in Poverty Bay, but has recently had to relocate to Gisborne as
a result of the movement of club members. The club was formed in
1910 and remains the oldest one in the Poverty Bay Union. Founded
by Apirana Ngata and others associated with the Young Maori Party
(YMP), the club continues to stress values running through the club
from these original members.[30] The YMP became the voice of Maori
in parliamentary politics from the early 1890s until the late 1920s
when it was challenged by an informal alliance between the Labour
Party and the Ratana Church. The club has been based on the same few
families and features some of the biggest names in Maori rugby,
notably the Nepia family. There are also strong community-building
elements to club organization, especially the key role that traditional
community leaders play in supporting and leading the life of the club.
Members hold that a vital element in the strength of the club is the total
team approach involving players, supporters and the community
networks that the club draws on.

In these three instances rugby plays significantly different roles in
Maori networks. Ranging from its use as a tool to assert traditional
social standing to a weapon in the Ratana mission to overcome what it
sees as the constraints of tribal affiliation to a community-building and
-maintaining agency, rugby in these networks has been adapted to a
series of Maori needs. These forms of Maori rugby do not feature in
colonialist frames of understanding. In this context Maori rugby is
controlled by affiliates of the New Zealand Rugby Football Union
(NZRFU) and is isolated from community relations. Although there
are Maori-specific competitions such as the Prince of Wales Cup,
Maori representative teams and Maori groupings within the NZRFU,
these formations are largely isolated from the social role of rugby in
Ngati Ruahine communities, in the Ratana Church and the community
focus on the YMP Rugby Club. These manifestations of Maori rugby
are well outside the colonialist frames of reference of most public
discussions of the game.

Rugby in New Zealand Colonialist and Popular Discourses

The first recorded instance of a Maori rugby player was Wirihana in a game in Wanganui in 1872, only two years after the first recorded game under the rugby rules in Nelson in 1870.[31] Clearly Maori involvement in the rugby world had early beginnings. The situation around Wanganui at this time did not suggest that all would be well in Maori-Pakeha relations. In the nearby Taranaki province Maori and imperial troops had been at war less than ten years beforehand. Political tensions were mounting. Maori under the leadership of Titokowaru had defeated colonial troopers in a number of battles and had threatened Wanganui only a few years before. For the time being there was a lull between the conflict resulting from the British invasion of the Waikato and the resurgence of conflict in the Wanganui–South Taranaki region.[32] Tensions and conflicts continued until well into the 1880s as the government's land-purchase programme undermined hopes for peace in the area. Te Kooti Arikirangi Te Turuki had recently been granted sanctuary in King Country where tribes from the Upper Wanganui were supporting restrictions on Pakeha access. By the end of the decade, even the so-called friendly Maori were placing increasing restrictions on Pakeha access to the river. Under these circumstances, it is hard to see Wirihana's involvement in a rugby match as the sign of a sea change in Maori-Pakeha relations or a more inclusive role for Maori within the developing colonial state. It also points to the complex and contradictory nature of colonial contact and relations between settlers and Maori.

Things have changed and the dominant view is now one where Maori are held, by many Pakeha at least, to be fully equal within the New Zealand state. Indeed, there are those who would argue that the on-going process seeking the resolution of historical injustices resulting from breaches of agreements recognizing native title is making Maori more than equal. These critics seem to be unsettled by social change and nostalgically seek a return to a long-gone world where New Zealand was held to have 'the best race relations in the world' – that is, before all these 'uppity' Maori started making a noise. The dominant role played by rugby in the received version of the New Zealand nation has played no small part in the common-sense acceptance of the equal-incorporation view.

Rugby writing, in its most common form as rugby journalism, has been crucial in facilitating and perpetuating this view. Perhaps the most significant writers influencing perceptions of Maori rugby in this regard are T.P. McLean, whose career as a rugby journalist spans over 70 years, and the late Winston McCarthy, who rose to prominence as a commentator in the 1940s and the 1950s. Both men have written extensively on rugby issues, with McLean producing many tour books and as a full-time journalist for the Auckland-based *New Zealand Herald*. McCarthy wrote only two books of note but, as the leading commentator for many years when radio ruled, shaped understandings of leading players and of provincial and national levels, including representative Maori teams.[33]

Public discussion of Maori rugby often claims a particular set of characteristics and a certain style for the game. Yet there is seldom any attempt to articulate those characteristics. Former All Black and current Member of Parliament Tutekawa Wyllie made one such attempt when he argued that:

> Maori play a particular type of rugby. It's spontaneous and exuberant. In rugby we celebrate the joy of living. So we're prepared to take risks and to do things just for the hell of it. In our day it wasn't whether we won or lost but the way we played the game. Winning isn't everything. What matters to our young people in rugby and in life is having a go and giving it your best shot. I don't know whether that's being coached out of our players. And I don't know whether New Zealand rugby has room now for our philosophy.[34]

This sense of Maori rugby as somehow freer than regular, All Black rugby that pervades so many discussions of the game is a colonialist subtext. It perpetuates the view that the natives' happy-go-lucky relationship with the world determines this performance. Few writers have gone as far as Waihori Shortland in a recent piece about growing Maori ex-All Black disillusionment over the NZRFU attitude to Maori rugby where he argued that:

> Maori rugby was a different game, with a different philosophy. It wasn't about grinding away to a master plan and being safe and efficient. It was about having a go – and enjoying all the triumphs and disasters that are a part of the approach. This was no place for the All Black selectors, unless they were there to share the fun and the spectacle.[35]

This idea of fun and spectacle recurs in discussions of Maori rugby. Former All Black Michael Clamp even went so far as to assert that 'there's a Maori traditional style that doesn't always win games'.[36] These claims to 'inventiveness'[37] could be seen as an attempt to position Maori rugby in a site not unlike that claimed in the past by the Barbarians Rugby Football Club. It is ironic that the 'noble savages' of the antipodes claim the style claimed by the club of Victorian gentlemanly amateurs in Britain.

The claims made by Wyllie and Shortland are seldom stated so boldly. In doing so, and in speaking from a Maori perspective to a largely Maori audience (*Mana* is a magazine aimed at profession-alizing Maori and hoping for a sizeable liberal Pakeha readership), they disarm some of the potential criticisms of the colonial ideology that underlie the position they adopt. The boldness of these generalizations is rare in serious journalism. More often writers individualize their commentary and in doing so expose the ideological frame. McCarthy, for instance, said of 1960s Maori All Black Mac Herewini, 'He had the typical Maori approach to the game, excellent hands, twinkling feet, a roguish dummy and was, perhaps, the most accomplished tactical kicker I have ever seen at any time... . Mac Herewini, like most Maoris [*sic*], has a delightfully puckish sense of humour.'[38] McCarthy's characterization is a clear restatement of the dominant image of the 'good' Maori, widely expressed during the 1950s and the 1960s, as opposed to the 'bad' Maori (often the same person) who was unreliable, lazy and had no aspirations. Such sentiments are not unfamiliar in other cultures, mainstream discussions of the African-American athlete during the same period being but one example.

Yet these observations on Maori rugby are relatively rare. In much rugby writing there is little about the commentary that distinguishes the style as particularly Maori in any way. Howitt spends the first 60 pages of *Haka*, admittedly a coffee-table book, presenting a report of the tour of Wales and Spain in 1982. In the manner of most rugby reporting, it consists of match reports and assessments of players and personalities. There are regular references to Maori rugby as a style or form, but little that might be held to explain or categorize it in terms of traits or characteristics. Howitt, like many others, proposes a form with no content. Maori rugby players are seen simply as other players, although the discussion is very masculinist, as if there was an unspoken agreement that they will not be identified as having Maori traits (except the ability to sing well – better than the Welsh! – and to perform exceptional haka).[39]

This ambivalence suggests that there is an unwillingness to develop or tease out ideas about Maori rugby for fear of exposing the colonialist discursive frame. This risk is great, because only 'good' Maori are ever likely to be admitted to the fold of masculinity, as being 'decent blokes'. The traits and characteristics of Maori rugby are simply left to float in the ether to be learned as knowledge of rugby increases. Implicit in this characterization of Maori rugby as 'free' and 'inventive' is the criticism that All Black rugby, or Pakeha rugby in general, is dull, staid and rigidly controlled. There is a considerable truth in this implication. One of the dominant characteristics of All Black–Springbok rugby, for instance, was the emphasis on control by the forward pack and the kicking ability of the fly-half (first five-eighth in New Zealand), particularly during the 1970s and the 1980s. There is a great tendency in New Zealand rugby writing to counter this implication with direct criticism of Springbok rugby as turgid.[40]

One of the earliest and most explicit instances of the ambiguity of Maori rugby can be seen in the 1888–89 New Zealand Natives tour of Britain and Australia. Originally planned as a Maori tour, the membership of the touring party was expanded to include five New Zealand-born Pakeha, hence the applicability of the label 'native' – they were not born at 'home'. Indications are that this is not strictly correct: Greg Ryan argues that Patrick Keogh, one of the Pakeha additions, was born in Birmingham and migrated to New Zealand at the age of four or five, while Mac McCausland was born in Victoria before moving to New Zealand when he was 15.[41] This tour is downplayed in the history of New Zealand rugby for a number of reasons. It predated the formation of the NZRFU, although its promoters were able to secure the support of the provincial rugby unions. As shown above, Sinclair downgrades the significance of the tour by arguing that the Native team was not fully representative, with the result that he sees the performance of the 1905 All Black tour of the British Isles and France as more significant.

It is more significant that this tour even took place. Ryan argues that the tour is important for a number of reasons, including factors relating to the significance of colonial sports in New Zealand, and others relating to the tour itself.[42] The introduction of football and cricket to New Zealand in the 1870s was seen as a sign of conformity to British standards and lack of racial deterioration in the colonies. More particularly, the Maori adoption of rugby and its popularity in Maori communities became proof of assimilation, co-operation and racial harmony. This was part of a growing discourse of colonial harmony that allowed zones of resistance to British rule, such as the Poverty Bay, King Country, South Taranaki and Urewera regions, as well as Maori opponents of land sales, to be marginalized and constructed as rebels. For Ryan, the 1888–89 tour is important because there was a high rate of success over a large number of games on a long trip. This importance is enhanced because it was a predominantly Maori team touring 'home', which should be seen as a sign of colonial security in the British ambit and of security of British might on the edge of empire. Finally, the composition of the team reflects on the racial attitudes of the time.

Ryan's stress on the sporting success of the tourists challenges the dominant position of the 1905 All Blacks in the mythology of New Zealand rugby, in that a predominantly Maori team played more games against British rugby with a stronger base, the Northern Union having not yet split from the establishment. The success rate was not so good, but the tour was longer, included many more games and was much harder. The success of the 1905 All Blacks, and especially of the 1924 'Invincibles' are an integral part of Pakeha masculine history. The Pakeha colonials beat the team *from* 'home' *at* 'home'. Of greater significance, however, is the way the tour reflects British imperial might. The tourists were the subject of significant press commentary in Britain. The *Daily Telegraph*, for instance, pointed to the Maori as a superior sort of 'native' and Britishness as a superior sort of colonialism when it suggested that:

> the spectacle of the noble Maori coming from different parts of the earth to play an English game against English players... is of the very essence of peace and bears a message of kindly import and goodwill towards men.[43]

Not long after *The Times* drew attention to the power and superiority of the British colonial mission, noting that:

> the colonizing race that can imbue the aboriginal inhabitants of the colonized countries with a love for its national games would seem to have solved the problem of social amalgamation in those countries.[44]

Despite this high praise, Ryan also stresses that there was concern about the players' abilities to live up to the expectations that they were 'civilized'. This was a particular one in Britain, where, although the public school ethos and traditions exerted considerable influence, rugby's strengths were outside those areas of dominance. Public school old boys were simply not present everywhere and sporting success took on different values where their influence was lacking.

In the north of England winning became a sign of community value and worth.[45] Elsewhere, including colonial New Zealand, sporting success was becoming a way to assert community identity. In this context there is a tendency in the colonialist discourses surrounding this tour to find fault in the Natives' standards of civilization, as well as to suggest that the high standards achieved by the Natives (especially the Maori members of the team) could be undermined by the ethos of northern working-class rugby. As the tour progressed, the Natives were held to be rough players, like the northern players. The result was that the Native team was caught in the class tensions of English rugby between what became the Northern Union and the public school ethos of the London-based RFU.

The fear of both the promoters and of many British observers was that this Native team would not be 'native enough'. Ryan pays particular attention to this problem in his consideration of the tour. Popular media discussion of Ryan's work focused on this question.[46] The tour promoters had hoped to use the exoticism of the Natives as a drawing card.[47] Ryan specifically points to commercial tours by Maori, arguing that the English were not used to seeing Maori. In stressing visits by Hongi Hika (1820), Moehanga (1807), Tamihana Te Rauparaha (1852) and others as late as 1864, as well as a commercial tour in 1829–30 by Whiti and Ariki Toa of Ngati Maru, Ryan sees as crucial to the impetus of the tour that its promoters expected to enhance the draw and their income by playing on Maori exoticism. The promoters were unsuccessful in this. It seems that the English expectations were for something far more exotic (the popular press featured images of pseudo-Sudanese 'fuzzy wuzzies' and South Seas 'cannibals') that did not eventuate when it turned out the Maori team (Natives) were just 'dusky' players of the English game. Ironically, the specifically Maori elements of the tour, such as the haka, were seen as silly or a 'pantomime', with suggestions that it was a gimmick.[48] Even those elements of the tour were soon abandoned, as Ryan argues that the tourists realized that to make money and fund the tour they would need to rely on a tight schedule and superior playing. It is not correct to suggest, as Ryan does, that the responses to the 'Maoriness' of the team were the result of 'ignorance and misunderstanding' rather than racism.[49] To adopt this position is to misunderstand the nature of colonialist discourses and the ambiguous position of Maori success in rugby. It is also a failure to recognize the implications of the tension between the haka as 'gimmick' and the role of the types of haka used before sports matches in issuing a challenge.

Over a hundred years later questions relating to haka are much different. The journalist Hugh Barlow poses the question as being not whether a test match would be the same without the haka, but whether haka would be the same without the All Blacks.[50] The particular haka used by the contemporary All Blacks, *Ka Mate*, has been described as the most abused and maligned of all haka.[51] Yet despite this maligned status, *Ka Mate* is the only haka many Pakeha have ever heard; and perhaps some believe it is the only haka. It is also a potent cultural icon, especially when seen by those abroad. It is not understood by many that haka of the type performed before sports matches have a particular purpose. Called *ngeri,* these haka are short and are used to flex sinews and summon blood to prepare for battle. In this way a haka is a suitable test-match prelude. Early colonists, especially missionaries, attacked haka as filthy or debasing in their efforts to 'civilize' the Maori. Haka became a potent symbol of Maori power and a popular folklore of haka has emerged. Stories are told of the Pioneer Battalion, the Maori unit during World War I, performing haka before battle, and of the fear expressed by German soldiers at the sounds of the challenge. Walker has suggested that haka were first used in sports settings by the 1888–89 Natives team, adopted by the 1905 team and used ever since. In this way, he says, a 'tradition was born from the amalgamation of two cultures'.[52]

The use of haka in All Black contexts is still not straightforward. Writing in the early 1990s, Robert Macdonald criticized the use of haka by all Pakeha teams touring South Africa. In citing Macdonald, Zavos disagrees, arguing that the use of haka, which he says was adopted in the 1890s when racist attitudes were widespread, is a sign of a colour-blind, non-racial rugby community.[53] Walker's assessment of adoption by amalgamation is perhaps too generous. A more valid reading informed by the perspective advanced by Zavos would be to see this use of haka as an integral part of the amalgamation of sporting and martial motifs at the base of Pakeha masculinity and as an incorporating discourse building a hegemonic colonialist discursive frame.

This ambiguous relationship between Maori and dominant masculinity is clearly seen in other aspects of the 1888–89 Natives tour. The 'Maoriness' of the team was not sufficient to make them exotic enough to draw crowds and their style of rugby was not seen as civil, or genteel, enough for them to be treated as legitimate players within the dominant framework of public school and imperial athleticism. The promoters of the tour struggled to make money, the tour was lengthened, more games were added and costs were cut.[54] Sinclair's construction of the parameters of hegemonic masculinity clearly and explicitly excludes the 1888–89 tour as an icon in favour of the 1905 tour. This logic seems flawed: Sinclair's desire to promulgate a particularist nationality within the Empire suggests that the earlier tour should be a more potent icon, given the success enjoyed by the 1906 Springboks during their tour of Britain. His case would be strengthened by arguing that the 1888–89 tour was earlier, longer, harder and relatively successful.

Other writers have been more generous than Sinclair. McLean has labelled the Natives tour an 'immovable cornerstone of all New Zealand rugby'.[55] Although stressing its importance, especially in terms of significance to Maori, he also places his understanding of the role of Maori rugby firmly in the hegemonic discourses centred on the myth of the best race relations in the world. In discussing the 1888–89 tour, he argues:

> That, surely, was one of the romantic developments of all sport – the mingling, within so short a space, of natives and newcomers in an expedition which, while not truly representative, identified New Zealand Rugby to the world long before any other nation's game had become known outside its own shores. How different might have been the history of South Africa, one cannot help thinking, if the peoples native to that country had been permitted and encouraged, as were Maoris, to join the sport brought in by the foreign settlers.[56]

His argument is a common case in rugby writing. He sees rugby as a tool not for making one people, but 'into two peoples mutually growing and mingling and concentrating their efforts into the good of one community – of which a not insubstantial part was to turn out to be Rugby.'[57] More recently Zavos has made the same case in a discussion of the form and nature of the anti-apartheid movement – the dominant focus of which was rugby contact with South Africa. He argues that rugby has traditionally been more inclusive than the anti-apartheid movement. In doing so he quite properly points to the exclusion of Maori from hierarchies of the state, from leadership positions in the Church (failing to note that the Anglicans have had a Maori Bishop of Aotearoa for many years) and argues that neither of the major anti-apartheid organizations (HART – Halt All Racist Tours – or CARE – the Citizens Association for Racial Equality) ever 'had Maori in leadership positions'.[58] In making this argument, Zavos assumes that HART and CARE equalled the anti-apartheid movement. This was not the case. These organizations certainly provided the structural core, but every major protest action since the 1960 All Black tour of South Africa saw the development of broad oppositional coalitions where Maori played key leadership roles.

After the Natives tour of 1888–89, Maori were poorly represented in nationally representative teams for quite some time. McCarthy notes that, even though the first tour arranged by the NZRFU in 1893 included four Maori, three of whom were in the 1888 tour, it is difficult to find much about early Maori players, even just after World War I.[59] Furthermore, few Maori played nationally representative rugby between 1894 and 1910 when the first official Maori team was selected. This question of identification is vexed. McCarthy reveals elements of the nature of New Zealand's particular colonialist discursive mode with his recurrent comments on players who did not appear to be Maori. This question of physical appearance poses questions for the understanding of Maori rugby as a style: if a player is not obviously Maori, does an audience understanding of playing style, within the terms of the generic codes for Maori rugby, change?

The dominant ideological theme running through these popular discussions of Maori in/and rugby is one shaped by and shaping colonialist perspectives. There is seldom any discussion of questions of masculinity or even any hint that masculinist issues may be of concern. In maintaining these silences, popular rugby writing grants legitimacy to the all-one-people view of New Zealand. McCarthy does so in his recurrent mention of Maori players who do not appear to be Maori, Zavos stresses rugby's inclusiveness, while McLean stresses the 'natural gifts of strength, courage and audacity' that have seen Maori readily and successfully 'assimilated into rugby and [become] proficient at rugby'.[60] In these ways the potential challenge to the hegemonic masculinity of Maori rugby proficiency is circumvented.

Of the contemporary rugby writers, Zavos is perhaps the most proficient exponent of this hegemonic discourse.[61] Zavos draws on his childhood experience, blending hegemonic masculinist and colonialist ideologies with the nostalgic frame of reminiscences of youth. As a young journalist, the realization of the significance of being Greek and playing first-class cricket came as an epiphany. This significance is framed in terms of his years of practising cricket (or rugby for other non-Anglos) as being about outsiders becoming insiders:

> The sports arena was my path, perhaps my only way, to respectability and self-knowledge. Thinking about this, I realized that sporting achievement is – or should be – colour blind, because it is (or should be) focused on what a person does, not his or her background, culture, class, religion or looks. Kids who try to make it in society through sport, know this instinctively.[62]

He extrapolates from this to argue for the social merit of rugby as a force of good, claiming that 'rugby in New Zealand, from the 1880s, provided the paradigm for how New Zealand society should have opened itself up to the Maori community last century and this century'.[63] This ideological segue from immigrant Greek to indigenous Maori subsumes enormous difference. In practising his cricket to become an insider, Zavos's relationship with the dominant Anglo community was fundamentally different and the terms for the negotiation of inclusion were to be phrased in ways other than those for Maori. Maori were included in New Zealand. They are indigenous and cannot be naturalized elsewhere. When Maori signed the Treaty of Waitangi with the Crown in 1840, newly arrived Lieutenant-Governor William Hobson proclaimed, 'He iwi tahi tatou, we are all one people.' This dominant ideology creates a different relationship between Maori and Pakeha than that between Maori and non-Pakeha Tauiwi.[64] Accordingly, this attempt by Zavos to create a parallel between migrant sporting success producing social inclusion and Maori sporting ability or success is flawed.

Zavos holds firmly to the notions of a rugby community that operated a doctrine of inclusion rather than assimilation, integration or bribery. Despite this, he is unable to see the contradiction between this assertion and the evidence he marshals to build his case. The elision of this evidential contradiction is a key tactic in the construction of hegemonic discourses. It allows the naturalization of a common-sense view through the assertion of a view that the simple power of claim overrides that contradiction. For instance, he cites King's claim that 'apart from warfare, the one national activity to which Maoris [sic] contributed in a measure resembling their full potential was rugby football',[65] which he endorses by pointing to the leadership roles Maori have held in rugby from the outset. To grant this extra credibility, he draws a parallel between Maori as All Black captains and Frank Worrell's captaincy of the West Indian cricket team. There is no recognition of black exclusion from leadership positions in West Indian cricket before Worrell in the 1950s, or of the political struggle over cricket and colonialism in the West Indies.[66] He continues to invoke the suggestion from writers such as King that rugby provided a place where a positive sense of 'Maoriness' existed in Maori communities, and where Pakeha could see Maori activity they understood and of which they approved, or Sinclair's argument that rugby stimulated national pride and brought people together. Zavos caricatures and attacks Phillips as anti-rugby, claiming that Phillips sees the sport as the cause of brutalized Pakeha male. In making this assertion he asks why rugby did not do the same to Maori men. In another instance of evidential elision, he points to Maori who held positions of power in rugby (as team captains, but significantly not managers or coaches) but claims that Phillips argues rugby was a cause of Maori exclusion from social power. There is a narrow focus here where social power is equated with positions of responsibility or leadership in a rugby team. At a time when New Zealand is starting, gradually, to come to terms with a history of dispossession and invasion that is colonialism and its consequences in high rates of Maori poverty and other poor social indicators, this argument is ingenuous in the extreme. Overall, Zavos sees rugby as always having been a force for unity in New Zealand. This is an excellent case of masculinist and colonialist hegemonic discourse. Significantly, he ignores both the social context and the role rugby plays in that framework. He does not ask about the implications of King's comment that Maori only held high public profile in rugby and war, or in what spheres of public life Maori were consequently not high profile. In asking what characteristics of these spheres facilitate Maori elevation and success, attention returns to colonialist discourses of the noble savage and the warrior.

King points to the problem that Zavos ignores: in Maori rugby Pakeha could see activity in areas that they both understood and of which they approved. Maori, by their savage nature, were supposed to fight – in war or its peacetime substitute, rugby football. Neither required intellectual work or significant social competence, but rather brawn and physical ability. In nineteenth-century social and racial thought, significant elements of which continue in the present, Maori were childlike, in need of guidance and direction, incapable of full social membership or citizenship. They were a warrior people and had fought courageously, but of course unsuccessfully, against the might of the British Empire. The tales of colonization are peppered with rhetoric of Maori ability, chivalry and bravery. None of the myths quite admit that for the most part Maori were militarily superior to the British, that they were economically dominant in much of the North Island for the 1840s and the 1850s, that at the end of the wars in which the British are held to have defeated Maori there remained an independent zone larger than Belgium in the middle of the North Island, or any of the other indicators of Maori strength.[67]

These myths of empire are at the core of Pakeha understandings of Maori abilities and their place in the world. They are also the basis of Pakeha hegemonic masculinity such that any rereading of the image of Maori *vis-à-vis* this image threatens that hegemony. Maori rugby success could be admitted comfortably but for one cultural characteristic: as the defeated people, as the colonized they are gendered female by colonial discourses. This suggests a range of significant questions about Maori rugby and empire relating more broadly to the presence of a potent indigenous community[68] and suggests that, following the work of Sara Mills,[69] seeing colonialism as a cultural process as much as an assertion of metropolitan might is important in future analyses of sport and imperialism. In addition, a reconsideration of the process of sports diffusion which factors in emulation and accomodation as well as penetration and assimilation in colonial and imperial settings would also seem an important approach to adopt in the further study of such phenomena. Indeed, in much of the Empire the colonies were governed by small British elites who relied on the support of indigenous agents to maintain political power. An approach that focuses on a hegemonic process suggests that colonists do not have diabolical powers of control and grants the colonized a sense of agency. Analyses based around hegemonic processes and the notion of a cultural war of position can help to develop an understanding of the significance of events where the colonized and formerly colonized beat their former colonizers, and often in settings that signal allegiance and superiority. It can also explain ways that sport is often a symbolic weapon in struggles for cultural political power as well as a tool in the manufacture of national(ist) consciousness. Finally, it can help to account for why the integrative consequences of modern sport are more powerful than the divisive effects.

The broad policy approach toward Maori during the latter part of the nineteenth century focused on assimilation. It was intended that a Maori elite would be developed that was able to function fully in the Pakeha world. This elite was to be British. Critical evaluations of Maori masculinity are non-existent in New Zealand scholarship, for the main part because Maori are faced with a huge array of public policy issues towards which most attention is directed. Accordingly, current works in the area have a tendency to produce implicit questions simply because there is so much to be done. In suggesting possible limitations to recent work in this area, the intention here is to clearly indicate possibilities for research that connect with trends in scholarship in other communities and (post-) colonial environments. For the time being, in New Zealand the more appropriate question may be the extent to which martial imagery of 'native tradition' may be used to legitimate sporting forms and styles adopted. The haka and the noble savage can be seen as valid icons of masculine Maoriness, in

Pakeha terms. It is likely that the brutality retained in the savage part of nobility allows the legitimation of masculinist sporting endeavours.

In short, then, Maori rugby prowess is constructed and legitimated in terms approved by Pakeha masculinity. As the cases of the Ngati Ruahine hapu, the Ratana Church and the YMP Rugby Club show, this is not the only way Maori rugby is legitimated and is not its only social role. The potency of these dominant masculinities limits the application of Maori rugby in other contexts and prevents significant disruption of masculinity's homosociality. Maori men can never be admitted to this legitimate masculine world on terms other than those determined by its cultural mores. They can be admitted as rugby players and as soldiers. It is the rare Maori man who is legitimate in terms of masculinities' codes who has neither of these practices in his background. As the colonized group, dominant masculinity classifies Maori as woman. They disrupt the group by bringing a different set of social and cultural practices that are well outside the expected norms. Pakeha masculinity cannot manage that degree of disruption – its defence of homosociality and colonialist discursive frames is too intense.

NOTES

I am grateful to John Bale for his comments on an earlier version of this paper.

1. Terry McLean, 'Maoridom's Mighty Warriors', *Tu Tangata*, 9 December 1982, p. 5.
2. New Zealanders of European descent.
3. J.O.C Phillips, 'Rugby, War and the Mythology of the New Zealand Male', *New Zealand Journal of History*, Vol.18, No.2 (1984), pp. 83–103; *A Man's Country: the Image of the Pakeha Male. A History* (Auckland, 2nd edn, 1996). Phillips's case is outlined in his essay 'The Hard Man: Rugby and the Formation of Male Identity in New Zealand', in John Nauright and Timothy J.L. Chandler (eds), *Making Men: Rugby and Masculine Identity* (London, 1996), pp. 70–90, which is in large part excerpted from *A Man's Country*.
4. Frank Sargeson, 'The Hole that Jack Dug', *The Stories of Frank Sargeson* (Auckland, 1964), pp. 243–50.
5. Sargeson, 'The Hole that Jack Dug', pp. 247–8.
6. E.W. Taylor, *Why the All Blacks Triumphed* (London, 1906), p. 37, cited in Phillips, 'Rugby, War and the Mythology', p. 91.
7. Nicholas Thomas, *Colonialism's Culture: Anthropology, Travel and Government* (Cambridge, 1994); Sara Mills, *Discourses of Difference: An Analysis of Women's Travel Writing and Colonization* (London, 1991).
8. Thomas, *Colonialism's Culture*, p. ix.
9. James Belich, *The New Zealand Wars and the Victorian Interpretation of Racial Conflict* (Auckland, 1986).
10. See Ranginui Walker, *Ka Whawhai Tonu Matou* (Auckland, 1989); and Lindsay Cox *Kotahitanga: the Search for Maori Political Unity* (Auckland, 1993).

11. Family and extended family.
12. Thomas, *Colonialism's Culture*, p. 28.
13. Mills, *Discourses of Difference*, p. 58.
14. Ibid., p. 59.
15. Homi Bhabha, 'Of Mimicry and Man: the Ambivalence of Colonial Discourse', in Annette Michelson, Rosalind Krauss, Douglas Crimp and Joan Copjec (eds), *October: the First Decade* (Cambridge, MA, 1987), pp. 318, 320, 322.
16. Thomas, *Colonialism's Culture*, p. 64.
17. Keith Sinclair, *A Destiny Apart: New Zealand's Search for National Identity* (Wellington, 1986), p. 13.
18. Sinclair, *A Destiny Apart*, pp. 143–55.
19. Sinclair's figure is wrong, there were five Pakeha on the tour.
20. Greg Ryan, *Forerunners of the All Blacks: the 1888–89 New Zealand Native Football Team in Britain, Australia and New Zealand* (Christchurch, 1993).
21. See Christopher Pugsley, *Gallipoli: the New Zealand Story* (Auckland, 1984), especially the Foreword by Lt-Gen. Sir Leonard Thornton, pp. 7–8.
22. For a discussion of these issues in contemporary contexts see Paul Spoonley, 'Constructing Ourselves: the Postcolonial Politics of Pakeha', in Margaret Wilson and Anna Yeatman (eds), *Justice and Identity: Antipodean Practices* (Wellington, 1995), pp. 96–115 and Malcolm MacLean, 'The Silent Centre: Where Are Pakeha in Biculturalism?', *Continuum*, Vol.10, No.1 (1996), pp. 108–20.
23. These problems are posed in a number of analyses working within a hegemony theory approach. A competent summary of the issues is presented in Jeremy MacClancy, 'Sport, Identity and Ethnicity', in MacClancy (ed.), *Sport, Identity and Ethnicity* (Oxford, 1996), pp. 1–20.
24. There is a useful overview and discussion of the issues in this debate in James Belich, *Making Peoples: a History of the New Zealanders from Polynesian Settlement to the End of the Nineteenth Century* (Auckland, 1996), pp. 217–23.
25. Trobriand cricket was memorably portrayed in Gerry Leach's 1975 film *Trobriand Cricket*. See Edmund Leach, 'Review of "Trobriand Cricket"', *RAIN*, No. 9 (1975), p. 6; H.A. Powell, 'Cricket in Kiriwana', *The Listener*, 4 September, 1952, pp. 384–5; Annette Weiner, 'Review of Trobriand Cricket', *American Anthropologist*, Vol.79 (1975), pp. 506–7.
26. I am grateful to Emma Wethey for this information. The best translation of *hapu* is 'sub-tribe' while *iwi* is best understood as 'tribe'. Neither of these words does justice to the subtlety of the terms and neither properly conveys the significance of this shift from *hapu* to *iwi* status.
27. Mereana Hond, of the Taranaki Iwi Muru Raupatu Working Party and Te Kawa a Maui/School of Maori Studies, Te Whare Wananga o te Upoko o te Ika a Maui/Victoria University of Wellington, has explained the significance of coastal rugby to the Taranaki *iwi* to me.
28. Ann Parsonson, 'The Pursuit of Mana', in W.H. Oliver and B.R. Williams (eds), *The Oxford History of New Zealand* (Wellington, 1981), pp. 140–67. Parsonson has written an entirely new chapter for the second edition, although this first edition chapter remains one of the most incisive commentaries on Maori-Pakeha relations during the nineteenth century.
29. See for instance J. McLeod Henderson, *Ratana: the Origins and the Story of the Movement* (Wellington, 1963), p. 66.
30. Anon 'Kia Kaha … Kia Toa – YMP', *Turanganui a Kiwa – Pipiwharauroa*, No.1 (October 1993), p. 10.
31. David Somerville, *Encyclopedia of Rugby Union* (London, 1997), p. 59.
32. For a discussion of these events, see Belich, *The New Zealand Wars*, especially

pp. 235–57, 267–75; Belich, *I Shall Not Die: Titokowaru's War, 1868–1869* (Wellington, 1989); and Belich, *Making Peoples*, especially pp. 229–46; Judith Binney, *Redemption Songs: a Life of Te Kooti Arikirangi Te Turuki* (Auckland, 1996), especially pp. 209–311.

33. Winston McCarthy, *Haka!: the All Black Story* (London, 1968); and McCarthy and Bob Howitt, *Haka: the Maori Rugby Story* (Auckland,1983).

34. Waihori Shortland, 'Paradise Lost', *Mana*, No.1 (January 1993), p. 47.

35. Ibid., p. 46.

36. Michael Romanos, 'South Africa Tour Clouds Clamp the Champ', *Tu Tangata*, No.22 (February 1985), p. 13.

37. Bob Howitt, 'The Nathan Influence', in McCarthy and Howitt, *Haka*, p. 137.

38. Winston McCarthy, 'When the Game Went Flat', in McCarthy and Howitt, *Haka*, pp. 114–15.

39. Bob Howitt, 'The 1982 Tour of Wales and Spain', in McCarthy and Howitt, *Haka*, p. 16.

40. Among the many instances of this criticism, see Spiro Zavos, *Winters of Revenge: the Bitter Rivalry between the All Blacks and the Springboks* (Auckland, 1997); the tendency is even more apparent in Graham Hutchings, *A Score to Settle: a Celebration of All Black–Springbok Rugby, 1921–1996* (Wellington, 1997).

41. Ryan, *Forerunners of the All Blacks*, pp. 13, 29 and 136.

42. Greg Ryan, 'Rugby Football and Society: the "New Zealand Native" Tour of 1888–89', *Historical News* (October 1992), pp. 12–14.

43. *Daily Telegraph*, 28 September 1888, cited in Ryan, 'Rugby Football and Society', p. 13.

44. *The Times*, 4 October 1888.

45. Ibid., see also James Martens, 'Rugby, Class, Amateurism and Manliness: the Case of Rugby in Northern England, 1871–1895', in Nauright and Chandler, *Making Men*, pp. 32–49.

46. Eirwen Harris, 'Race Used to Exploit First Rugby Tourists', *Dominion Sunday Times*, 27 July 1990.

47. This is discussed in some detail in Ryan, *Forerunners of the All Blacks*, pp. 43–55.

48. This haka was not the currently used *Ka mate* but included a more comprehensive cultural performance. The reference to the haka as 'pantomime' was a comment by the British rugby administrator Frank Marshall, cited by Ryan in *Forunners of the All Blacks*, p. 52.

49. Ibid., p. 53.

50. Hugh Barlow, 'More to a Haka than Meets the Eye', *Dominion*, 28 June 1996.

51. Timoti Karetu, *Haka! Te Tohu o te Whenua Rangatira: the Dance of a Noble People* (Auckland, 1993), cited in Barlow, 'More to a Haka'.

52. Ranginui Walker, 'Te Karanga: Haka History', *Metro* (Auckland), October 1996, p. 125.

53. Spiro Zavos, 'Kea Kaha', *Metro*, January 1992, pp. 74–80.

54. Ryan, *Forerunners of the All Blacks*.

55. Terry McLean, 'Whither Maori Rugby: a Background to Rugby's Special Affinity for the Maori', *Tu Tangata*, 9 December 1982, p. 18.

56. Terry McLean, 'Maori Rugby Emerging as a Force', *Tu Tangata*, 9 December 1982, p. 11.

57. Ibid.

58. Zavos, *Winters of Revenge*, pp. 192–3.

59. Winston McCarthy, '1888 and All That', in McCarthy and Howitt, *Haka: The Maori Rugby Story*, pp. 62-80.

60. McLean, 'Maori Rugby Emerging', p. 13.
61. Zavos, *Winters of Revenge*, pp. 74–80.
62. Ibid., p. 77.
63. Ibid., pp. 77–8.
64. Immigrants, or strangers. Properly speaking, all migrants could be considered Pakeha, but the term has developed to label an ethnic group of European descent even though for most this is at best a fictive ethnicity. Tauiwi, usually used to mean strangers, has come to be applied to all non-Maori as a collective, which then comprises Pakeha, tangata Pasifika (people of the Pacific) and other groups. This creates a deep seated tension between notions of multiculturalism and biculturalism largely resulting from poor analyses of the basis of tensions in ethnic relations. The dominance of liberal and individualist analytical frames individualizes tensions in ethnic relations rather than seeing the problem in the institutions of colonialism. New Zealand professes to be building a bicultural nation. This is a common element of much government policy and is key to the process of settling claims against breaches of the Treaty signed in 1840 between Maori and the British that facilitated British colonization. For discussion of these issues, see Hauraki Greenland, 'Ethnicity as Ideology', in Paul Spoonley, Cluny Macpherson, David Pearson and Charles Sedgwick (eds), *Tauiwi: Racism and Ethnicity in New Zealand* (Palmerston North, 1984), pp 86–102; Pearson, *A Dream Deferred: the Origins of Ethnic Conflict in New Zealand* (Wellington, 1990); Andrew Sharp, *Justice and the Maori: Maori Claims in New Zealand Political Argument in the 1980s* (Auckland, 2nd edn, 1997); Sharp, 'Why Be Bicultural', in Margaret Wilson and Anna Yeatman (eds), *Justice & Identity: Antipodean Practices* (Wellington, 1995), pp. 116–33; and MacLean, 'The Silent Centre'.
65. Michael King, *Maori: a Photographic and Social History* (Auckland, revised edn, 1996), p. 199.
66. See for instance C.L.R. James, *Beyond a Boundary* (London, 1995); Hilary Beckles and Brian Stoddart (eds), *Liberation Cricket: West Indies Cricket Culture* (Manchester, 1995); Stoddart, 'Cricket, Social Formation and Cultural Continuity in Barbados: a Preliminary Ethnohistory', *Journal of Sport History*, Vol.14, No.3 (1987), pp. 317–40; Stoddart, 'Sport, Cultural Imperialism and Colonial Response in the British Empire', *Comparative Studies in Society & History*, Vol.30, No.4 (1988), pp. 649–73; and Stoddart, 'Caribbean Cricket: the Role of Sport in Emerging Small-nation Politics', *International Journal*, Vol.43, No.3 (1988), pp. 618–42.
67. For an overview of these issues, see Belich, *Making Peoples*, on the myths of war, pp. 229–46; and *The New Zealand Wars*, pp. 291–335; on the Maori economy, pp. 213–17.
68. There are a number of useful case studies in J.A. Mangan (ed.), *The Cultural Bond: Sport, Empire and Society* (London, 1992).
69. Mills, *Discourses of Difference*, pp. 67–107.

2

Rugby, Carnival, Masculinity and Identities in 'Coloured' Cape Town

John Nauright

Rugby, Race and Empire

As with the Maori in New Zealand, black South Africans also have a long history of participation in rugby. Yet, beyond these two societies and the South Pacific Islands of the British Empire, rugby never became as universal as did soccer and cricket in the rest of the Empire. Tony Mason recounts how modern football began in India with the Calcutta Football Club initially playing rugby between 1872 and 1876 and again briefly after 1884. Rugby never took off in India, however, as Indian clubs played soccer by the mid-1880s.[1] Mason does not tell us why rugby was abandoned, although he does note that the interests of the majority of British troops stationed in India were focused on soccer by the 1880s since many clubs and competitions had developed in Britain. Only in Yorkshire and parts of Lancashire was rugby played in a similar fashion with cup competitions and moves towards professionalism.

Rugby became one of the main sports included in private school sporting actitivies throughout the Empire in the latter part of the nineteenth century, but by the early twentieth century most missionaries and officials concentrated their efforts on soccer and cricket as sports best utilized as part of the moral education and as social outlets for indigenous populations. As a result we know much more about the social histories of cricket and soccer in the Empire and the diffusion of these sports among local populations, while what we know of rugby has, to date, been confined largely to the settler dominions of South Africa, New Zealand and Australia.[2] Yet rugby became a significant social and cultural activity among the Maori in New Zealand as we have seen, among Pacific Islanders and for black South Africans, particularly in the regions of the Western and Eastern Cape where missionary educational efforts were most pronounced by the latter part of the nineteenth century and where educated African and mixed-race or 'Coloured' elites emerged steeped in British imperial culture.

Unlike New Zealand and the Pacific Islands, black rugby players were denied access to international playing fields for most of the twentieth century after the beginnings of black rugby in the 1880s. Thus rugby for black South Africans more closely resembled West Indian cricket in structural terms than rugby in the south Pacific. Before the 1990s the historic exclusion of black rugby players from rugby structures controlled by whites or from participating in the same competitions as whites has meant that most white South Africans have assumed that rugby is not much followed among blacks who prefer soccer. Several recent studies of sport and of rugby in South Africa have begun to demonstrate that the history of rugby among black South Africans is nearly as long as for whites and their passion for rugby in the Western and Eastern Capes in particular has rivalled that of whites.[3]

In the context of this book I explore what happened within rugby and rugby culture when it diffused to black communities in South Africa, with an emphasis on the role of rugby in the predominantly working-class Coloured communities of Cape Town. In particular, rugby developed as a key site for the reproduction of a masculinity centred on codes of behaviour different from those prevalent among whites and in white rugby. Indeed, in discussing black rugby in South Africa, as with white rugby, while we can generalize about meanings at a broad level, it is only through detailed analysis of the local that differences are clearly evident. Rugby for much of its history was not only played in segregated competitions by blacks and whites, but within black South Africa several competitions emerged where others were excluded on the basis of race or religion. While early sporting structures among black South Africans tended to exclude on the basis of education or on cultural behaviour (centred on concepts of British 'civilization'), by the early 1900s separate organizations and competitions existed for Africans and 'Coloureds';[4] and, among Coloureds in Cape Town, two associations emerged, one that was dominated by Muslims and one that excluded them from playing. In this chapter I turn to explore how rugby developed as a cultural activity for Coloureds in Cape Town and how rugby, as played, developed particular masculine practices different from those present in white rugby, although clearly shaped by the form and content of rugby as a sport.

As with the analysis of sport in most societies at the local level, there are often few records and one must rely on hopes for reasonable reporting in the local media or on oral history. It is fortunate, however, that one of the Coloured rugby organizations in Cape Town has minute

books largely intact dating from 1918 (although when I examined them
in 1995 they were stored in the open in an adminstrator's garage). As
such, we can analyse debates and resolutions along with press reports
and oral history in constructing a sense of what rugby has meant in the
Coloured communities of Cape Town and what changes to the culture
of the game took place there. I provide a general history of Coloured
rugby and then focus on three incidents that illustrate the role of the
game as a definer of social distinctions and masculine expression. The
first of these examines the trans-gendered appeal of rugby as a social
and cultural activity in inner city Cape Town. Annual charity matches
became a focus of community carnivalesque expression only
surpassed by the annual New Year carnival celebrations themselves.
The second is an investigation of a player in the non-Muslim union
who was suspected of being a Muslim. The third looks at the nature of
violence attributed to Muslim teams and how this reinforced a sense of
masculinity in a community surrounded by non-Muslims, both
Coloured and non-Coloured. I conclude with a discussion of rugby's
history and culture in nostalgic memories of community as it existed
in Cape Town before the demolition of District Six in the early 1970s.

Performing Rugby and Performing Identity in Cape Town

Cape Town was the first European city established in Africa and was
founded soon after the Dutch East India Company set up a refuelling
station there in 1652 for their ships going to and from India and
Indonesia. By the early 1700s there was a thriving local community of
European settlers, slaves from Africa, Asia and Madagascar and
mixed-race people who began to appear soon after the Dutch arrival.
After the slaves were freed by the British (who took over the Cape as
a result of the Napoloenic Wars) in 1838, many flocked to Cape Town
to work on the docks and in other industries. Over 5,000 settled in two
areas on opposite sides of the city centre, the Bo-Kaap, which was
predominantly Muslim, and District Six, a polyglot of cultures and
races. District Six was South Africa's first real working-class area and
was already overcrowded when it was proclaimed as a district of Cape
Town in 1867. In 1936 the population of District Six stood at 22,440,
rising to over 40,000 by the early 1950s. Another 5,000 to 7,000 lived
in the Bo-Kaap. These two areas became the core for the early
development of rugby among Coloureds. White rugby in Cape Town
first appeared in the 1860s, with clubs being formed in the 1870s.
Coloured men soon followed with the first clubs being established in
1886. Two of the most famous clubs, Roslyns and Wanderers, were
founded in this year. In addition, the Western Province Coloured

Rugby Football Union (WPCRFU) was founded by Roslyns and three
other clubs in the same year and a national union also appeared, being
established at a meeting of delegates in Kimberley. Wanderers did not
join the WPCRFU but instead formed another union with new clubs in
1898, the City and Suburban Rugby Union (CSRU). The CSRU
banned Muslims from playing in its competition until the early 1960s
while the WPCRFU was predominantly, but by no means exclusively,
Muslim.[5] By the 1920s the cultural pattern of Coloured rugby in Cape
Town was becoming highly developed. Teams met on street corners to
discuss strategy, to select for upcoming matches, to analyse previous
matches and to socialize generally. Each team had a particular street
corner in the District or Bo-Kaap where players and keen followers
would meet. Official club and union meetings were often held in the
homes of better-off club members. Though the working class areas of
Cape Town were the areas where Afrikaans first developed as a
separate language, club and union meetings were nearly always held in
English, following formal structure and protocol.[6] Matches played by
WPCRFU teams were held at Green Point Common and later at the
stadium at Green Point Track in Green Point, within walking distance
of both District Six and the Bo-Kaap. District Six was a vibrant area of
cultural activity with sports playing an important part in it. Of all
sports, though, rugby was by far the most important. The former
school principal Gassan Emeran says that culture, politics and even life
itself revolved around rugby, which was a 'second religion' for the
Muslims of the District and the Bo-Kaap, while a former teacher
Magomoed 'Meneer' Effendi states 'rugby brought the whole
community together'.[7] The 'community' came together through rugby
most notably in the annual Rag charity matches that began in 1936.
These matches were held annually at the Green Point Track between
Young Stars and Caledonian Roses, usually with capacity crowds of up
to 10,000 and more in attendance. A whole day of activities was
planned around rag matches. Other than the Carnival that takes place
each New Year's in Cape Town, where troops dress up in bright
colours, carry colourful umbrellas and perform song and dance
routines, the Charity Rag match, as well as matches between the
WPCRFU and the CSRU, was the focal point of local community
celebration. In some years a women's match was played to start the
day, followed by each grade of team from the two clubs playing,
culminating in the highlight of the day, the first team match. In
preparation for the match each year women knitted special team
uniforms and scarves, cooked food and the players and supporters
learned new songs. In a classic piece of carnivalesque the two clubs

adopted the colours and team songs of the Universities of Cape Town (Eikies) and Stellenbosch (Maties), whose annual match was a highlight of the local white rugby calendar. The day also was modelled on the annual universities match. As with Carnival celebrations, Rag was a cultural event allowing for release, unfettered enjoyment and conviviality and was a focus for a community whose members faced discriminatory and sometimes hostile situations in daily life. As Bakhtin argues, for participants in carnival activities, they do not merely experience the event, but *'live* in it'.[8] Unlike Bakhtinian carnival, though, there was no social mixing among people who would usually be separated hierarchically, these celebrations remained of and for the Coloured communities of inner-city Cape Town. While Rag matches were causes for celebration and benefited local charity, the rugby playing itself was as vigorous as in other matches. In the 1968 match four players were sent off for punching, although punching was by no means common in reports of other Rag matches.[9]

Rugby, Community and the Carnivalesque

In his study of cricket and culture in the Caribbean, Richard Burton situates cricket within a series of cultural practices including street corner life and carnival. He argues that 'cricket, carnival and the intricate patterns of West Indian street culture become overlapping expressions of a single underlying social, cultural and psychological complex'.[10] Cricket in this context becomes a social drama where the line between participants and observers becomes blurred in an 'organic' performance ritual. Ultimately, cricket and carnival are seen by Burton as having the power to unite in Trinidad. While one must be careful in analysing cultural pehonomena as diverse as rugby and cricket and spatial places as far apart as Cape Town and Trinidad, it is useful to think about black rugby in the urban setting of Cape Town as having some features of carnivalesque similar to the status of cricket in Trinidad. In South Africa, however, neither rugby nor any other sport has been able to unite South Africans across racial divides generated by decades of segregation and apartheid, except for the momentary example of the 1995 World Cup that Booth discusses later in this book. Even that 'unity' proved illusory for it was achieved largely on the terms of the white power elite. Elsewhere I have examined the development of black sport generally and of 'Coloured' rugby in Cape Town in particular in broader studies of South African sport and rugby.[11] In this chapter I argue that the development of Coloured rugby in the largely working-class areas of Cape Town meshed with other urban Coloured cultural forms as an integral part of local popular culture whereby a sense of belonging and community was expressed in a society which, outside of specific residential spaces, was controlled by others. Thus a reading of Coloured rugby in Cape Town, as with West Indian cricket, as a popular cultural form, suggests that we can generalize about the nature of British sports when taken up by local populations in the Empire. Though many of the rules generated by the British were kept in sports, and for many educated by missionaries or in colonial schools playing British sports was part of an 'ideology of respectability', the cultural codes surrounding the playing and watching of sport changed dramatically when the games moved from British and settler middle- and upper-class hands to local and working-class ones. In South Africa sporting competitions were segregated and for many black South African men and some women the playing and watching of sport were important parts of everyday life and an escape from the broader society dominated by whites. Thus an element of carnival celebration entered into black South Africans' experiences of sport. As Julia Kristeva argues, following Mikhail Bakhtin, carnival 'is a spectacle ... [where a participant] is both actor and spectator'.[12] Bakhtin argued that in the middle ages carnival was significant in the lived experiences of ordinary people who were subjected to dictates of the Church, the feudal system and work ryhthms, but these people also inhabited an unofficial realm where the social order was mocked and parodied and where singing, laughter and dancing were important parts of social release and enjoyment.[13] Coloured rugby may be seen as a *ritual spectacle* in which Bakhtin included carnival pageants. Ritual spectacle was one of the three categories of 'folk carnival humour' where the official and serious tone of society was opposed in the feudal period in Europe.[14] The role of the carnivalesque in sport has not been explored as widely as it might have been. Malcolmson and others have shown how sporting and other recreational activities were integral parts of the social calendar in the England of the seventeenth and the eighteenth century, while Burton and Orlando Patterson have made the argument for linking carnival and cricket in the West Indies.[15] No one has, however, linked rugby and the carnivalesque. Indeed, rugby was initially instituted as a game that was supposed to teach the virtues of self-control, discipline and of corporeal subjugation to mental control. Yet, as the chapters by Light and by Carle and Nauright show, emotionality generated by the playing of rugby is at the core of Japanese men's and Australian women's rugby culture. As with cricket in many parts of the Empire, where the notion of batting for hours using the forward defensive stroke was anathema to non-English cultures, rugby as taught to public schoolboys did not remain a static form when played by men not raised in that environment. Even though rugby was seen to have pedagogical value and was encouraged by Coloured school teachers, its cultural manifestations were as different from Rugby School as Sabina Park is from the Long Room at Lord's. As we shall see, there was a distinct element of parody and carnival in Coloured rugby; but rugby was much more than just an outlet for social release and parody – it was an arena for the development of a physical masculinity, an arena for the demonstration of bodily achievement, a pedagogical site for the training of young men and one of the most important sites for the expression of local identity.

You Are What You Wear: Religion, Rugby and Community
While the annual Rag matches were significant in the local communities of the Bo-Kaap and District Six, for many followers of rugby, the matches between the WPCRFU and the CSRU displayed the best of local talent. Many players could not cross between the two unions since the CSRU did not allow Muslims (whom they then referred to as 'Malays') to compete in their competitions before the 1960s. So intense was the animosity against Muslim players among CSRU officials that any player found to be Muslim was expelled from the CSRU and clubs lost match points or were fined. Unfortunately, no documentation exists that explains the ban clearly since the relevant minute books were lost by the 1920s. Oral evidence from former CSRU officials suggests that it was related to the displaying of notions of respectability, civilization and Christianity. No animosity appeared to be levelled at WPCRFU clubs, however. In 1923 a letter from Roslyns requesting affiliation with the CSRU was discussed at the CSRU monthly delegate meeting. No mention was made of Roslyns being a predominantly Muslim club, only that if Roslyns were admitted the CSRU constitution would have to be changed.[16] In addition, the President of the WPCRFU occasionally attended CSRU meetings as a guest.[17]

CSRU records document cases of suspected Muslims playing in their competition. One particular case is most illuminating in showing the lengths to which CSRU administrators went to keep Muslim players out. In 1938 the CSRU President J.C. Jasson stated in his presidential address to the Union's Annual General Meeting on 10 March that 'I am perfectly satisfied that there are Malays [Muslims] playing for some of the clubs, and I recommend that we have a full dressed debate on that question.' In the ensuing debate Jasson asked, 'Are we going to forgo our birthright and allow Malays to play in our competition?' Several delegates spoke on the issue, one arguing that two clubs, Temperance and Thistles, had fielded Muslim players. The matter was put to a vote and the law banning Muslims remained intact.[18] In April the Progress club submitted a letter accusing the Thistles of playing a Muslim named T. Coosuim, registered as a Mr Ferreira, in a match against them on 16 April. At the Committee Meeting on 5 May the player was brought in for questioning. President Jasson asked his name, which was given as Gustav Ferreira. Ferreira/Coosuim then stated that he was born Christian and that none of his people were Malays. Another committee member alleged that he had seen Ferreira/Coosuim wearing a fez, a round red hat commonly worn by Muslim men in the Western Cape. Another member alleged that he saw the accused and his brother wearing fezzes in town. Jasson thought Ferreira/Coosuim was being evasive, but he was given the opportunity to produce a baptismal certificate and allowed to continue playing temporarily.[19] The matter was again taken up on 19 May when a baptismal certificate for Gustav Ferreira, born on 19 January 1906, was laid on the table. The matter was then adjourned.[20] The case reappeared in July, however, as letters and a statement signed before witnesses from a man named G. Ferreira from Kalk Bay were presented to the Committee Meeting. This Mr Ferreira claimed that he was the only G. Ferreira in Kalk Bay and that he was approached by a Mr R. Almachien for his baptismal certificate so that Toya Coosuim could play football in his name. Ferreira refused but the certificate was obtained from his Catholic Church. After allegations of intimidation, the meeting decided to appoint a committee of inquiry consisting of the President, the Chairman and a representative from Thistles and Progress to investigate at Kalk Bay.[21]

President Jasson submitted the committee's report on 4 August, stating that, after their trip to Kalk Bay, they were convinced that the evidence from Progress was correct but that to prove it conclusively they would have to go to court and pay ten guineas. The motion to exclude the player was passed by 8 to 1 with one abstention. Thistles were then penalized all the points they had earned while Ferreira/Coosuim played for them. The evidence hinged on connecting the accused with wearing a fez which led to a full investigation of his background. Law 22 of the CSRU was thus protected whereby no Muslim was allowed to play for any affiliated clubs. Although some Muslims began to play for CSRU clubs in the 1960s, as late as 1968 CSRU officials argued at a Special General Meeting that Muslims, led by G.N. Khan, head of the WPCRFU, and Abdullah Abass, were trying to take over the South African Rugby Union (SARU). In the

1960s SARU developed as the non-racial alternative to rugby organized through links to the whites-only South African Rugby Board (SARB).[22] In October 1967 tensions between Muslim and Christian Coloureds were marked enough to result in an editorial in the main newspaper aimed at the Coloured market, the *Cape Herald*, urging an end to 'ill-feeling between Muslim and Christian'.[23]

So why was there such apparent animosity towards Muslims in a society where Coloured people were marginalized? It is clear that several issues were involved. First, in efforts to demonstrate 'respectable' behaviour many black organizations in South Africa asserted their Christian backgrounds and beliefs. In addition, meetings were held in English even when the majority of members spoke Afrikaans, Xhosa or another language as their first language. While the WPCRFU leaders also behaved and conducted themselves in a 'respectable' manner, they adhered strongly to their religious practices as well. Other issues may have been involved too. The CSRU was able to purchase its own land on which to hold matches, although it was forced to relocate when its land was declared to be in a white area by the apartheid government. The WPCRFU continued to play at Green Point, but never purchased its own ground. In presenting its case to white officials, the CSRU needed to rely on being perceived as 'respectable' and, as such, made it clear that it was a Christian organization. Indeed, several clubs, such as Temperance, founded in 1895 by members of the St Thomas Church Temperance Society, emerged from links with religious organizations.[24]

Differences and 'Unity'

As the previous incident suggests, significant differences existed between different groups running Coloured rugby in the Cape Town area. These differences also appeared at regional and national level making a unified front in Coloured rugby difficult to achieve. In the early 1960s attempts to generate rugby unity nationally were made, instigated by black rugby officials hoping for a unified front and by the white SARB who hoped to bring all rugby competitions under its aegis. Two of the main leaders of Coloured rugby at the national level, Abdullah Abass and Cuthbert Loriston, disagreed over the approach. Loriston agreed to join the SARB structures, taking Western Cape country area unions with him and, initially, the CSRU. Abass held the support of the WPCRFU and other areas in South Africa in forming SARU, which remained outside the control of the SARB. The leaders of SARU demanded that any unified rugby structure would have to be formed on the basis of merit selection for all representative teams.

Such a merit-based, non-racial selection policy was not supported by
Danie Craven and other white rugby officials who refused to push the
apartheid government on issues of segregation, although no law
specifically banned mixed sport between blacks and whites. In 1970
attempts at unity in rugby resurfaced with Abass stating his
willingness to resign and calling on Loriston to do the same so that
personalities did not enter into the discussions.[25] By this time, however,
most black people involved in sports were reluctant to accept any unity
with whites as long as apartheid remained in force. In Cape Town
feelings ran particularly high once District Six, the heart of Coloured
Cape Town, was declared a white area by the National Party
government in 1966. The removal of residents in the early 1970s
substantially affected local culture and, in particular, sports since those
who played in competitions such as the WPCRFU had to travel far
greater distances to matches and players in one club no longer lived in
close proximity to each other. Many clubs went out of existence
although others appeared in new areas of settlement in the townships
of the Cape Flats. Although the future of rugby was threatened by the
vagaries of apartheid, the style of play and the role of rugby in local
communities remained strong, if not quite as vigorous as in the period
before 1970.

Violence, Intimidation and Trickery: Reshaping Masculinity

Rugby played a significant role in shaping masculine behaviour in the
predominantly Coloured areas of Cape Town. Masculinity surrounding
Coloured rugby was quite different from white rugby. Again an
element of carnival resistance emerged as players sought, through
complex skirting of the regulations or through intimidation, to gain
advantage over their opponents. In this context 'trickery' was highly
valued. Trickery was the ability to gain advantage without getting
caught and involved a range of intimidatory mental and physical
tactics. Indeed, some activities that would be openly condemned in
rugby circles elsewhere were highly prized in Coloured rugby. One
example comes from a match between a WPCRFU repre-sentative
team and Eastern Province. The WPCRFU player Rajab Benjamin
recounts that in the match his team was being destroyed by a fast
Eastern Province winger in the first half:

> one year we played in Port Elizabeth, Eastern Province and
> Western Province. Eastern Province had a wing, he was a high
> stepper wing. Every time when he come past he run away from
> our wing... So I said to the captain: 'You must make a change

man. You can't leave that wing here man. The man he is going to run faster and every time he is going to score in the corner. We are going to lose.' So he asked me 'What can we do?', so I say 'The only thing we can do is change me from my position, I am going to play there'. So he said 'OK'. I was open loose forward and I went to go and play in his position. The first time he came past, the second he is gone off the field. So there is no more tries coming from that side. So I got a whole run for myself and I scored ... it shows you that the technique you must use is your brains. You must use your brains.[26]

Other examples include front-row players using small knives to cut their opponents in the scrum and the use of threatened bodily harm before matches to try and 'psych out' opposing players. When this failed, clubs occasionally turned to age-old tactics of trying to limit the effectiveness of top players from opposing sides as the above incident indicates. In a 1969 club match between Leeuwendales and Caledonian Roses, the Leeuwendale star winger Armien Manuel was repeatedly subjected to what the press called 'rough handling' as the Callies tried to limit his impact on the game. One Callies player was sent off for an unfair challenge on Manuel and two Leeuwendale players followed as they retaliated. When Manuel finally had to go off due to injury, and with Leeuwendales down to 11 men, the team walked off the field in protest.

Intimidation was particularly present when WPCRFU teams played against the CSRU. In these matches the WPCRFU almost always won, although on paper the teams were never much different in talent. Gassan Emeran suggests that WPCRFU players were able to intimidate CSRU ones through a deliberate strategy involving several months of taunting – though violence surrounding such matches did not spill over the rugby field's boundaries.[27] Indeed, the *Cape Herald* in its report of the 1966 match commented on the vigorous nature of play, but also on the 'pleasant aspect' of seeing 'the opposing players fraternising happily on the field after their hard and tense struggle'.[28]

The vigorous nature of play in Coloured rugby was more aggressive than in white South African rugby. Rajab Benjamin recounts how he took a white rugby-playing friend who played wing for Western Province to see a Coloured match from the WPCRFU in the early 1960s. Roslyns were playing Rangers at the Green Point Track in Cape Town. The white player said that 'You know if I was a Coloured man I would never play rugby.' When Benjamin asked him why, he stated 'Look at how they are playing it!' Benjamin countered,

'No, but it is rugby man. That is how rugby should be played. After the match then they praise one another and they kiss, but they play the game hard, hard, hard.'[29] Indeed, two brothers named Jansen from the Retreat club in the CSRU died from injuries sustained in a match against Progress on 27 September 1930. An investigation was held, but no intent to harm was found.[30] Other incidents occurred periodically and when matches became too violent, union officials and the press reacted swiftly in castigating guilty players and teams. One WPCRFU match in 1969 between Silvertree and Caledonian Roses was reported as looking 'like chaos' when fights broke out during the match. The *Cape Herald* argued that whatever happened at the match it 'definitely wasn't rugby'.[31] Whatever the reason for such clashes, however, I have found no reports of violence spilling over from the rugby ground, supporting the argument by Benjamin that any violence stayed on the field and was forgotten as soon as matches ended. Thus we can see that a code of masculinity developed whereby any violence stayed on the field and did not spread into other aspects of daily life. Gangs who supported different sides may have clashed as a result of rugby, but there is no evidence of rugby clubs or players, sometimes meeting on adjacent street corners, targeting each other beyond the boundaries of the rugby pitch.

Despite the aggressive and comparatively vigorous nature of play, specific limits were set on violent behaviour by Coloured rugby unions, particularly if any player interfered with officials. In the early 1920s a series of incidents noted in CSRU records demonstrate that certain actions were severely punished. At the Committee meeting on 12 October 1922 two Thistles players were suspended for assaulting a touch judge; and a Wanderers player reported for striking and head-butting the referee in the face on 7 October 1922 was suspended for life.[32] P. Beaukman of Thistles was also suspended for life for striking a referee in 1923 although his role as a former club chairman was used in his defence.[33] In 1933 eight players were suspended or reprimanded, four for 'foul play', three for 'disturbance on ground' and one for striking a referee.[34] The CSRU had over 1,100 registered members at the time and ran three grades of competition among its nine clubs, so the instances of violent play, attacks on referees or disorderly behaviour at matches were minimal. At times crowds became unruly, but reported instances of large-scale violence were less frequent than in white rugby and appeared most often at large matches between the WPCRFU and the CSRU or in matches in the 1940s and the 1950s involving leading clubs with links to the most powerful gangs in District Six. Most examples of crowd problems reported in the CSRU minute books relate to isolated instances of drunkenness which Union officials were quick to eliminate through the banning of any offenders. The differing interpretations of acceptable levels of legitimate violence have led to problems in the post-unity era. Paul Dobson, head of the judiciary committee for the Western Province Rugby Union, stated in 1995 that disciplinary meetings before unity were held twice a season and since then they have been held twice a month with the majority of players alleged to have committed offences being Coloured players.[35] This is not to argue for one set of interpre-tations over another, but merely to suggest that, while the rules of rugby are uniform, the interpretation and the codes of player behaviour are not and are subject to local and cultural variations as other chapters here also highlight.

Conclusion: Rugby, Nostalgia and Identity in Post-Apartheid Cape Town

Through these vignettes and a brief historical discussion of a number of issues in local rugby, I have attempted to partly reconstruct the place of rugby in the Coloured communities of Cape Town over the past century. Both the CSRU and the WPCRFU joined with the non-racial sports movement in the 1960s and its rugby arm, SARU, thus remaining outside the white-dominated SARB and its Coloured affiliate the South African Rugby Football Federation, although CSRU participated in Federation competitions from 1963 until it was expelled in 1966. White, Coloured and African teams played in separate competitions under the general authority of the white SARB. As a result the two Cape Town unions were denied access to government funding, which went only to SARB affiliates, adding to the massive resources of SARB. The Cape Town unions were not completely isolated from white rugby as, on several occasions throughout the 1970s and 1980s, discussions were held between SARB and SARU. All the time Coloured rugby continued, although by the mid-1990s the rugby landscape and culture had changed dramatically. Two disruptions were crucial in altering local rugby. First, the removal of residents from District Six in the early 1970s spelled the end for many clubs and changed forever the shape of the local culture and of rugby. Two powerful clubs, the historic Roslyns and the financially-sound Montrose, were even forced to merge and become Cape Town United. In the 1990s, the unification of rugby, or more properly the absorption of non-racial rugby teams and structures into the formerly white-dominated structures of South African rugby, has further weakened historic Coloured rugby clubs so that few remain as participants in Western Province competitions. While the end of racial discrimination in rugby is to be welcomed, unity in rugby has come at a price for Coloured clubs, some dating from the 1880s and the 1890s.

Indeed, the price of sporting amalgamation has been so great that there have been numerous discussions held among old WPCRFU administrators and players about restarting their competition either formally or as a Sunday league. These talks have been fuelled by a nostalgic recollection of rugby culture and a longing for a community of the past and the role that many think rugby can play in combating juvenile delinquency.[36] These concerns have been encouraged by the broader processes of large-scale African migration into the Western Cape, the end of job protection for Coloured workers in the Western Cape and affirmative action policies that tend to favour Africans (at least, as many Coloureds perceive the situation). Finally, as a free market in property emerges, communities such as the Bo-Kaap have come under increasing pressures from outsiders looking for prime real estate near the centre of Cape Town. In this situation there is the danger of entire communities and histories disappearing, although local initiatives such as the creation of museums in District Six and the Bo-Kaap, a rugby museum in the Bo-Kaap, and the emerging work of local historians writing about black rugby players of the past have served to keep alive a vibrant history of local culture and local sport. This is imperative as some whites proffer the fiction that rugby has not been taken up seriously by black South Africans until quite recently. Despite the evidence of black sporting clubs and associations existing for over a century, comments by Springbok rugby players illustrate the ignorance among most South African whites about black South Africans' sporting history. In 1994 the Springbok player Uli Schimdt stated that rugby was not in the culture of blacks and it was not natural for them to play, they should rather stick to soccer.[37] The former Springbok captain, National Party minister and minister in the first government of national unity Dawie de Villiers said in 1980, 'Don't forget that the Blacks have really known western sports for [only] the last ten years ... they have not reached the same standard [as whites].'[38] It is imperative in the light of these comments that much more work is done on the history of black rugby and the cultural role of rugby for black South Africans, particularly in its historic areas of strength in the Western and Eastern Capes.

In the case of rugby in the Coloured communities of Cape Town a rich picture of rugby in local, social and cultural history is emerging although records are by no means complete. It is clear that rugby provided a carnivalesque atmosphere for participants and fans, was seen as an activity to promote respectability, to make men and to provide Coloured men with opportunities to control non-work activities in their daily lives. Here a different rugby culture developed where play was more vigorous than in white rugby and where differences in spectating culture emerged out of the working-class cultures of Cape Town.

NOTES

1. Tony Mason, 'Football on the Maiden: Cultural Imperialism in Calcutta', in J.A. Mangan (ed.), *The Cultural Bond: Sport, Empire, Society* (London, 1992), pp. 143–4.
2. For recent discussions of cricket in this context, see Brian Stoddart and Keith A.P. Sandiford (eds), *The Imperial Game: Cricket, Culture and Society* (Manchester, 1998).
3. For detailed discussions of black South Africans in rugby see Albert Grundlingh, Andre Odendaal and Burridge Spies, *Beyond the Tryline: Rugby and South African Society* (Johannesburg, 1995); John Nauright, *Sport, Cultures and Identities in South Africa* (London, 1997); and David Black and John Nauright, *Rugby and the South African Nation: Sport, Cultures, Politics and Power in the Old and New South Africas* (Manchester, 1998). For a general overview of race and sport in South Africa also see Douglas Booth, *The Race Game: Sport and Politics in South Africa* (London, 1998).
4. 'Coloured' originally referred to all people not classified as European. From 1904 onward the term has referred to essentially the same groups of people in South Africa. For more discussion of this see Ian Goldin, *Making Race: the Politics and Economics of Coloured Identity in South Africa* (London, 1987), pp. xxv–xxvii. 'Coloured' was a term that the official state used to classify South Africans of mixed-race ancestry. Some people defined as 'Coloured' have also been known as Cape Malays, people descended from slaves brought to the Cape from what are now Malaysia, Indonesia and Madagascar. Many of these people themselves use the term 'so-called Coloureds' as a self-description. The racial terminology developed during segregation and apartheid is problematic; the general reference to mixed-race South Africans as 'Coloured' in this chapter will have to suffice until new terminology is developed. When I refer to 'black' people generally this refers to all South Africans not wholly descended from the peoples of Europe.
5. The first known evidence of Muslim players in any CSRU team dates from 1961. Minute Book, Perserverance Rugby Football Club, 1961.
6. CSRU Minute Books which exist from 1918 onwards are written in English with comments inserted denoting whenever a person spoke in Afrikaans.
7. Meneer Effendi interviewed by John Nauright, 10 December 1994.
8. Quoted in Sue Vice, *Introducing Bakhtin* (Manchester, 1997), p. 152.
9. *Cape Herald*, 6 July 1968.
10. Richard D.E. Burton, 'Cricket, Carnival and Street Culture in the Caribbean', in Hilary McD. Beckles and Brian Stoddart (eds), *Liberation Cricket: West Indies Cricket Culture* (Manchester, 1995), p. 90.
11. See Nauright, *Sport, Cultures and Identities*; and Black and Nauright, *Rugby and the South African Nation*.
12. Julia Kristeva, 'Word, Dialogue, and Novel', in *Desire in Language: a Semiotic Approach to Literature and Art* (Oxford, 1980), p. 78.
13. For a discussion of Bakhtin's thoughts on carnival see Vice, *Introducing Bakhtin*,

pp. 149–99. For Bakhtin's main writing on carnival see Mikhail Bakhtin, *Rabelais and His World* (trans. Hélène Iswolsky) (Bloomington, IN, 1984).

14. Vice, *Introducing Bakhtin*, p. 151.
15. Robert Malcolmson, *Popular Recreations and English Society 1700–1850* (Cambridge, 1973); Burton, 'Cricket, Carnival and Street Culture', Orlando Patterson, 'The Ritual of Cricket', in Andrew Salkey (ed.), *Caribbean Essays: an Anthology* (London, 1973), pp. 108–18.
16. CSRU Minute Books, Monthly Delegate Meetings, 28 September 1923. Discussion of letter from Roslyns requesting afflilation from 1924.
17. CSRU Annual Report, March 1924.
18. CSRU Minute Books, Annual General Meeting, 10 March 1938.
19. Ibid., Committee Meeting of 5 May 1938.
20. Ibid., Adjourned Committee Meeting, 19 May 1938.
21. Ibid., Committee Meeting of 21 July 1938.
22. Ibid., Special General Meeting of 3 March 1968.
23. Howard Lawrence, 'Ill-feeling between Muslim and Christian', *Cape Herald*, 14 October 1967, p. 8.
24. 'Temperance Celebrates 70th Anniversary', *Cape Herald*, 28 August 1965, p. 18.
25. *Cape Herald*, 6 June 1970.
26. Rajab Benjamin and ex-Montrose players, interviewed by John Nauright, Cape Town, 26 December 1994.
27. Gassan Emeran interviewed by John Nauright, Cape Town, 18 January 1995.
28. 'W.P. – City in Robust Clash', *Cape Herald*, 13 August 1966, p. 9.
29. Rajab Benjamin interviewed by John Nauright, Cape Town, 26 December 1994.
30. CSRU Minute Books, Committee Meeting of 2 October 1930.
31. 'They Call This Rugby!; Fists Fly in Kagee Cup Clash', *Cape Herald*, 23 August 1969, p. 12.
32. CSRU Minute Books, Committee Meeting of 12 October 1922.
33. Ibid., Committee Meeting 6 July 1923.
34. Ibid., List of Suspensions 1933.
35. Conversation with Paul Dobson, January 1995.
36. This attitude about the educative and social role of rugby came out in all the interviews with former officials and players of both the WPCRFU and the CSRU. The rise in crime in Cape Flats townships has been substantial in the 1990s with little extant infrastructure to combat it. Many see sport as an alternative, though this is not without its problems as well.
37. *Cape Times*, 26 October 1994.
38. Quoted in Grundlingh, Odendaal and Spies, *Beyond the Tryline*, pp. 24–5.

3

Recognition through Resistance: Rugby in the USA

Timothy J.L. Chandler

Introduction

American rugby has yet to find its own chronicler but it has long been accepted by football historians that McGill's playing Harvard in 1874 signalled the beginning of organized rugby football on the North American continent. It is fitting that it was an inter-university match, that has been taken as the signal of this beginning since universities have always been the seedbeds and backbone of the game in the USA. In view of the game's subsequent history in North America, however, it would have been far more fitting if the universities credited with this beginning had not been established and 'establishment' schools, had not been Eastern schools, and, in the case of the US school, had not been 'Ivy League'. In the light of subsequent history, it would have been far more fitting if a 'new', West Coast institution, such as Berkeley or Stanford had received the credit. This is for two reasons: first, because the game was really developed and consolidated in the West under (English) Rugby Football Union (RFU) laws; and secondly, and perhaps more importantly, because Stanford and Berkeley have been perceived as 'other' in relation to Harvard. They have been the 'other' Harvards – the 'Harvards of the West', and it is this sense of 'otherness' which has also typified the position of rugby in relation to America's own football. In the USA (and to a lesser extent in Canada) football has long meant 'Gridiron'; and all of the great university rivalries mimic the (invented) traditional East Coast rivalry between Harvard and Yale. By contrast, American collegiate rugby's most enduring rivalry is between Berkeley and Stanford – a West Coast rivalry.

In this chapter I argue that the 'otherness' of rugby football made it little more than a novelty, and very much a recreational sport, on almost all college campuses in the USA until the 1960s, with the minor but significant exception of the decade following the 1905 football crisis when deaths and injuries in football reached alarming proportions and alternatives to the game were sought. In its 'otherness' rugby developed an image as an activity that was casual, amateurish,

boozy and boisterous – an activity that was delighted in as much for its
pre- and post-match revelry as for its on-field skills. Unlike the
gridiron game, rugby eschewed the technical rationality of playbooks,
professional coaches and rigid organizational structures. It was not the
establishment game. What support it did get in terms of on-field skills
came largely from outside and from outsiders. Major support came in
the form of British and colonial assistance that included antipodean
tourists going to or returning from Britain; Oxbridge graduates touring
the United States looking to broaden their horizons and spread the
rugby creed; and expatriot British or colonial rugby players living,
studying or temporarily employed in the United States, looking to
continue to play the game they loved. As we shall see, the social
aspects of the game were developed in this manner also and were then
furthered through such activities as Spring Break tournaments in
Bermuda, and later, tours to Britain.

The fact that the game was always a student-organized and student-
run activity meant that it never challenged football's place in the
American college sporting calendar. This also meant that, as an
activity, it was marginalized by university administrators because
rarely, if ever, did it receive any significant institutional support.[1] It
was with the growing unrest on college campuses during the 1960s
that the game began to find additional support from among the student
body. The 1960s saw the place, role and value of football (along with
almost everything else) increasingly questioned by students. With its
rigid discipline inculcated by a seemingly endless array of
authoritarian coaches – most of whom were trying to make sense of a
whole new generation of student athletes who wished to question their
authority and adopt a very different set of standards and principles
from their own – football and its purveyors came under increasing
scrutiny from students across the country. This was particularly the
case in California, home of two of the best-known rugby playing
universities, Berkeley and Stanford. Unlike the outcome of the
administration-led debates of 1905 when, as we shall see, a number of
institutions and particularly those in California gave up football for
rugby, nowhere was football officially replaced by rugby in the 1960s.
However, to the extent that athletically-inclined students (who wished
to combine an alternative macho physicality with the 'drug culture of
the beer keg') chose to be associated with the student-centred culture
of rugby rather than the administration-centred culture of football, the
game of rugby flourished as the rapid increase in the numbers of
college teams and clubs during this period shows.[2] At the same time,
the 'ruggers' maintained and even enhanced their image as 'party-

animals'. During this period California and Texas proved to be key areas of rugby growth. Such growth was not confined to these states, however, as the development of new clubs and leagues in the Mid-West, notably in Illinois, Wisconsin and Minnesota, bear witness. Additionally, in the East, where the Ivy League schools continued to provide the majority of players for the burgeoning Eastern Rugby Union[3] (ERU) teams, the game took root in Massachusetts, New York and Washington, DC.

With the formation of the USA Rugby Football Union (USARFU) in 1975, the development of rugby took on a more planned and controlled look. Competitions at club and collegiate level began. The foundation of a national team, the Eagles, that played its first international match against Australia in 1976, and followed this up with test matches against France and then the old rival Canada, suggests that longstanding external links had helped a somewhat isolated rugby-playing community to gain further contact with the rugby playing world. The development of the USARFU enabled American rugby, with its then 1,200 clubs and 80,000 players, to prepare to challenge the established rugby-playing powers for the first time since 1924 when the United States had won the Gold Medal in the rugby competition at the Paris Olympics. The formation of the USARFU also enabled the rugby-playing world to unite with the United States. A major push for this began with the RFU's 1970 Centenary Congress to which 43 countries, including the USA, sent delegates. The Congress was part of the RFU's efforts to globalize the game. Accordingly, club championships were instituted in the USA and following this, in 1980, the first collegiate championship was held.

Within the USA since 1975 the challenge of both association and rugby football to the gridiron game has caused turf wars of a new sort in colleges and universities – turf wars for time and space, for facilities and equipment. Furthermore, the growth of women's rugby, while less prominent than women's soccer, has also added to the problems surrounding the implementation of Title IX,[4] as all women's sports look to gain equal access to the 'goods' of sport. Yet, in the face of football's longstanding hegemony in educational institutions, rugby, both men's and women's, continues to be 'other'.

Background

English colonists who came to America inevitably brought their games with them and, despite disapproval from some quarters, introduced 'football-type games as early as 1609 in Virginia and before the mid-seventeenth century in Boston'.[5] It is certainly the case that East Coast college students were playing a form of football in the early years of the nineteenth century. These were intramural affairs. Thus in the 1820s students at Princeton were playing a game called 'ballam' and similar activities could be found at Harvard, Yale, Amherst, Trinity and Brown in the 1840s. It appears that the rules were local but that the game, wherever played, was rough. College administrators banned it on a large number of campuses because of its roughness. However, as Maltby notes, football was actually organized in a number of the secondary schools before it was organized in the colleges, thus forming an interesting parallel with the game's development in England.[6] By 1860 Boston schoolboys played the game, as did the boys from the high schools and the Latin schools in the area. Together they formed what is thought to be the first football club in the USA, the Oneida Football Club of Boston. They also appear to have popularized the game at the Ivy League schools in the same way that boys from Rugby School took their game to Oxbridge.[7] At this point the game was student-organized and student-funded on college campuses. There was no official interest from any of the faculties. While it is unclear exactly how or when contacts between institutions were made, it appears that students at institutions such as Princeton and Rutgers decided to compete against each other, similarity of rules and geographical proximity no doubt being important features.[8] Yale and Columbia followed suit and, by 1873, representatives from these four institutions met in New York to codify their rules. These rules were in fact closer to the rules of London's Football Association than they were to the then current rugby rules. Harvard chose not to attend, preferring to continue its own Boston game in which the handling of the ball was allowed.

Suffering from a shortage of opponents against whom to play the handling game, Harvard looked to McGill and scheduled two games in the spring of 1874. McGill travelled to Cambridge, Massachusetts and played the first game by Harvard's rules and the second by McGill's rugby rules. As a result of these encounters the Harvard players decided that they liked McGill's game better. Thus the following year Harvard adopted the rugby rules.[9] By 1876 Princeton, Yale and Columbia had joined Harvard as members of the Intercollegiate Football Association (IFA) playing by rugby rules. Rugby's days were numbered, however, as detractors criticized it for its roughness, particularly regarding the scrummage. Disagreements among the IFA members and the increasing influence of Walter Camp saw the growth and development of America's own football in the 1880s.[10] Rugby was no longer the brand of football played in the elite East Coast colleges.

Similar discussions took place in other parts of the country, such as Minnesota, in the 1880s,[11] but football generally won the day over rugby as it came increasingly to be stamped as an American innovation at a time of rising nationalism following the 1876 centenary.

It is, then, somewhat ironic that the next big boost to rugby was to come in the decades on either side of 1900, also as a backlash against violence and roughness. On this occasion, however, it was gridiron football that was being criticized. The outcry over football's violence led a number of important colleges and universities, among them Columbia, to drop American football. Others, and most notably Berkeley and Stanford, chose to replace it with rugby. As Roberta Park[12] has ably displayed, the success of the two major West Coast universities in trying to foster the conversion to rugby of other schools and colleges was limited, despite significant efforts by two powerful university presidents and other important members of these two universities' communities. While in the short term their efforts encouraged other Californian schools such as the University of Southern California (USC), St Mary's and Santa Clara, as well as the University of Nevada to adopt rugby, Berkeley and Stanford's influence did not spread much further. Such influence did permeate downwards to the local high schools, however, a number of which adopted rugby, thereby providing a supply of players to enable both universities to continue to play when the rest of the country had moved ahead with football.

At Stanford and Berkeley rugby was able to take hold because both universities had forged links with their West Coast neighbours to the north. British Columbia in Canada was a strong rugby-playing area. Throughout this period it was a force in West Coast rugby because it continued to attract British emigrants; it had its own private schools that were founded on the rugby-playing English public-school model, and when West Coast teams were looking for new opponents travel up and down the coast was easier than travelling across the continent. This West Coast link, which continues today, has been an important source of opponents for the Californians. It has also given them an indirect link to British rugby, one which led to California's being seen as a good place for touring teams from Australia and New Zealand to break their journey on the way to and from the British Isles. Links formulated in the same way between Australia and New Zealand rugby and British Columbia rugby are also strong.

The impetus to adopt rugby at Stanford and Berkeley came from their respective Presidents, David Starr Jordan and Benjamin Ide Wheeler. Both men had been active as undergraduates at Cornell and

Brown, respectively. Both were interested in the education of young men of character, and perhaps in English rugby football; they, like De Coubertin and others, saw the possibility of developing manly moral character in their young charges. They were supported in their efforts by the faculty athletic representatives of their respective institutions – Jordan by Frank Angell, who had played rugby at Oxford, and Wheeler by George Edwards. As Park notes 'what both [presidents] desired for their students was vigorous, wholesome sport, not specialized and commercialized athletics'.[13] While face-to-face discussions were held only between representatives of these two institutions, letters were circulated to others on this matter. Furthermore, the significance of the debate over football was serious enough to attract the attention of President Theodore Roosevelt, himself a disciple of hardy athletic endeavour.[14] Having made their decision to give up football and adopt rugby, Jordan and Wheeler had the problem of influencing opinion in favour of the game beyond the walls of their own institutions. They were extremely fortunate in the fact that they were able to secure the visit of the 1905 New Zealand All Black team, which had just completed its stunningly successful tour of Britain, to play an exhibition match against a team from British Columbia on the Berkeley campus. The game was so successful that it was agreed to play a second match three days later at the San Francisco Recreation Grounds. The New Zealanders won both games handily, but in doing so put on an exhibition that persuaded many that rugby was a fine game and that Jordan and Wheeler's decision was a good one.[15] For those who agreed with the decision, rugby was considered a better game than football for a number of reasons, the most obvious of which were: that it was neither professional nor commercial; that it did not require professional coaches and lengthy hours of training; and that it was an appropriate game for manly and moral young gentlemen. For those who disagreed with the decision the major reason was that an English sport which some considered 'effeminate'[16] was replacing a 'red-blooded' American game. This argument continued in later years in rather more forcible terms when rugby was thought to be not just 'not-American' but 'un-American'.

Rugby's future as a major fall activity at West Coast institutions was limited. Its days at Berkeley and Stanford, as *the* code by which 'the big game' between the two institutions was played, were numbered. Geographically isolated and yet wanting and needing to be seen to compete with the major East Coast schools both academically and athletically, Berkeley chose to sever athletic ties with Stanford in 1915 in order to return to playing the American game. Berkeley felt that it could not afford to be seen as 'other' when it came to the country's most important college sport. As an academic institution it had ambitions outside California, and with football's fortunes having been revived through a series of rule changes and the increasing intervention of faculty and administration in the running of athletics, Berkeley felt that it was time to abandon rugby (and Stanford) and return to football. The changing patterns of control of college sport in the years after 1905 and the increasing importance of university administrators in the organization and control of athletics have been well documented,[17] as commercialization and professionalism became increasingly significant issues on college campuses. Where it did survive the revival of football, rugby remained a student-run activity on almost all campuses. Its 'minority' status meant that it maintained its student-organized, student-financed and student-led profile, one which it holds today on almost all American college campuses. This independence left room for a number of important developments. First, it meant that the game was maintained on college campuses only because of the efforts of students, and thus was developed alongside, and in conjunction with the culture of students. Secondly, unlike so many other college sports, it did not become a coach-centred activity. It maintained its status as 'other' and thus had the potential to be a site of resistance to the athletic mainstream. Such a status also made possible the opportunity to display resistance to the authoritarian approach adopted by so many coaches in college sport following the success of Amos Alonzo Stagg, Knute Rockne and others to build a university's reputation (and enrolments) on the back of sporting success. As we shall see, the culture of 'otherness' was to become a significant contributing factor to rugby's growth in the period after World War II and, more particularly, in the 1960s.

In the period after World War I the game survived only in small pockets on the East Coast but displayed a little more resilience on the West Coast. Stanford returned to playing football against Berkeley in 1919 – the war having had an impact on both campuses. Rugby appears to have continued intermittently on both campuses, although it was certainly no longer a major enterprise on either. Thus, while official rugby records do not exist at Stanford for the years 1918–32, they are extant from 1933 to the present day.[18] Such a situation is probably not unusual as the game at both the college and the high school level declined increasingly in the inter-war years. There were fewer institutions involved in the game and there were fewer individuals available to foster and promote it. However, the continued external links between California and British Columbia, the efforts of

touring teams and the continued exchanges between university
students in the British Isles and the United States meant that there was
always the possibility of the game's receiving new impetus and
motivation from outside. Certainly the gold medal successes of US
Olympic teams in both the 1920 and 1924 Games may be ascribed, in
part, to the influence of Oxford-educated men such as Frank Angell
whose Stanford team represented the United States in 1924. Such
success, however, appeared to bring neither greater recognition of, nor
increased interest in, the game from within the United States.
Nevertheless, the Stanford team's tour to Europe in 1924 was the
forerunner of many others, all of which helped to foster and sustain the
game in the 'rugby-isolated' United States. For other than touring
teams there was little in the way of opposition for teams on the West
Coast, and despite there being less isolation on the East Coast, with its
far greater density of colleges and its major cities such as New York
and Boston, the game was having to compete for contact-sport athletes
with an ascendant football. As such, rugby continued as a minority
activity, organized and run by students, largely beyond the gaze of
university officials and outside the interests and concerns of the
Amateur Athletic Union (AAU) and, subsequently, the National
Collegiate Athletic Association (NCAA).

Evidence of the game's continuity between the wars is sparse and it
appears that it was only because of the efforts of a few dedicated
students in the coastal rugby-playing enclaves that the game continued
at all. Rugby was alive, although not particularly well, at Harvard,
Yale, Penn, Brown and Princeton. Similarly, on the West Coast at
Stanford, Berkeley and Southern California the game continued with
the additional help of contacts with Canada. It is also clear that there
were a number of clubs, many of them formed by British, New
Zealand, Australian and Canadian ex-patriots in association with
graduates of rugby-playing American universities, that were started to
enable these émigré rugby enthusiasts to continue playing their chosen
game. Examples include the Olympic Club and the Hollywood Club in
California both of which played important roles in the founding of the
Southern California Rugby Football Union in Hollywood in July 1933.
The New York Rugby Football Club (NYRFC), founded in 1929, was
instrumental in the development of the game in the East in the 1930s
and in the founding of the ERU in 1934. The importance of the
NYRFC in the eyes of rugby's governing body the RFU is displayed
in the acceptance of the NYRFC for membership in the RFU in 1932.[19]

That was also a significant year in rugby in other parts of the United
States, the original Mid-West Union (MWU) being founded then in

Chicago. Who or what was behind the founding of the MWU is not entirely clear, although the organizing of matches and providing officials were likely to have been important factors. Another reason may have been one similar to that for the founding of the ERU. The ERU was almost certainly formed to provide a structure for a training side to play Cambridge University on its United States tour in the spring of 1934.[20] The ERU was initially made up of nine teams. It was therefore necessary to organize a union to help to select and train a competitive, representative team to take on the might of Cambridge, which boasted a very strong team at this time.[21] Again, it appears to have been the influence of external forces that helped to stimulate and encourage the growth and development of rugby and its increased organizational structure within the United States. American rugby, it appears, is not a home-grown product.

Despite such efforts at furthering rugby's future in the United States during the 1930s, interest in the game waned as the effects of the depression and World War II greatly impeded its progress. Few more than 30 clubs competed on a regular basis in the US in 1950, yet by 1980 in excess of 1,000 clubs were participating. How can such extraordinary growth be explained? To suggest that the growth of the game was steady and planned in this 30-year period would be misleading. Its development was uneasy, unsteady and haphazard. The influences were varied, uneven and sometimes unusual. One such example is provided by the history of the Dartmouth College Rugby Football Club. This was founded in 1951. A number of East Coast schools had seen a revival of the game in the post-war years. In rugby-playing Bermuda officials were attempting to promote tourism by attracting students to spend Spring Break on the island by offering a College Rugby Week. Dartmouth organized a team in order to be able travel to Bermuda and participate in this tournament against their East Coast college rivals and other local teams.[22] Throughout the 1950s this tournament was a significant annual event for both rugby-playing and rugby-spectating students alike. Indications of the growing strength of, and interest in, the game in American colleges and universities can be seen in the beginning of tours by their teams to the British Isles. Again through the efforts of an outsider – in this case a British-born student Richard Liesching – Dartmouth toured England in 1958 and in subsequent years visited Ireland, Wales and Scotland. The tour to England received official sanction when the Dartmouth team became part of President Eisenhower's 'People to People Sports Committee'. This was one of the few times that rugby has not been seen as 'other'. As official ambassadors, the tourists received considerable press coverage – a typical headline proclaiming 'Ike's Boys Love Rugby and Beer'.[23] If such an example is in any way typical of the development of the game in the USA, then the impact of individual players, as well as the influence of touring must all play a part in the growth of the game in the period after 1950. I also argue that beer played an increasingly important part in the growth of the game in the years that followed.

Growth in the 1960s

The greatest period of growth in the game took place from the mid-1960s onwards when numbers of both university and club teams burgeoned. The development of many of the club teams at this time was not dissimilar to that of the Washington Rugby Football Club (WRFC). The impetus for the WRFC came from an ex-patriot Irishman Fred Forster who was feeling the lack of a rugby club in the nation's capital. He had previously spent time in California where rugby had been available to him. It is indicative of what he had learned about American rugby in California, and the on-going influence of 'outsiders' and particularly of New Zealanders, that soon after his arrival in Washington he decided to call the New Zealand Embassy to try to make contact with other players to form a club. The WRFC was founded in 1963 and the first match was played against a team from the Baltimore Rugby Club. Other contests followed soon after.[24] During the course of the 1960s schedules for the WRFC and clubs like it became more settled and regular, largely due to the development of local and regional unions. However, limited numbers of opponents of similar standard made it necessary for colleges and then clubs to travel further to find appropriate opposition outside their own immediate area. Tournaments became popular as a way of bringing teams together and promoting the game. This was particularly true for the seven-a-side game. Thus the NYRFC held its first Thanksgiving Weekend Sevens Tournament in 1959. This has since become an annual event, attracting teams from across the USA. Through the efforts of members of the WRFU, clubs were founded at the US Naval Academy, George Washington University and the University of Maryland during the 1960s providing something of a snowball effect in the growth of the game in the 1970s. The ERU, which was founded with a membership of nine clubs in 1934 and had grown to 29 by 1960, boasted over 590 clubs in 1995. Much of this growth may be put down to the efforts of clubs such as the WRFU to promote the game within the colleges, with the colleges then reciprocating by providing the next generation of players for the clubs.

It was as likely that clubs would be formed by university alumni who wished to go on playing the game after completing their degrees, as it was to have graduates join existing clubs. Thus perhaps the best known and most successful club in the United States is the Old Blues from California. In essence, this is the alumni club for Berkeley's rugby-playing graduates. Similarly, the Old Mission Beach Athletic Club (OMBAC) of San Diego that was founded in the 1950s was revived in the 1960s by a group of graduates from San Diego State University.[25] In the Mid-West the Chicago Lions Club was founded in 1964 with the majority of players coming from the University of Chicago where, because there was no football programme, rugby had lived without threat. In Minnetonka, Minnesota, two Dartmouth alumni, in collaboration with a former Irish international and a former professional football player, formed a club in 1960.[26] The continued growth of club rugby in the United States since the late 1960s has been fuelled by the growth of the game on the campuses. It is important to note that of the 100,000 people involved in rugby in the United States in the late 1990s 95 per cent are college educated, almost 50 per cent of whom have graduate degrees. Nor is it unimportant to note that two-thirds of those involved in rugby have a household income in excess of $50,000 per annum, enabling clubs to extract significant membership fees from its predominantly middle-class membership in order to maintain a sound financial base.[27]

Alternative Masculinity

It is important to understand what happened on college campuses in the United States during the late 1960s and the early 1970s that helped to promote the growth of this 'un-American' game. As we have seen from the days of Dartmouth's Spring Break tours to Bermuda and their English tour in 1958, the social side of rugby had always been important. Rugby tours were almost as much about beer and bawdy songs as they were about rugby. Furthermore, rugby was still very much a student-organized and student-structured activity. These two factors were vital as student unrest began to gather momentum on campuses across the country. In major college sports such as football and basketball the impact of this unrest has been well documented.[28] Athletes began to resist the highly-regimented behaviour which was required of them; they disliked the autocratic coaching styles of their coaches; they wanted greater freedom of expression but found that, even in simple things such as hair length, they were limited by a coach's authority.[29] Many students sought athletic alternatives that better met their needs for freedom of expression and gave them a measure of control over their sporting activity. Playing rugby meant that they did not have to submit themselves to the control of a coach and an institution, because rugby was only a student-controlled club sport and not an administration-controlled intercollegiate sport. If there was a rugby coach at all, that coach was a student appointment, often a graduate student. For those who wanted their athletic alternative to be a contact sport, rugby provided an activity that had many of the features of football – it involved running with the ball, it involved catching and kicking, and it involved tackling.[30] While there were undoubtedly other reasons why students gravitated towards rugby, all of them found in the player-oriented and relatively unrestricted atmosphere of the game the opportunity to be involved in a 'macho' game which had an attendant freedom from authority and a 'legitimate' drug-culture. Playing rugby brought with it the opportunity to be involved in (excessive) beer drinking as an integral part of the game.[31]

While Western cultures have long advertised alcohol usage as an almost exclusively male activity, the consumption of beer with fellow males seems to be 'a potent resource for the enactment of conventional masculine identities…[so that] "drunkenness may be an aspect of the concept of masculinity"'.[32] Thus, while the consumption of alcohol has been closely associated with ideals of masculinity, aggression, endurance, toughness, the propensity for macho behaviour and even violence, we know that such behaviour does not necessarily require the presence of alcohol.[33] However, in the case of American rugby, and particularly college rugby, we have a situation in which a male bonding activity (sport) noted for its sexist, racist and homophobic discourse[34] is supplemented by the effects of alcohol which have been identified as providing release from and /or resistance to the confines of one's social and cultural constraints.[35] In other words, rugby may have provided an outlet for aggression and feelings of threatened masculinity in the face of potential emasculation for many of the young male students who swelled the ranks of college rugby clubs during this period of rapid growth. The cultural disruption of traditional masculinities so prevalent in American culture from the late 1960s onwards may well have foreshadowed a period when a combination of rugby and beer provided, at least potentially, not only a legitimate source of release from this disruption but, more importantly, a 'sanctioned' source of resistance to it. Rugby's dual roles as site of resistance (to the control of the authoritarian coach) and as site of release (since beer was a socially-sanctioned drug), may be posited as one of a number of explanations for the remarkable growth of rugby during this period. The significance of these roles in the continued attraction of rugby on college campuses, and particularly the influence of alcohol, may be seen in the current efforts being made by the USARFU to influence the image of rugby on campuses across the country. Since taking over control of collegiate rugby in the mid-1980s the USARFU has been looking to control all aspects of the collegiate game. In its Charter the collegiate committee of the USARFU notes a number of particular responsibilities in the areas of communications, development, programmes and image. Included under the area of image are the following goals:

> Develop image enhancing program for college rugby programs
> Develop an alcohol policy for collegiate rugby clubs and players[36]

Such statements lend support to the notion that college rugby has long been and continues to be a centre of sociability and conviviality for many male (and increasing numbers of female) college students, and that what happens off the pitch (which almost always includes beer) plays a large part in the attraction of the game.[37] At the same time such a situation obviously invokes criticism from the USARFU as sending the 'wrong' message about the game. Herein lies the paradox that faced the USARFU in the 1970s and the 1980s and that appears not to have been completely resolved even today: if the 'off-the-field' activity is central in attracting people to the game and increasing numbers 'on-the-field', to what extent is it beneficial to the growth of the game to try to limit off-the-field activity? The fact that the USARFU considers alcohol to be a problem only gives credence to the argument that (excessive) beer drinking and its 'entailments' have always been part of the attraction of rugby, particularly among students.

Following Wenner's argument for the 1980s' phenomenon of the sports bar, an additional explanatory factor for the growth of rugby on college campuses in the 1970s was that, for a significant number of students, rugby functioned at the nexus of 'a holy trinity of alcohol, sports and hegemonic masculinity'.[38] As Wenner notes, not only do both sport and public drinking serve as masculine rites of passage, the places and spaces in which they take place often also serve as places of refuge from women.[39] It is perhaps not without interest that, in almost all American college rugby and much American club rugby during this period, beer was (and in many cases still is) brought to the pitch and dispensed before, during and after the games and was strictly 'for the boys'. Did 'drinking with the boys' before and after the game bring about the two mutually reinforcing effects which have been posited for such activity: that of furthering the male image of alcohol and of making the men engaged in the activity seem more manly? Certainly such projections fit well with public perceptions of both rugby and drinking. Furthermore, following Donnelly and Young's analysis, it could be argued that part of the culture of American rugby from the mid-1960s onwards was about 'drinking like a man' in order to be accorded the status of having reached manhood both on and off the pitch. The rugby culture and the rugby environment were unique in comparison with those of other sports. The rugby environs are an example of Oldenburg's 'third place' – a place of same-sex association where 'regular, voluntary, informal, and happily anticipated gatherings of individuals beyond the home (first place) and work (second place)' can take place.[40] The rugby field and its environs (which have always included a particular bar or pub) carried a male territorial imperative in the turbulent times of the 1960s and the 1970s – times that were particularly turbulent for young college-aged males as young women questioned, ever more loudly, the patriarchal nature of American society.

Anecdotal evidence gathered from a range of players and coaches, who were part of college or club rugby from the late 1960s to the mid-1980s[41] and data gathered from the analyses of Donnelly and Young[42] offer a remarkably consistent picture of rugby in the United States as a place for displays of comradeship, drunkenness, vandalism, nakedness and general rowdyism. Similarly, the picture of rugby as a 'counter-cultural site' is also confirmed. However, to suggest that these were the only reasons for the game's growth during this period would be an oversimplification. Motives for joining rugby clubs were varied. For while some joined for the social aspects of the game, some for the opportunity to show a disdain for coach-centred sport, and some because of the contrast rugby offered to football (rugby as other); there were many others who were attracted simply because they liked contact sports but were perhaps neither quick enough nor fast enough to be successful at football. For them rugby was enjoyed as a replacement for, rather than an alternative to, football. Others joined initially from being pressed to make up numbers on a team only to find that they enjoyed the game. There were multiple motivations for joining a club but, whatever they were, more students were responding to them in the 1960s and the 1970s than ever before.

In their analysis of rugby's development between 1965 and the mid 1980s, Donnelly and Young highlight the importance of the middle-class, amateur, English influence on American rugby's cultural form.[43]

There is little doubt that such an influence did affect the cultural form of American rugby. Based largely on materials drawn from the available histories of club and college teams but also on other available anecdotal evidence, however, I argue that there was (and continues to be) an equally important 'colonial' influence on American rugby in its growth period. We have already seen the influence of New Zealand and Australian and even Fijian-born players on the development of the game at both college and club level. Those of Irish, Welsh and Scottish heritage also had an impact on American rugby, all of whom would have brought some rather different influences to bear than their English counterparts. This is not to deny that there were what Donnelly and Young refer to as 'cultural bubbles' where the influence of one particular cultural group (in this case middle-class Englishmen, many of them graduate students) helped to 'freeze' the rugby culture they had brought with them, in the values of the rugby culture they helped to develop in American college and club rugby.[44] There undoubtedly was a strong middle-class English influence on American rugby. Nevertheless, the role that such individuals played on the game's cultural form in the United States is open to further debate because, as Young himself has argued, 'rugby subculture is a form of resistance to middle-class norms on the part of (mostly) middle-class males...'[45] As such, class may be as important a factor within nationalities as between them in this issue. Rugby may well have provided an opportunity for working-class English (or Welsh or Irish) males to poke fun at rugby's hegemonic middle-class norms. At the same time it was providing a site of resistance to cultural assimilation for all rugby-playing non-Americans while they were studying or working in the United States. Playing rugby enabled them to maintain their identity as non-Americans, in the same way that playing rugby provided opportunities for their American teammates to be 'un-American'. Rugby helped both in maintaining an old identity while providing the key to a new one for all the 'ruggers'. It helped to maintain an old identity for those from overseas who found themselves either temporarily or permanently in the United States, and it provided a new identity for those who needed a site of resistance to the America of which they were a part. In other words, different motivations and different meanings could be brought by a range of teammates to the same field at the same time.

Different motivations could also be brought to the bar after the game. To suggest that rowdy behaviour, singing and drinking were always central to all of the players after the game is as limited a view as suggesting that rugby itself was always a site of resistance. At different times, in different places, and for different individuals, such behaviour may have symbolized cultural resistance, hegemonic masculinity, homosociality, conviviality or just simple high spirits. It is probably the case that rugby players' activities both on and off the field did not always relate to resistive effort, the domination of women and/or homosexuals, or their own formation as a gendered group. All of these are distinctive features of rugby subculture. Yet what makes the US version unique is that these behaviours were manifested so much more publicly than in most other rugby-playing cultures. The lack of clubhouses meant that public spaces such as bars or pubs became the centre for all pre- and post-game activity. Any analysis needs to take account of the fact: that the vast majority of clubs were welcomed in these public places; that while some customers took their business elsewhere, others came to the pubs and bars because of the rugby teams; that while some women were offended by the behaviour of the 'ruggers', others enjoyed the banter and rowdiness and the 'free entertainment' provided by the players; that the rugby players provided an excuse for poking fun at middle-class norms for other customers of these hostelries; and that while some women resented being thought of as 'rugger huggers' others knowingly and willingly took on the roles of 'nurse' or 'big sister' within the teams and clubs. Again, available anecdotal evidence suggests that while 'rugger-huggers' were not uncommon, there was also a small but identifiable group of women who took the opportunity provided by 'the suspension of middle-class norms' in the post-match pub environment to display sexual aggression towards a player or players. At the college level, at least, this often appears to have had the effect of transforming the environment from one in which the players felt in control of their male bastion to one in which their manhood was called into question and where they no longer felt in control of their sexual destiny. Further evidence is obviously necessary in order to test such an hypothesis, but such a possibility does offer a warning against viewing rugby culture as entirely male-controlled and completely monolithic.

The World in Union?

It is clear that rugby's organizing bodies in the United States did perceive that there was an 'image problem' and as such there was increasing pressure to 'clean up' the image of the game off the field from the late 1970s onwards. At the same time the game was being promoted increasingly strongly at the local level. Organizational structures continued to grow at all levels. College leagues such as the New England College League were formed in the 1970s and, critically, the USARFU was formed in Chicago on 7 June 1975, with its four constituent territorial unions (Pacific Coast, Mid-Western, Western and Eastern), to manage rugby throughout the United States. External influence continued to play a part in this development. Tours by English clubs such as Roslyn Park and Richmond became more common in the 1970s as travel became easier and less expensive and as first the RFU and later the International Rugby Football Board (IRB) looked to promote the game world-wide. The launching of an American national side, the Eagles, in 1976 saw the return of United States teams to international competition for the first time since the 1924 Olympics. The Eagles played their first international match against Australia in Anaheim, California on 31 January 1976, in keeping with their longstanding antipodean rugby links. Following a rematch of the 1924 Olympic finals against France, played in June 1976, the Eagles went to Vancouver to take on their old rival Canada. As previously noted, the growth of the game at the national level has been supported by its expansion at the regional and local levels. Accordingly, states such as Texas have seen a massive growth in the game over the past 25 years, and the game has also seen significant development in the Mid-West in areas such as Wisconsin and Minnesota. Nevertheless, the strengths of the game remain on the coasts, and most notably in California. The Old Blues won the first Men's Club championship in 1979 and have won the title on nine other occasions. The first Women's Club Championship, also held in 1979, was won by Florida State University. It was not until 1980 that the first Men's Collegiate Championship was contested. It was won by Berkeley – a perennial powerhouse in the competition along with close rival Stanford. While 1981 marked the first Men's High School Championship, the Women's Collegiate Championship was not established until 1991 when it was won by the US Air Force Academy. Until that time women's collegiate teams had competed in the women's club championship. The strength of women's rugby in the USA in 1991 was evidenced by the victory of the US women's team in the first Women's World Cup.

Rugby was adopted by Stanford and Berkeley as an antidote to the violence, commercialization and professionalism of college football. The official professionalization of the game in 1995/1996 opened the gates to the commercial exploitation of rugby union, with all the concomitant problems and difficulties which have accompanied that decision (see also Chapter 9). As the world leader in commercialized (commodified) sport, one wonders how long it will be before American commercial expertise is brought to bear more fully on rugby. Perhaps we have seen the first signs of the 'Americanization' of the game with the founding of the Professional Arena Rugby League (PARL). PARL features seven-a-side rugby union played in an arena. The first game between the Dallas Outlaws and the Los Angeles Road Warriors was played in the Reunion Arena in Dallas in August 1998. The fact that the new league is not associated with the IRB or the USARFU suggests the possibility of the development of another form of rugby. Like its counterparts box lacrosse and indoor soccer, arena rugby seems to be building a separate administrative structure and marketing organization (PARL) to support it. We can perhaps summon up a vision of rugby's future in the United States from PARL's invitation to fans to participate in 'a riot featuring 40 minutes of hard-hitting rugby showcased with stunning cheerleaders, fan participation, and a rock concert at half time'.[46] It is certainly possible that American rugby will be seen as 'other' by the rest of the rugby-playing world if PARL's invitation is widely accepted. As if in response to this development, however, on 14 October 1998, in Berkeley 'USA Rugby and Fox Liberty TV Networks entered into an agreement to explore the possibility of a professional rugby competition in the United States'.[47] Spring 2000 is targeted as the inaugural season for this city-based competition which will attempt to build on the interest generated by the 1999 Rugby World Cup. It is likely that, initially at least, the league will consist of eight franchises centred in New York, Washington, Los Angeles and San Francisco – rugby's American powerbases.[48] If the globalized form of the game finally does gain recognition through television exposure in the United States, making American rugby fully 'part of the Union', it seems likely that arena rugby, a local, Americanized form of the game, will itself become 'other'.

NOTES

1. The one notable exception to this seems to be the University of Southern California where football coaches were supportive of rugby until the 1970s.
2. In the 1950s there were few more than 30 clubs; by 1980 there were more than 1,000.
3. The Eastern Rugby Union was originally founded in 1934.
4. Title IX of the Education Amendments of 1972 governs sex discrimination in educational institutions that receive federal funds. Women's athletic programmes have had to fight for equal opportunities and equal funding despite the passing of this amendment.
5. M. Maltby, *The Origins and Early Development of Professional Football* (New York, 1997), p. 3.
6. Maltby, *Origins*, p. 5.
7. See T.J.L. Chandler, 'Games at Oxbridge and the Public Schools, 1800–1880: the Diffusion of an Innovation', *International Journal of the History of Sport*, Vol.8,

No.2 (1991), pp. 171–204. Also Chandler, 'The Structuring of Manliness and the Development of Rugby Football at the Public Schools and Oxbridge, 1830–1880', in J. Nauright and T.J.L. Chandler (eds), *Making Men: Rugby and Masculine Identity* (London, 1996), pp.13–31.

8. Maltby, *Origins* , p. 6.
9. The editor of the *Harvard Magenta* (1874) wrote that the Canadian game was 'better than the somewhat sleepy game played by our men'.
10. M. Oriard, *Reading Football: How the Popular Press Created an American Spectacle* (Chapel Hill, NC, 1993).
11. R.Wagner, 'Rugby in Minnesota' (http://members.aol.com/wags40/old.html).
12. Roberta Park, 'From Football to Rugby – and Back, 1906–1919: the University of California–Stanford University Response to the "Football Crisis of 1905"', *Journal of Sport History*, Vol.11, No.3 (1984), pp. 1–36. See also B. Morse, *California Football History* (Berkeley, CA, 1937).
13. Park, 'From Football to Rugby', p. 12.
14. D. Mrozek, *Sport and American Mentality 1880–1910* (Knoxville, TN, 1983).
15. Park, 'From Football to Rugby', p. 15.
16. This was the opinion of the famed Harvard coach William T. Reid, Jr.
17. See, for example, Ronald Smith, *Sports and Freedom* (London, 1988).
18. For a complete listing of extant records see 'Stanford Rugby Football Club History' (http://www-leland.stanford.edu/group/rugby).
19. See 'New York Rugby Football Club – History' (http://www. inch.com/~. nyrugby/); also A. Woodley, 'New York RFC, 1930–1979: Its Founding and Early Days' (New York, 1979).
20. See D. Sliom, 'Washington Rugby Football Club: a Brief History' (http://www3_nsainc.com/wrfc/history.html).
21. Cambridge University's 1934 match-winning team contained eight former or future internationals.
22. See 'Dartmouth College Rugby Football Club History' (http://www. dartmouth.edu/student/athletics/rugby/history.html).
23. Ibid.
24. See Sliom, 'Washington Rugby'.
25. See 'Old Mission Beach Athletic Club History' (http://www. ombac. org/rug_his.htm).
26. See Wagner, 'Rugby in Minnesota'.
27. See the official USARFU website (http://www.usarfu.org).
28. See, for example, H. Edwards, *The Sociology of Sport* (Homewood, IL, 1973).
29. For a description of US collegiate athletics during this period see, for example, J. Scott, *The Athletic Revolution* (New York, 1982).
30. P. Donnelly and K. Young, 'Reproduction and Transformation of Cultural Forms in Sport: a Contextual Analysis of Rugby', *International Review for the Sociology of Sport* , Vol.20, No.1 (1985), p. 30.
31. Ibid.
32. B. Gough and G. Edwards, 'The Beer Talking: Four Lads, a Carry Out and the Reproduction of Masculinities', *The Sociological Review* (1998), p. 409.
33. See P. Lyman, 'The Fraternal Bond as a Joking Relationship: a Case Study of the Role of Sexist Jokes in Male Group Bonding', in M. Kimmel (ed.), *Changing Men* (San Francisco, CA, 1987).
34. See, for example, M. Messner and D. Sabo (eds), *Sport, Men and the Gender Order* (Champaign, IL, 1990).
35. See A. Tolson, *The Limits of Masculinity* (London, 1997).
36. See the USARFU website. Alcohol policies have been adopted by many of the

territorial and regional unions such as the Mid-Atlantic Rugby Football Union.

37. Donnelly and Young, 'Reproduction and Transformation', p. 27.
38. L. Wenner, 'In Search of the Sports Bar: Masculinity, Alcohol, Sports and the Mediation of Public Space', in G. Rail (ed.), *Sport and Postmodern Times* (Albany, NY, 1998) p. 302.
39. Ibid.
40. R. Oldenburg, *The Great Good Place: Cafes, Coffee Shops, Community Centers, Beauty Parlors, General Stores, Bars, Hangouts, and How They Get You through the Day* (New York, 1989), passim.
41. Anecdotal evidence was elicited from a number of informants known to the author. Their observations mirror those offered by Donnelly and Young as coming from a variety of non-academic observers of American rugby during this period. See 'Reproduction and Transformation', p. 31 and also J. Wright, 'A Ruffian's Game for Gentlemen: Rugby Football in Sociocultural Contexts', doctoral dissertation, University of Delaware, 1993.
42. Donnelly and Young, 'Reproduction and Transformation', passim.
43. Ibid.
44. Ibid., p. 27.
45. K. Young, 'Get 'em off: the Performance, Organization and Control of Rugby Behaviour', in Donnelly and Young, 'Reproduction and Transformation', p. 31.
46. *Rugby World* (October 1998) p. 90.
47. See website – http://rugbyclubs.com/us_news/.us981014.htm
48. For a comprehensive listing of US rugby club sites see website (http:// darkwing. uoregon.edu/~benc/sites/sites.html).

4

Learning to Be a Man: French Rugby and Masculinity*

Thierry Terret

There they are, 30 good-looking boys fighting ferociously for the ball. They know that holding it for even a few seconds can mean a severe injury. Never mind! ... Their passion for that ball is stronger than anything. They want it! They want it! ... And their muscular bodies leap, and their quivering hands tense, and their crazed eyes follow the ball, always the ball, follow its whirling flight and its deceptive bounces. But the ball, like a woman, seems to play with their desire.[1]

At the beginning of the Third Republic in 1870 France was unfamiliar with modern sports; only academic pursuits such as fencing and horseback riding, traditional games and gymnastic exercises enjoyed a certain amount of success. The development of sports occurred mainly through the influence of England, especially in areas with the largest British communities – in Paris and ports along the English Channel and the Atlantic Ocean.[2] Rugby football was no exception. It was played as early as 1872, in Le Havre, by British residents who formed the Le Havre Athletic club. In 1877 French college students and British textile merchants working in Paris created the English Taylors' Club, followed two years later by the Paris Football Club. Encouraged by these examples, other French students in the capital founded the Racing Club of France in 1882, the Stade Français in 1883 and the Olympic Club in 1888.[3]

In Bordeaux, in the south-west, the Bordeaux Athletic Club (BAC) and the Stade Bordelais were created under similar circumstances, at the initiative of a group of students and British nationals. The two clubs merged in 1900. Other teams, such as the Stade Athlétique Bordelais (SAB) and the Burdigala, soon joined them, allowing the creation of a south-western championship[4] at a time when soccer and rugby went their separate ways in France.[5]

*Translated from the French by Karen Tucker, MA; 75612.26@compuserve.com

Rugby's development was marked by geographical, social and gender restrictions, which had three decisive consequences. First, the sport reflected the diversity of values that different social groups attached to physical effort. Rugby was considered above all a student activity and expressed a form of excellence and ideal masculinity for French society. For certain visionaries rugby could thus serve as an educational vehicle furthering the goals of the French Republic's schools. Secondly, rugby gave the south-west the opportunity to confront Parisian domination openly, to compete on its own soil against the capital which, since the Revolution of 1789, had never stopped pitting its centralist and authoritarian Jacobin tradition against the decentralist Girondist position that was particularly strong in Bordeaux. Finally, beyond the rivalry between Paris and the provinces rugby also offered the opportunity to forge and exhibit a masculine ideal at a time when, between 1870 and 1914, the country was going through the longest 'night before combat' in its history as it prepared to take back Alsace and Lorraine from the Prussian enemy. By acting out an on-going collective battle, rugby had a remarkable 'capacity to activate community and national identities'.[6] It would be hard to imagine such an identification not being linked with the intensification of values related to masculinity, since conquering and persuading were major themes in a society dominated by men and haunted by the spirit of *revanche* (revenge). Until recently, in fact, hunting and war were the two activities most exclusively male throughout history.[7]

Paradoxically, however, the history of the relationship between sport and gender has hardly been studied in France. A number of studies have opened up new perspectives on the subject,[8] but most remain surprisingly marginal compared with the wealth of research in the English-speaking world.[9] Moreover, the work that has been done focuses exclusively on the contribution of sports to the construction of feminine identity or the role of women in the history of sports. In this field gender is limited to the feminine, and it must be acknowledged that masculine identity has not been the subject of research investigating its relationship with sports. This observation can be extended to all French research on gender, which is clearly characterized by the valorization of the feminine and, simultaneously, by a lack of concern for history,[10] compared with approaches that are more sociologically, psychologically or biologically oriented.

The history of French rugby has, however, been the subject of many successful works,[11] even if researchers have rarely dealt specifically with masculine identity. They have, instead, focused on collective identity, the process of territorialization and, more generally, the relationship between rugby, politics and culture. Only anthropological, and to a lesser extent, ethnological approaches have attempted to investigate rugby's role in expressing values perceived as highly masculine.[12] These studies, however, present at least two problems.

The first results from the methodology used, which simultaneously compares the players' social status, game position, geographic origin and style of play in order to demonstrate practices that differ significantly across opposing systems – for example, socio-economically disadvantaged forwards from the south-west of France who emphasize strength and solidarity against intellectual Parisians in backline positions who stress speed and individuality. Thus, Christian Pociello, using statistical findings, analyses the social divisions of rugby's several aspects by interpreting them as the expression of different and legitimate systems of violence and opposition.[13] While such an approach may seem seductive, Pociello was nevertheless reproached for implicitly basing his analysis on stereotypes, especially masculine stereotypes, without having discussed their validity.[14] Moreover, these studies try to demonstrate how ways of expressing virility find especially fertile terrain in rugby through its practice and institutions, but they place masculine identity in a contemporary context. In modern Western societies, however, masculine identity has undergone a series of profound transformations and crises; probably the two most significant of these occurred at the beginning of the twentieth century[15] and during the years 1970–80.[16] In other words, there is little relevance in studying the relationship between rugby and masculinity during a given period using characteristics analysed in a different context such as ours. Consequently, my goal is to show how the initial development of rugby in France at the turn of the century generated and drew sustenance from specific values associated not only with masculine identity but also with middle-class and peasant populations. These values overlapped with both regional and national identity issues.

Masculine Identity and Identities

After accurately distinguishing between 'maleness', a biological concept, and 'masculinity', which focuses on men's psychological attitudes and characteristics, Robert Stoller concludes that 'masculinity consists of the preoccupation with being strong, independent, tough, cruel, polygamous, misogynistic and depraved'.[17] This identity is largely constructed in opposition to the other gender which, historically and socially, has been defined by the double principle of female subordination and male domination, a principle considered as a form of symbolic violence *par excellence* by Pierre Bourdieu.[18] There are, however, different levels of tolerance for violence even within patriarchal societies. It is therefore appropriate to consider how the criteria defining masculinity differed among groups in order to understand how rugby, at the time it became established in France, offered a specific way to construct a sense of masculinity that affected some groups more than it did others.

Jacques Defrance has demonstrated that, at the end of the nineteenth century, 'physical excellence'[19] was socially defined in at least four ways, identified by the intersection of the athlete's socio-economic status with the degree of physical commitment required to produce the ideal body. With this model the four ideal types of men may be identified by means of different physical activities. For the aristocracy, 'man' was defined by grace, style and the elegance of his demeanour, values cultivated by careful grooming and the academic arts. In the eyes of the bourgeoisie the ideal man was individualistic and thrived in activities where intense effort was given full expression through achievements and record-making perfor-mances. On the one hand the lower classes of society favoured an ideal of self-control, formalized by medical doctors and developed in schools, which dominated school and military physical education regimens, and the field of medicine. On the other, the lower classes fostered an ideal of physical strength expressed by more traditional symbols of masculinity found either in gymnastic exercises or in the practice of acrobatics, wrestling and tightrope walking.

The first two of these coexisting models of masculinity went through a period of serious questioning. After an initial crisis at the end of the seventeenth and the beginning of the eighteenth century,[20] masculinity experienced its strongest shock waves in France at the end of the nineteenth century. This crisis involved only the dominant classes, the aristocracy and the urban middle class, at a time when 80 per cent of the French population was still rural, and resulted from transformations in male–female relationships.[21] At the start of the Third Republic men agreed on the importance of women in the family; they now considered a woman 'the foundation of the family, where her influence is more decisive than the father's. Her health is an absolute necessity, even more important than his. The strength of the generations she gives birth to depends on it.'[22] Benefiting from a number of social advances, especially in the areas of education[23] and civil rights, women demanded changes in their everyday relationships with men without necessarily going through the political process.[24] They then encouraged the new generation of the dominant classes to reinforce signs of their self-assertion through different activities and a variety of roles and social positions.[25]

At the same time, these dominant sectors of French youth were overcome by pessimism, discouragement and a crisis of confidence after the defeat by Germany in 1870, as evidenced by Agathon's dark analysis.[26] The author saw little besides sports that could maintain the spirit of conquest, military virtues and a warlike atmosphere:[27] nothing could be 'more helpful for the renewal of the country than a generation that is athletic, realistic, non-ideological, chaste and capable of handling economic challenges ...'[28]

In France it was precisely these young middle-class and aristocratic men, first from Paris, then from Bordeaux, who made up the first rugby teams and founded clubs in the most prestigious high schools – Condorcet, Lakanal, Michelet in Paris and Bordeaux High School and Talence High School in the south-west. Thus in Toulouse, the Stade Olympien des Etudiants de Toulouse was established by former high-school students dispersed among the colleges in the city.[29] More generally, it was these young graduates whose efforts led to the institutionalization of most sports and who were ardent defenders of amateur sports and a certain vision of the Republic.[30] Recruitment was exclusive. Pierre de Coubertin himself, promoter *par excellence* of this bourgeois sport,[31] refereed France's first championship final – between the Racing Club and the Stade Français at Bagatelle Park in Paris in 1892.

In this sense, rugby did not diverge from the models inspiring these young men. Between 1882 and 1892, when rugby first became a recognized sport, the players developed a non-violent and spectacular style of play by combining the aristocratic demand for elegance with the bourgeois emphasis on individual performance.[32] Rugby thus provided the opportunity to demonstrate the qualities of dexterity, speed and quick decision-making that were the prerogatives of the upper classes. In contrast, strength was a value that was neither admired nor sought after. The rugby player was a fast-moving athlete who knew how to fake and spin around, to trip and break away – a playing style that pleased French reporters, who showered praise on the athletes. True tackles were rare. The rugby of these young bourgeois men was similar to *la barrette*, a traditional French game known since the middle of the nineteenth century in which, as opposed to rugby, a player had only to brush against the ball carrier and yell '*touché*' to stop play.[33] As long as contact was not essential, attack strategies favoured individual over collective effort, just as in defence, where players were reluctant to tackle below the waist, physical contact was limited. Rugby was an extension of track and field sports, and the players were mainly runners and jumpers who moved easily from track and field to team sports, sometimes during the same meets. In late-nineteenth-century France, rugby was not so much a collective sport as an individual one, pitting the intelligence of the athlete against the anonymous strength of the group. In general, it preserved the values of its first players who were reluctant, for example, to get dirty or find themselves on the ground in a physically subordinate position.[34] Certain forwards even refused to participate in scrums, which were less glamorous because they were more anonymous. The style of play seemed distant from that observed in England,[35] most likely because the masculine ideal was different on the two sides of the Channel. Anglophiles such as de Coubertin and Paschal Grousset tried unsuccessfully to promote the English example and introduce it in French high schools,[36] but the French rugby player had not yet broken with the dandy of the *belle époque*. When men wished to impress, they were likely to choose elegance over masculine strength.

Beyond the process of social distinction that led an individual, during the game itself, to display behaviours that were the most revealing and the most likely to signal membership in a high social class, rugby also offered other attractions for a dandy trying to demonstrate his manhood. It allowed him to affirm his break with childhood and, as a result, his submission to patriarchal authority. This was especially the case because fathers were perceived as being responsible for the change in mores and the crisis in masculine identity. Secondly, the player identified himself as male by emphasizing his differences *vis-à-vis* women and creating places from which they could naturally be excluded or reduced to the role of spectator. Pierre MacOrlan, the brilliant author of *La Clique du Café Brebis* (The Gang at the Ewe Café), published in 1918, evoked the spirit in which the young men of his generation played rugby; they were concerned with distinguishing themselves socially, displaying courage, liberating themselves from their families and seducing women:

> At the age of 16, we knew how to discipline ourselves and, despite the malicious sweetness of a young girl's beautiful eyes, we knew how to focus on winning the match for the team. But, upon reflection, each of us could understand the value of this renunciation. At night, around the table where steam rose from the tea cups ... our big sisters and our big sisters' friends sang our praises ... Because, despite everything, a rugby player is

someone more mysterious and more distinguished than a gymnast, in shirt-sleeves, fearful because he stained the knees of his pants during a fall. The girls vaguely sensed that these young men, outfitted in the English style and attentive to the referee's whistle, were no longer under the control of their parents, at least for 80 minutes. Girls, even middle-class girls, prefer those men who know how to achieve the sort of freedom they do not wish for themselves.[37]

This richly evocative passage clearly defines how, for MacOrlan, rugby contributed to the forging of masculine identity from a social, moral and biological perspective. First, man is defined within the framework of social status; the rugby player is a decision-maker, as opposed to those who, in 'shirt-sleeves', shine only through brute force. With respect to moral values, he is also the man who tolerates pain and glorifies his courage. Finally, man is defined by what he is not (a woman) or by what he is no longer (a child), resulting in two mirror definitions: manhood in opposition both to childhood, since rugby is a true initiation marking a distancing from his parents, and to womanhood, since rugby provides a man with the opportunity to conquer her while displaying his autonomy.

At the beginning of the twentieth century young women of good family were again increasingly seeking strong, rather than handsome, men.[38] As opposed to preceding generations, it appears that they were receptive to a more virile masculinity and the subdued rugby of that period could hardly resist such pressure and would eventually move toward a rougher form of play, thus joining the images of combat valued at other levels of society.

Rugby: Male and Regional Identity

As rugby opened up to other social classes, the definition of man, whose identity was partially constructed through rugby, was also transformed. This change went hand-in-hand with a process of geographical and social diffusion that over several years turned rugby into a repository of regional identities and helped to develop a certain idea of what constituted a 'real' man.

The establishment of rugby in south-western France owed a great deal to the presence of the British, especially the wine merchants, who brought with them a culture that found particularly favourable conditions in this region. Such was the case in the Bordeaux area, where a Scottish businessman, J.J. Shearer, was instrumental in introducing rugby. Shearer, along with Tom Potter and Jim Crockwell, brought the sport to Pau in 1888, and he introduced rugby to Bayonne together with the Welshman Owen Roe.[39] Several men from Bordeaux were instrumental in disseminating rugby throughout the region. Thus Pierre Fabre, who attended high school in Bordeaux, left for Bayonne to get his *baccalauréat*[40] and ended up launching one of the best clubs in the country. Other Bordeaux men founded clubs in Agen (1900), Bergerac (1902), Oloron (1903), Casteljaloux (1904), Mauléon et Saint-Sever (1905), Périgueux, Habas and Cambo (1906), Mont-de-Marsan, Hendaye and Soustons (1908) and Marmande (1911).[41] However, other major centres of rugby, such as Toulouse,[42] did not benefit from the presence of men from Great Britain or Bordeaux.

Bordeaux's early start in disseminating rugby meant that the city had a great influence on newcomers during the early years. Crowned first south-western champion, the Stade Bordelais then set its sights on the university students of Paris and challenged the Stade Français. Stade Bordelais was defeated, but its players proved that the Parisians were not the only ones who could handle a rugby ball and that it was a force to be reckoned with.[43] At that time l'Union des Sociétés Françaises de Sports Athlétiques (USFSA), the main French national sports federation, completely ignored clubs in the provinces beyond Paris; they used only players from the capital, for example, to make up the French national team. The USFSA was founded in 1887 to co-ordinate track events, and was originally made up of the large Parisian clubs, the Racing and the Stade Français. The original federation was transformed two years later into a expanded organization. Run by Georges de Saint Clair, an aristocrat who actively lobbied on behalf of sports, the federation co-ordinated all athletic sports in France, which, at that time, were limited to lawn-tennis, track and field, and rugby football.[44] It remained an elitist and overwhelmingly Parisian organization. In rugby the French national championship played since 1892 included only Parisian clubs; among these the Stade Français especially stood out. It would not be until 1899 that the USFSA accepted the idea of a yearly final opposing the capital's champion against the best club from the provinces.[45] As a result, the new French championship pitted the Stade Bordelais against the Stade Français, and the team from Bordeaux won the first such match on its home field.

This highly symbolic final between a club from the south-west and one from Paris would be repeated many times as southerners – from Bordeaux, Bayonne, Tarbes, Perpignan and Toulouse[46] – gradually rose to dominance, as the results from 1900, outlined below, show:

1900: Racing Club of France (RCF) defeated Bordeaux
1901: Bordeaux defeated Stade Français (SF)
1902: RCF defeated Bordeaux
1903: SF defeated Toulouse
1904: Bordeaux defeated SF
1905: Bordeaux defeated SF
1906: Bordeaux defeated SF
1907: Bordeaux defeated SF
1908: SF defeated Bordeaux
1909: Bordeaux defeated Toulouse
1910: Lyon defeated Bordeaux
1911: Bordeaux defeated University Sporting Club of France
    (SCUF Paris)
1912: Toulouse defeated RCF
1913: Bayonne defeated SCUF
1914: Bayonne defeated Tarbes
1915: no championship
1916: Toulouse defeated SF

The geographical dominance of the south-western clubs became even more pronounced after 1918, when the Parisians disappeared from the list of winners. Until World War II the hegemony of the Aquitaine and Languedoc clubs remained unchallenged as the two south-western teams regularly opposed each other in the French championship final. Only Lyon managed for a time to match them when it played the final in 1910 and 1931, and twice against Narbonne in 1932 and 1933.

There are historical explanations for the rivalry between certain regions and the capital that some people attribute to the invasion of the 'Barons of the north',[47] in the case of the south-west, but that more likely had its origins in the revolutionary period. The centralist position of the Parisian bourgeoisie who overthrew the monarchy in 1789 was in direct opposition to the notion of decentralized power, which was advocated by Bordeaux. The contradictions between the Jacobin and Girondist[48] would subsequently engender intense hostility.

At the beginning of the century the Parisian 'enemy' allowed regional teams to overcome parochial rivalries. This was exemplified by an incident that occurred just before the French championship final in 1909 between Bordeaux and Toulouse, the two great teams of the south-west. The Bordeaux players, upon arriving at the Toulouse train station, were greeted by Toulouse supporters with cries of 'Long live Bordeaux!' to which they responded, 'Long live Toulouse!'[49] And at the end of the match, won by Bordeaux with a score of 17–0, the spectators shouted, 'Long live the provinces!'[50] Such regional solidarity led to the obvious conclusion that 'the shores of the Garonne'[51] are becoming the place of choice for rugby in France.[52]

South-westerners used every opportunity to remind their teams about the Parisian menace. In 1907 the newspaper L'Express du Midi warned the Stade Toulousain's managers to keep their players in shape at a time when the Parisian teams were improving their performance at international matches.[53] The final that Toulouse won in 1912 against the Racing Club led to a virtual deification of the team: a red statue of the Virgin Mary wearing the local colours was set up to thank the players and their supporters.[54] It should be noted that the regional press had very explicitly decided what was at stake some time earlier: 'Bordeaux and Toulouse will avenge … all the provinces for the great injustices they have too long endured and for the unjustified humiliations that Paris believes it can inflict.'[55]

Provincial honour was at the centre of the dispute, along with its cortège of symbolic figures. The male values expressed by rugby were, in this case, values of resistance: a true man rebels in order to be free. The player embodied man's athletic ability, in a cultural and symbolic sense, to resist central authority and to be his own master.[56] Rugby was thus seen as cultural revenge for the political domination that Paris imposed on the provinces, especially in those provinces most sensitive about their identity.

Gradually, with the diffusion of rugby, this intensified regionalism would find a somewhat different mode of expression, although it would by no means disappear. Rugby spread from Bordeaux to the large cities and suburbs, then fanned out through the valleys until it reached every village. Most clubs still active today were established during this pre-1914 period. The top rugby teams, however, were all situated in the south-central part of the country, an area more rural, more traditional, less urbanized and industrialized than the north, and whose economic and cultural opposition to the capital was blatant.

This limited diffusion, which was unusual in the history of French sports,[57] eventually led to a village-centred rugby that was more noticeable in the Aquitaine region than around Toulouse and that brought in its wake a renewed enthusiasm for the game.[58] Because this phenomenon involved a more rural, middle- and working-class population, it resulted in the emergence of a new male ideal. This becomes apparent when one contrasts the types of player recruited in the suburbs and small towns and villages with those recruited by the major Bordeaux and Toulouse teams before 1914. The intellectual and industrial middle classes still predominated on these urban teams. For example, the Stade Toulousain championship team of 1912 included seven university students, one manufacturer, one pharmacist, one city hall secretary, one salaried employee, two veterinarians and two soldiers. Similarly, the 1909 Stade Bordelais team included two merchants, two manufacturers, one shopkeeper, one farmer, three chemists, one chimney sweep, one university student, one teacher, one person with a law degree and two soldiers.[59] The symbolic battles taking place on the playing fields at the beginning of the century only intensified the conflict between the southern ideal of the strong man and the northern ideal of the urban intellectual.

Anti-Paris sentiment was most intense in the south-west, since this rural area suffered at the beginning of the century from a crisis that affected the livelihoods of peasants in the wine-growing regions. Their migration toward the large urban centres prompted a renewal of the most traditional values, which at times took on a political slant.[60] It is reasonable to believe that rugby served as a way for a male peasant to affirm his virtues at a time when they were being called into question. However, in contrast to the first stage of rugby's establishment in the middle class, peasants defined manhood in a completely different way. It was strength, land and solidarity that upheld the peasant man's honour and set him in opposition to the 'city people', especially the most vain among them – the Parisians. Rugby was a way peasant men could overcome their inferiority complex and take advantage of the morphological and muscular capital they had developed through work.[61]

The new man, as embodied by the player, found clear expression in the change in playing style that journalists reported and the spectators expected. Pech and Thomas comment that, after 1912, regional journalists started putting less emphasis on impressive individual breakaways, sometimes even criticizing the lack of solidarity among the players. The positive descriptions of scrums and rolling mauls and the disappearance of dribbling indicate that the playing style that was valued, and thus met the expectations of readers, had profoundly moved in the direction of a game where strength prevailed over style.[62] From then on, rugby noticeably joined other elements of south-western popular culture. It was – and still is – portrayed as an illustration of the south-west's 'natural' temperament.[63] Rugby playing went hand-in-glove with other aspects of regional life, such as bullfighting, hunting, festivals (the *bandas*)[64] and the love of good food. Another symbol of the south-west was the '*castagne*', a Gascon noun meaning 'fight' which has a large number of declensions and metaphors that clearly reveal the cultural importance of fighting.[65] Finally, this part of the country was already well-known for its machismo. Rugby appears to have become a means of reinforcing all these cultural symbols. It regularly provided the occasion for enormous meals and the recounting of conquests and seductions.[66] The press, for example, followed with avowed pleasure the feminine conquests of Ramondou, who played for Toulouse at the beginning of the century.[67] Emile Lesieur, a Basque and French international player before 1914, recalls that he went to see a girlfriend in London every time the team played in England, much to the chagrin of the managers, who nevertheless tolerated his escapades. Perhaps they realized that he really believed it when he said that 'it helped my game, since I'm an extremely nervous person'.[68] In short, in the country of bullfighting and *fois gras*, rugby was defined as 'a gathering of fifteen guys who have balls'.[69]

It is thus not surprising that the rugby player was increasingly valued for playing like a warrior and demonstrating his virility. Manhood had previously been displayed through style; now men tried to impress by being effective (winning the match) and courageous. Masculine honour required the defying of your adversary and the seeking out of physical combat without worrying too much about the rules. Since you could not truly be a man in the south-west without playing rugby, questions of honour and pride increasingly took centre-stage during scrums.

Male Identity and Education: the Rugby Missionaries
Rugby moved in another direction, however, at a time when the sport was experiencing an intensification of identity issues. This direction, openly educational, also played a role in rugby's limited geographical implantation. It created another definition of masculinity by evoking the concept of a continually evolving man.

It must first be understood that during the Third Republic the school system was made up of two entirely separate entities: 'the people's school' and 'the school for prominent citizens'.[70] While all children, starting in 1882, were required to attend school until the age of 13, the people's school was reserved for the children of the working class. After receiving their primary school certificate, the most gifted of these children could study in a teachers' college to become primary school teachers. The school for prominent citizens taught children of the middle class who considered high school an inevitable rite of passage. The teaching profession was not identical within these two systems. The people's school emphasized the basics, reading, writing and arithmetic and physical discipline, while the school for prominent citizens stressed academic knowledge and initiative. Physical education was also radically different. In the people's school, before 1914, 'the teaching of gymnastics, so important for the physical development of young people, is imperative today because of our military structure and the adoption of required military service'.[71] Inspired by the Swedish method, gymnastic exercises emphasized physical development and practice.[72] The school for prominent citizens had a greater tolerance for sports, although they were not valued as highly as they were in England. High school, however, became the only place where sports managed to develop, albeit with some difficulty.[73] As a result, rugby became an activity sponsored by high-school clubs, especially in the south-west, without being taught in the strict sense of the term. Rugby often took root in local communities in much the same way. In Toulouse, for example, the first club to devote itself to rugby was none other than the Fédération Athlétique du Lycée de Toulouse (Athletic Federation of Toulouse High Schools), whose members joined the Stade Toulousian once they became university students.[74] In general, rugby was spread by high-school students in the large cities of the south and the south-west – Bayonne, Toulouse, Perpignan and Montpellier.[75] Of the 13 rugby clubs in Toulouse in 1912, eight were high school or university teams.[76] This made rugby unique considering that, since 1892, the number of community clubs belonging to the USFSA had permanently exceeded the number of school clubs until the ratio reached ten to one by 1914.[77]

Besides the recruitment of players among the upper middle class – and we have already seen what type of man was sought – it is also interesting to consider the case of the primary school because here too the south-west showed much originality. Before 1914 sports could clearly not be offered to children during their years of mandatory schooling. Only a type of gymnastics that was analytically measured and controlled could meet the disciplinary and health requirements required by the law as well as by military, medical and political authorities. State schools did not value an athletic model, but rather an hygienic one opposed to any practice posing a physical or moral risk. Authorities, including sports advocates, did not see how sports could offer any educational benefit for young people.[78] Rugby, violent and uncontrollable, was the antithesis of everything deemed desirable for the man of the future.

Some people did speak highly of the merits of sports, however, for young children as well as teenagers. Among them was Philippe Tissié, a physician who advocated a more modern conception of physical education. Tissié wanted to develop outdoor activities without abandoning Swedish gymnastics. This Protestant republican born in the south-west strongly believed in preserving the heritage of regional cultures and considered games a cultural repository: 'The soul of a people is revealed in games ... Tell me how you play and I will tell you who you are.'[79] He distinguished three types of game: recreational games, major games such as *la barrette* and sports such as rugby. In his view, rugby was not educational; like other sports, it offered:

> real dangers for young people who participate; even the training it requires should not be encouraged because it involves outdoor acrobatics, which is worse than anything! We have to fight such athletic tendencies, because children and teenagers should limit themselves to sports, that is to say, athletic games, that are less rigorous ... .[80]

Dr Tissié later asserted that 'sport provokes reflexive impulses in the individual that do not correspond to the French temperament and generates troublesome consequences with respect to the longevity of its players'.[81] He believed that *la barrette*, to the contrary, was a type of recreational game and was especially appropriate for primary and middle-school students. The prevailing educational orthodoxy, encouraged by the strong influence of medical circles hostile to excessive exercise, reinforced this choice of a sport that could be adapted, euphemized and better controlled. In the schools of the Third Republic, *la barrette* was to rugby what gymnastic dancing, called calisthenics, was to dance and what physical education exercises were to athletic sports.

Tissié wanted the children of the working class to benefit from the type of physical education that had been offered to the sons of the middle class for about 12 years.[82] He took advantage of his role of inspecting primary schools between 1896 and 1907 to organize *barrette* matches. This 'football without violence'[83] spread throughout the south-west with the support of regional education commissioners, the middle class and the local press. In 1888, wishing to improve his efficiency, Tissié created a regional organization called the *Ligue Girondine d'Education Physique*. This group was in direct competition with the two national organizations founded only weeks earlier by de Coubertin (*Comité pour la propagation des exercices physiques dans l'éducation*) and Grousset (*Ligue Nationale d'Education Physique*).[84] The Gironde league aimed to promote the playing of outdoor games that respected regional traditions.[85] Two years later Tissié launched the idea of '*lendits*'. These annual outdoor events brought together hundreds of students for several days in June, offering them a variety of traditional and athletic activities. The highest local authorities attended and supported the events, at least until 1903, when a change in education commissioner suddenly led to the closing of Tissié's organization.[86]

These '*lendits*' invariably ended with a *barrette* match, whose rules were formalized in 1892 and distributed throughout the region two years later.[87] Very quickly, Tissié continued his proselytizing at a higher level, even within the *Ecoles Normales d'Instituteurs* (teachers' colleges) by means of a series of conferences. As a result, most of these institutions, which stuck strictly to convention and republican ideals[88] in their training of primary school teachers, ended up organizing sports clubs. In the south this would serve as an opportunity to further develop rugby, which was played in such clubs as the *Normalienne rochelaise*, the *Union sportive normalienne d'Angoulême* and the *Union Sportive de l'Ecole Normale de Toulouse*.

The rugby played by these college students received unexpected additional support from the split that would soon divide the two forms of football, one that would oppose the rugby of the Republic to the soccer of the church. In response to the church and the former monarchy uniting against the Republic, an anti-clerical movement developed, reaching its peak after the Dreyfus affair and the fall of General Boulanger. In 1905 a definitive law codified the division by separating church and state in all areas of public life. Among other things the Catholic side reacted by launching an effort to proselytize youth, which was formalized in 1898 by the creation of the *Fédération Gymnique et Sportive des Patronages de France*. The new organization was responsible for promoting the creation of Catholic youth fellowships and co-ordinating their activities. Sport was quickly perceived as a means to attract new members; ignoring it would have amounted to leaving the field open to the anti-clericalists: 'The enemy is here, ready to welcome the child entrusted to you and enroll him in these gymnastic, shooting and physical exercise clubs where it [the 'enemy'] knows how ... to admirably disguise its destruction of any religious thought.'[89] For each secular school there soon arose a Catholic youth fellowship, and the church soon assigned these groups new goals:

> The task assigned to a federation entirely dedicated to male sports was to 'make men' at a time when the clergy, aware of a certain feminization [in the church], focused their efforts on masses, retreats, pilgrimages and movements, etc. for men only.[90]

In the south-west parish youth fellowships spread rapidly at the beginning of the century[91] and, in reaction, secular groups sprang up 'to stop the rise of clerical activity'.[92] This competition led federation leaders to make certain political choices, which resulted in the division of the two sports: clerical circles adopted soccer while secular republican militants claimed rugby. The clergy considered soccer 'gracious, scientific [and] it creates a very precise feeling of distance, a perfect knowledge of its role [whereas rugby] quickly becomes jerky, fumbling, brutal and easily degenerates into fist fights; one seeks in vain a guiding principle'.[93]

Within the context of this intense rivalry that divided France and the imminent conflict with Germany, turn-of-the-century teachers were virtual tools at the service of the Republic. The 'black Hussars', as Jules Ferry[94] himself called them, were charged with defending republican values, which at that time radically opposed the clerical tradition. For those teachers most receptive to the virtues of sports (although few were), rugby became a formidable educational tool for forging men in the republican sense of the term – in other words, individuals whose bodies were at the service of the nation rather than religion. Religious schools staked out their positions in reaction; as one example, they abolished rugby competitions. This is what happened in 1908–09 in the Bordeaux area. While several private middle and high schools had sports clubs that played rugby under the auspices of the *Union Régionale des Patronages Sportifs du Sud-ouest*, a regional federation of Catholic youth fellowships, the Union suddenly ended all rugby matches to the benefit of the soccer association, regardless of the position taken by the directors of the schools concerned.[95] As a result each school asserted its position, the Catholics accusing the secular schools of having chosen the violent and dangerous sport of rugby, the secular schools accusing the Catholics of exploiting and perverting sports for their anti-republican and reactionary ends.

Of course, teachers used many means other than sports to build a republican France. Gymnastics was still the main component of physical education. Only regions where the rivalry between church and Republic was strongest were really affected by this rivalry – essentially rural areas and areas set among mid-sized mountains. Although situated in the heart of rugby country, the strongly Catholic Basque enclave remained either closed or hostile to the invasion of rugby for a long time. Nevertheless, teachers, respected by rural and traditional peasant society and having close social and cultural ties with their students, played an important role in disseminating rugby throughout the south-west, even after World War I when there was a relative decline in anti-clericalism.

The values developed through rugby, in the view of secular schools, culminated in the creation of a republican, or anti-clerical, individual. However, this was a rugby that was euphemized by means of *la barrette*, at least in principle. It is likely that educators saw in this game a way to affirm masculine values against male deviance. *La barrette* contributed to an ideal in which man dominated his natural aggressiveness and put his virility at the service of the group or leader.[96] As Tissié stated a little later, 'The war generation is undisciplined. The spirit of submission has been weakened by the long absence of the father ... To discipline your muscles is to discipline your mind and, by this braking mechanism itself, inhibit unhealthy impulses.'[97] School rugby played a role in defining the ideal man as someone who was master of his strength. Self-control and basic physical effort were valued as more likely to develop cardiopulmonary capacity: 'Scrums have become less frequent, leaving more room for running, which has greater effect on the physical development of adolescents than scrummaging, which requires more shoving'.[98] But could such statements last in the light of rugby's evolution outside academe? The men who played *la barrette* hardly met the expectations of the game's enthusiasts. And rugby was conquering France, not for its educational virtues but because of its ability to generate strong feelings of pride and reflect some of society's dominant values. While *la barrette* became increasingly a woman's game, men turned toward forms of play that were more aggressive.

Rugby between the Two World Wars: Man and Race
Soon after World War I the USFSA fell apart under multiple pressures and several single-sport federations were subsequently created. One of these, the *Fédération Française de Rugby* (FFR), took over the destiny of the sport in October 1920. One of its first objectives was to make French rugby more visible on the international scene. Of course, several federations went in the same direction from 1920 to 1924; during this period France played 24 international matches, not counting the Olympic Games.[99] However, rugby, along with soccer and track and field, was one of the best represented sports at the international level. Rugby matches quickly achieved remarkable popularity in the country and games played against teams from the British Isles drew tens of thousands of spectators to the stadiums. Major games even started to be broadcast on the radio in 1923, and the government, participating in the craze for the sport at the international level, suggested the filming of games that might further the nation's image:

France's victory over Ireland in rugby football in Dublin in 1920, the first victory abroad for a French rugby team, had enormous repercussions. The political newspapers and numerous magazines in England and America devoted very long, illustrated articles to... these events... .In similar cases, it would be most useful if propaganda films could include some episodes of important matches in which France is favoured to win.[100]

Barely a few months after the armistice, in a France intoxicated by victory and the worship of its soldiers, rugby became an instrument of nationalism with which players and spectators completed their construction of a male ideal corresponding to the ideal of national pride. As a result, there were no longer losers or victors of the Great War, only the French and others, in a state of confusion heightened by the dramatic intensity of rugby matches. The French opposed the Americans at the 1924 Olympic championship in Paris. The French, favoured to win, nevertheless lost the match before a stunned crowd. The American flag was torn up and the Welsh referee forcefully insulted. Olympic rugby did not survive this incident, being removed from the games by the International Olympic Committee.

> That was the period of 'rrrace' with three R's[101] and it was said that if Perpignan had won, it was because of the superiority of its 'rrrace,' remembers Alfred Sauvy, former head of the Racing Club. Anyone who lost a match was treated like a coward and considered unworthy of the French race, the race of victors.[102]

Although being a man meant being a patriot above all, a Frenchman who declared his superiority over others, rugby's influence was not limited to national pride. On the contrary, local identities were also shaped by the game. Indeed, the FFR was built on a foundation that remained very Parisian. International matches almost never took place outside Paris. However, the social and regional orientation followed by rugby before 1914 continued. While the number of affiliated clubs reached a record of 894 in 1924, their expansion was especially large in the south-west and rural, and working-class populations increasingly identified with the game. Organizing a championship that required players to qualify by region helped to create a concrete structure that intensified identity issues: France against foreign country, province against Paris, town against town. While these three levels differed, they all reflected rugby's ability to inflame group pride.

These developments led to an extraordinary accentuation of rough play and brutality in the game. The honour of the community, whether team, village or region, demanded the expression of strength and virility, even at the price of unspeakable violence. Intimidation became the rule, affecting players, referees and spectators. The following report, for example, appeared in the sports press and concerned a Carcassonne–Perpignan match: 'Excited by the spectators' shouts, their brains overheated by the sun, a vindictive spirit developed to an extreme degree, producing unprecedented scenes.'[103] French rugby then got caught up in a spiral in which not being looked down on as being physically weak was all that mattered. Fights multiplied and a torrent of insults would follow the first punch. In 1927 a player lost his life during a match between Quillan and Perpignan, a few weeks after several players from Perpignan had been attacked by their adversaries.

The federation was powerless to contain this drift towards violence. After the second fatal accident, in 1930, the courts held the FFR legally responsible. No longer recognizing the federation's authority, 12 of the most prestigious clubs left the FFR to create an amateur rugby association, the *Union Française de Rugby Amateur*, in the hope of putting rugby out of its agony. This split illustrated a renewed social spirit among players and managers, said contemporary commentators. For the clubs that broke away:

> rugby borrowed from sportsmanship, returning to an 'aristocratic' ideal that privileged sociability over belonging to the same class (age group and social class); in the other model, the sport borrowed from ritual, which united men ... belonging to the same local environment, to the same community.[104]

The two definitions of masculinity discussed earlier lay just beneath the surface of these two conceptions of rugby: masculinity expressed through an impressive style and attitude, and masculinity reduced to the display of virility.

To a certain extent, however, it was too late. The opportunity was too tempting for the directors of the International Board to pass up; they could flaunt their superiority and denounce the character of the French game and the type of man it was shaping. The Five Nations Tournament, which had admitted France in 1910 – no doubt because the French team presented absolutely no risk to British hegemony[105] – expelled the country in 1932 and kept it out until after World War II:

> After reviewing the documents provided by the French federation and dissident clubs, we are forced to decide that, given the

unsatisfactory state of the game of rugby football as it is managed and practised in France, neither our federations, nor the clubs under their jurisdiction, can organize or honour matches with the French team or the French clubs, at home or abroad, unless and until we are satisfied that the game is managed and played in an appropriate manner.[106]

French rugby not only engaged in violence, but also in the soliciting and purchase of players among clubs. The FFR had no other choice but to exclude the guilty parties, and disqualified players soon rose up in opposition to the Federation. The end of official relations between the FFR and the English Rugby Union facilitated contacts between some of the French dissidents and the English Rugby League. This rift was formalized in 1934 with the birth of the French Rugby League (*jeu à treize*), officially professional, which recruited from the same territory as Rugby Union.

Conclusion: What Type of Rugby for What Type of Man?
It thus appears from this review of rugby's origins in France that the sport's relationship with masculinity demonstrated the diverse ways men defined themselves. The identity process for different men was not identical, and the type of rugby favoured by students, educators and south-westerners was not exactly the same. In this sense rugby's masculine ideal could not be reduced to a simple intensification of the traditional attributes of virility, such as strength. In fact, as long as honour was at stake it was difficult for men at the beginning of the century not to take advantage of every opportunity to accentuate the very signs of their existence through a game of opposites: young middle-class men from the great Parisian and Bordeaux high schools against their parents; men from the provinces against Parisians; the French against foreigners; republicans against clericalists; educators against sportsmen, and so on. A man's character was forged more through resistance than through simple virility. These forms of opposition took shape precisely during periods when the integrity of the group was challenged, such as during the crisis of masculinity among the middle class at the end of the nineteenth century, the crisis in rural life a short time later, the crisis in the church at the same time and the ethnic crisis. Rugby, whose potential to bring people together is a precious tool for the formation of identities, eventually did play a role of defence and resistance among male populations that felt the most aggrieved.

NOTES

1. Roger Fournier, *Dans le Temple du Dieu Rugby* (Vienna, n.d.), pp. 131–2.
2. Jaccques Thibault, *Sport et éducation physique: 1870–1970* (Paris,1972); Richard Holt, *Sport and Society in Modern France* (London, 1981); Pierre Arnaud and Jean Camy (eds), *La naissance du mouvement sportif associatif en France* (Toulouse, 1986). Jacques Dumont, Gilles Pollet and M. Berjat, *Naissance du sport moderne* (Lyon, 1987).
3. In fact, the Racing and Stade Français clubs, the two oldest French sports clubs still active today, benefited from the dissolution of the Paris Football Club.
4. Jean-Paul Callède, *Du Stade Bordelais au SBUC (1889–1939)* (Talence, 1993).
5. *Les Sports Athlétiques*, No.94 (1892).
6. Paul Irlinger, 'Le sport au pluriel ou les singularités du rugby', in Christian Pociello (ed.), *Sport et société* (Paris, 1981), p. 363.
7. Elisabeth Badinter, *L'un est l'autre* (Paris, 1986), p. 266.
8. See, in particular, Serge Laget, Françoise Laget and Jean-Pierre Mazot, *Le grand livre du sport féminin* (Belleville, 1982); Annick Davisse and Catherine Louveau, *Sport, école, société: la part des femmes* (Paris, 1991); and Pierre Arnaud and Thierry Terret, *Histoire du sport féminin* (Paris, 2 vols, 1996).
9. There are many examples. It is sufficient to mention here a good overview by Jennifer Hargreaves, *Sporting Women* (London, 1994).
10. Other than the French translation of the books by Margaret Mead, *L'Un et l'autre sexe* (Paris, 1966, lst edn, 1948) and the book by G. Falconnet and N. Lefaucheur, *La fabrication des mâles* (Paris, 1975), there have been some notable exceptions over the past 15 years that should be mentioned, such as the special 'masculine/feminine' editions of the journal *Actes de la recherche en sciences sociales* (No.83, June 1990 and No.84, September 1990) in which Pierre Bourdieu does an excellent analysis, or the special edition of the journal *Le Genre Humain* (No.10, 1984). See also Tony Anatrella, *Le Sexe oublié* (Paris, 1990), Geneviève Delaisi de Parseval, *Les Sexes de l'homme* (Paris, 1985) and *Des hommes et du masculin* (Lyon, 1992), Annelise Maugue, *L'identité masculine au tournant du siècle* (Paris, 1987), as well as the intelligent analysis by Elisabeth Badinter, *XY: De l'identité masculine* (Paris, 1992).
11. Among the most complete are those by Jean Dauger, *Histoires de rugby* (Paris, 1965), G. Pastre, *Histoire générale du rugby* (Toulouse, 5 vols, 1958–72), Henry Garcia, *La fabuleuse histoire du rugby* (Paris, 1992), Jean-Pierre Augustin and Alain Garrigou, *Le rugby démêlé* (Bordeaux, 1985), Jean-Pierre Bodis, *Histoire mondiale du rugby* (Toulouse, 1987), and Jean-Pierre Augustin and Jean-Pierre Bodis, *Rugby en Aquitaine, histoire d'une rencontre* (Bordeaux, 1994).
12. Two authors have, for the most part, covered these issues: Christian Pociello, *Le rugby ou la guerre des styles.* (Paris, 1983) and Sébastien Darbon, *Rugby, mode de vie. Ethnographie d'un club. Saint-Vincent-de-Tyrosse* (Paris, 1995) and *Du rugby dans une ville de foot* (Paris, 1997).
13. Pociello, *Le rugby*, p. 219.
14. This critique of Pociello's work was discussed at length by Sébastien Darbon in 'Quand les boeufs jouent avec les gazelles', *Ethnologie Française*, Vol.25, No.1 (1995), pp. 113–25.
15. Maugue, *L'identité masculine*.
16. Christine Castelain-Meunier, *Les hommes aujourd'hui. Virilité et identité* (Paris, 1988). See also Alain Laurent, *Féminin-Masculin. Le nouvel équilibre* (Paris, 1975).
17. Robert Stoller, 'Faits et hypothèses, Bisexualité et différence des sexes', *Nouvelle*

revue de psychanalyse (Paris, 1973), p. 151. For a more general overview see Stoller's, *Recherches sur l'identité sexuelle* (Paris, 1978).

18. Pierre Bourdieu, 'La domination masculine', *Actes de la Recherche en Sciences Sociales*, Nos. 83, 84 (June, September 1990).
19. Jacques Defrance, *L'excellence corporelle, 1770–1914* (Rennes, 1987).
20. Michael Kimmel, 'The Contemporary "Crisis" of Masculinity in Historical Perspective', in Harry Brod (ed.), *The Making of Masculinities* (Boston, 1987).
21. Badinter, *XY*, p. 25; Maugue, *L'identité masculine*.
22. *Journal Officiel de la République Française*. Annales du Sénat, 10 June 1879, Annex No.206.
23. Françoise Mayeur, *L'éducation des filles en France au XIXth siècle* (Paris, 1985). Two examples are the establishment of high-school programmes for girls in 1867 and the creation of *Ecoles Normales d'Institutrices* (institutes to train women to become primary school teachers).
24. 'Les suffragistes françaises ne sont pas les suffragettes anglaises', commented *Le progrès* on 25 May 1913.
25. This is obviously not a phenomenon unique to France, but the timing of such a change varied in Britain and the United States.
26. Agathon, *La jeunesse d'aujourd'hui. Le gout de l'action, la foi patriotique, une renaissance catholique, le réalisme politique* (Paris, 1911).
27. Ibid., pp. 33–4.
28. Ibid., p. 113.
29. *La Dépêche*, 23 December 1899.
30. Eugen Weber, 'Gymnastics and Sports in Fin-de-siècle France: Opium of the Classes?', *American Historical Review*, Vol.76, No.1 (1971).
31. Jean-Marie Brohm, 'Pierre de Coubertin et l'avènement du sport bourgeois', in Pierre Arnaud (ed.), *Les athlètes de la République* (Toulouse, 1987).
32. Such cultural ties between the middle class and aristocracy were common at that time. See Theodor Zeldin, *Histoire des passions françaises*, Vol.1., pp. 28–9.
33. *Grande Encyclopédie du XXème siècle*.
34. Henry Garcia, *La fabuleuse*, p. 144
35. Compare, for example, descriptions of French games by E. Saint-Chaffray in *Football (rugby)* (Paris, 1894), with descriptions of English games by Edward Gwyn-Nicholls in *The Modern Rugby Game* (trans. Albert Caudron, 1912).
36. See several classics by Pierre de Coubertin for examples: *L'éducation en Angleterre* (Paris, 1888); *L'éducation anglaise en France* (Paris, 1889); *Une campagne de vingt et un an (1887–1908)* (Paris, 1909). See also Philippe Daryl, *La renaissance physique* (Paris, 1888). For information on Grousset see the remarkable analysis by Pierre Alban-Lebecq, *Paschal Grousset et la Ligue nationale d'éducation physique* (Paris, 1997).
37. Pierre MacOrlan, *La Clique du Café Brebis* (Paris, 1918).
38. Amélie Gayrand. *Les jeunes filles d'aujourd'hui* (Paris, 1914).
39. Jean Lacouture, *Voyous et gentlemen. Une histoire du rugby* (Paris, n.d.), p. 60.
40. High-school exit examination which must be passed in order to gain entry to higher education.
41. Jean-Pierre Augustin and Jean-Pierre Bodis. 'Le rugby français, ses champs d'action et son autonomie jusqu'en 1939', in Thierry Terret (ed.), *Histoire des sports* (Paris, 1996).
42. Paul Voincvel, *Mon beau rugby* (Toulouse, 4th edn, 1948).
43. On the history of rugby in Bordeaux see Jean-Paul Callede, *Du Stade*.
44. Georges Bourdon, in René Blum (ed.), *Encyclopédie des sports* (Paris, 1924).
45. This included any club from outside the Paris metropolitan area.

46. All these cities are located within a 250km radius (156 miles) in south-western France.
47. See, for example, Pociello, *Le rugby*; and Bodis, *Histoire*.
48. La Gironde is the name of the *département* (administrative district) whose major city is Bordeaux.
49. See Augustin and Bodis, 'Le rugby français'.
50. *La Petite Gironde*, 1909, quoted in Augustin and Bodis, 'Le rugby français'.
51. River in south-west France which passes through Toulouse and Bordeaux.
52. *L'Express du Midi*, 27 March 1909.
53. Ibid., 14 January, 19 February and 2 April 1907.
54. *Le journal des sports*, 22 April 1912.
55. Ibid., 10 April 1909.
56. We see this in a number of other settings also, but most notably in the north/south split in English rugby. See J. Martens, 'Rugby, Class, Amateurism and Manliness; the Case of Rugby in Northern England, 1871–1895', in John Nauright and Timothy J.L. Chandler (eds), *Making Men: Rugby and Masculine Identity* (London, 1996), pp. 32–49.
57. See Terret, *Histoire des Sports*.
58. This provides an interesting parallel with the growth of rugby in Wales and specifically in the Welsh valleys. See Dai Smith and Gareth Williams, *Fields of Praise: Official History of the Welsh Rugby Union 1881–1981* (Cardiff, 1980).
59. R. Pech, and J. Thomas, 'La naissance du rugby populaire à Toulouse, 1893–1914', in Arnaud and Camy, *La naissaince*, pp. 104–5.
60. Two examples are strikes by wine-making workers in the south in 1906 or the 1907 'beggars' rebellion'. See Georges Duby and Armand Wallon, *Histoire de la France rurale* (Paris, 1976).
61. See the 1966 biography by R. Mathé, *Emile Guillaumin*, quoted by Zeldin in *Histoire*, p. 164.
62. See the sports literature which formalized these changes after the war: J. Dedet, *Le Football Rugby, Théorie et practique du Football Rugby* (Paris, 1922); F. Michot, *Le Football Rugby* (Paris, 1922).
63. Numerous contemporary examples of this turning inward of rugby culture are provided in Pociello, *Le rugby français*.
64. The *bandas* are groups of musicians who entertain at parties and festivals in south-western France. Each village has its own group. Along with bullfighting, *bandas* are highly specific to the region.
65. Pociello (see *Le rugby français*, p. 132) was interested in this indigenous language and identified the relationship between fighting-related metaphors and characteristics of regional life.
66. See *Le Journal des sports*, 6 November 1909, which describes the nine-course meal served to the Toulouse team after an international match. For a description of the importance of banquets in sports culture during that period see Jean Camy, 'Fêtes et banquets: quelques formes de sociabilité festive dans les sociétés sportives vers 1900,' in Pierre Arnaud (ed.), *Les athlètes de la République* (Toulouse, 1987).
67. *Le Journal des sports*, 2 February 1909.
68. Testimony of Emile Lesieur in *Le monde hebdomadaire*, 2 March 1980.
69. *Le Journal des sports*, 10 January 1912, quoted in Pech and Thomas, *La naissance*, p. 117.
70. Antoine Prost, *Histoire de l'enseignement en France, 1868–1968* (Paris, 1968).
71. *Journal Officiel de la République Française (JORF)*; Annales du Sénat, 18 March 1870, Annex No.55. On this subject see Pierre Arnaud, *Le militaire, l'écolier, le*

gymnaste (Lyon, 1991).

72. Ministère de l'Instruction Publique, *Manuel d'exercices gymnastiques et de jeux scolaires* (Paris, 1891).
73. See Thibault, *Sport et éducation physique*.
74. Jean-Pierre Bodis, 'Les origines du rugby à Toulouse,' in *Cent ans de rugby à Toulouse* (Paris, 1991). See also Pech and Thomas, 'La naissance du rugby populaire'.
75. Jean-Pierre Bodis, 'Rugby et enseignement en France jusqu'au début de la seconde guerre mondiale,' in Pierre Arnaud and Thierry Terret (eds), *Education et politique sportives* (Paris, 1995). See also Jean-Pierre Augustin and Alain Garrigou, *Le rugby démêlé*, pp. 42–3.
76. Pech and Thomas, 'La naissance du rugby populaire', p. 106.
77. Pierre Arnaud, 'Les deux voies d'intégration du sport dans l'institution scolaire', in Arnaud and Terret, *Education et politique sportives*.
78. Even de Coubertin believed that gymnastics was the only appropriate form of exercise for children younger than 14, and that sports should be reserved for those who had already learned how to use their bodies instrumentally. See, for example, Coubertin's *Pédagogie sportive*, 1919 (Vrin, 1971).
79. Philippe Tissié, *Les Basques et leurs jeux en plein air* (Bordeaux, 1900).
80. Idem, *L'Education physique* (Paris, 1901).
81. Idem, in *Revue des jeux scolaires et d'hygiène sociale* (1933), p. 72.
82. Idem, in *Revue des jeux scolaires* (January 1901).
83. Idem, *L'Indépendant* (10–11 May 1903).
84. See Alban-Lebecq, *Paschal Grousset*.
85. The role of the *Ligue Girondine* in rugby's development is illustrated by the name of the current semi-finalist in the European Rugby Cup, the *'section paloise'*, originally called *'Section Paloise de la Ligue Girondine d'Education Physique'*.
86. See Thibault, *Sport et éducation physique*.
87. Pierre Seurin, 'Le rôle de la Ligue Girondine d'Education Physique et du Docteur Tissié dans l'introduction et le développement du rugby dans le Sud-ouest français', *Actes du congrès de l'HISPA* (Louvain, 1976).
88. Gilles Laprévote, *Les Ecoles Normales Primaires en France, 1879–1979* (Lyon, 1897).
89. Dr Michaux, *De l'éducation physique dans les patronages* (Paris, 1897).
90. Michel Lagrée, 'Sport et sociabilité catholique en France au début du XXème siècle', in Arnaud and Camy, *La naissance du rugby*, p. 314.
91. See Jean-Pierre Augustin, 'Les patronages, la socialisation politique et le mouvement sportif: L'exemple du sud-ouest de la France', in Arnaud and Camy, *La naissance du rugby*.
92. G. Brun, 'Les sports et l'éducation physique. Rapport au XXXème congrès national à Tourcoing', *Bulletin de la Ligue* 232 (July–December 1910).
93. *Le Patriote*, 27 February 1914.
94. Minister of Public Education in 1879, who made public schools secular, free and mandatory.
95. Jean-Paul Callède, 'Gymnastique et sport à Bordeaux', in Arnaud and Terret, *Education et politique sportive*, pp. 79–80.
96. There are some obvious parallels with the pedagogical uses of rugby in other school systems. See the chapter by Light and also Chandler, 'The Structuring of Manliness', in Nauright and Chandler, *Making Men,* for a review of the pedagogical uses of rugby in the English public schools.
97. Philippe Tissié, *L'éducation physique rationnelle* (Paris, 1922), pp. 12–13.
98. Ligue Girondine d'Education Physique, *Règles de la barrette*, 1889.

99. Pierre Arnaud and Alfred Wahl, *Sports et relations internationales dans l'entre-deux-guerres* (Metz, 1994).
100. Archives diplomatiques de Nantes (Diplomatic Archives of Nantes), Services des Oeuvres Françaises à l'Etranger, No.85, around 1920. The entire text can be found in Pierre Arnaud, 'Des jeux de la guerre aux jeux de la paix', in Arnaud and Terret, *Education et politique sportives*, pp. 323–5.
101. A reference to the rolling 'r' of the south-western accent.
102. Quoted by Augustin and Bodis, 'Le rugby français'.
103. Géo André, *Le Miroir des Sports* (Paris, 1925).
104. Jean-Pierre Augustin and Alain Garigou, *Le rugby démêlé*, pp. 74–5.
105. Until 1920 the British did not even rank the 'Froggies.' In French rankings the French regularly came in last.
106. Quoted by Augustin and Bodis, 'Le rugby français'.

5

Rugby: The Game for 'Real Italian Men'

Gherardo Bonini

On 1 April 1997, commenting on his country's historic victory over France on Italy's most popular national evening news broadcast, an Italian sports journalist defined rugby as the game for 'real men'. Since this was the first occasion on which Italy had defeated a full French national team such rhetorical flourish was perhaps to be expected and was, indeed, common. In Italy however, such a view is, in fact, quite widely held both within rugby circles and outside them. Rugby is thought of as a masculine domain and the preserve of the manly.[1] Continuous confrontation with French rugby is one of the leitmotivs of the history of Italian rugby as is the struggle to gain television coverage in a country where association football (*calcio*) is a 'secular religion'.[2] The significance of Italy's first victory over France was that it provided a springboard for further broadening the appeal of the game. While the Italian national rugby side's performances have continued to improve greatly during the 1990s, which has led to the inclusion of Italy in the Five Nations Championships beginning in 2000, and to the Italian team being feared as a 'wildcard' in the 1999 Rugby World Cup, the victory over France was a huge symbolic leap forward for Italy. For many Italians 'emotional nationalism' is present in all sports and therefore an international victory over the old enemy France is, indeed, worthy of epithets such as the one cited above. Despite such pronouncements and the continuing outpourings of nationalist fervour surrounding other recent Italian rugby successes, rugby remains in the shadow of soccer, although it does have an intensely loyal following.

Unlike rugby in such countries as England, New Zealand and South Africa, Italian rugby has suffered by comparison because of a lack of well-established school and, to a lesser extent, university rugby programmes. Historically this has placed the development of Italian rugby at a comparative disadvantage. Although the game originally developed in universities, no educational institution has taken it up as a formal part of the education of social elites, except for a brief period during the rule of the Fascists in the 1930s. Rugby is rarely a part of

Italian high school physical education programmes and the development of young players has been left to clubs that provide courses and training for young men who wish to take up the game. At the university level regional committees organize sport based on student preferences and rugby is rarely included. Rugby's pedagogical role as a 'maker of men' has long been understood and accepted but it has not been fused with class-based masculinity as in England. It is one of a number of sports such as basketball, ice hockey, boxing and, of course, soccer that are thought to be manly pursuits in Italy. This chapter explores the historical development of Italian rugby and its role in the shaping of masculinity, the promotion of Fascist ideology and regional and national identities during the twentieth century. The issues of professionalism, women in rugby and the role of the media are briefly explored in looking at contemporary changes in Italian rugby.

From Pioneers to Rugby Soldiers

Through the efforts of some very single-minded university students who had developed a passion for rugby while studying in France, the game was brought to the two largest cities in northern Italy, Milan and Turin, in 1909.[3] The game had been played in France since the 1870s as Terret has demonstrated in his chapter. By 1910 France entered what became the Five Nations Championship. In the spring of 1910 the first matches featuring an Italian team were played against the famous French team Racing Club de Paris and also against a Swiss team named Servette. The club that instigated these early matches, Rugby Club Torino, was unable to continue and disbanded in 1911 after a match against the footballers of Pro Vercelli.[4] Although other matches against French teams were played after 1910, the outbreak of World War I interrupted the possible diffusion of the game beyond the limits of the few clubs in the north-eastern cities. These early matches were sparsely attended as contests were often hastily arranged and did not follow any organized schedule. Rugby was initially less popular than other sports among the *iniziati*, those familiar with British culture, due to the violence its rules allowed. Contact with French players was not able to distance rugby from its links with a particular British masculinity. Although rugby was not widely adopted this was not due to a bias against British sports; indeed, rowing, soccer, equestrian sports and target shooting were popular among university students, but only a few chose to take up rugby.[5] By the mid-1920s only a few rugby clubs existed in Italy and the game largely stagnated. After World War I there were sporadic attempts to expand the game. These efforts were largely unsuccessful, however, and, as such, there was never enough impetus to generate the development of an organizing and co-ordinating body for the game in Italy. By the 1920s cycling was Italy's most popular sport although soccer began to challenge cycling for supremacy during this and the following decade.[6] By contrast, rugby's support was confined to the elite and it was played mostly in universities. Unlike soccer and cycling, rugby was unable to attract a widespread following.[7] Problems over agreement on a common set of rules also hindered rugby's development and diffusion. A national organization to co-ordinate its running and administration did not appear until the formation of the Italian Rugby Federation (FIR) in 1928.[8]

In 1922 Benito Mussolini and his Fascist party took control of the government and set about organizing all facets of Italian life. The Fascists thought that physical development, especially of the male body, was important to the (re)generation of the Italian nation and the emergence of Italy as a world power. Sport was thus significant in Fascist aims to create a revitalized Italian masculinity. Under the aegis of the Italian Olympic Committee (CONI), empowered by the Fascists to centralize the control and activities of sporting federations, a propaganda committee for rugby was established in 1927.[9] The committee's charge was to develop *palla ovale*, the oval ball game. The Fascists gave rugby an Italian name because the word 'rugby' belonged to the English, contemptuously labelled by the Fascists unoriginally as 'perfidious Albion'.[10] As a dramatically new and different regime, the Fascists went about rewriting history as part of the process of legitimization. Fascism was being heralded as the ultimate form of government to which all countries should aspire. The Fascists claimed the Roman Empire as the cradle of the universe. Indeed, all forms of knowledge were given Italian origins including those cultural practices from abroad. England, as the country with the reputation for exporting its sports and games and 'teaching the world to play', could not be allowed to claim rugby football as its own. Football's roots were Roman and then Italian according to this view of sports history.[11] The rugby code was no exception. All the Fascists needed to do was to construct a 'true history' of rugby within football in order to claim it as their own. Thus, on the occasion of two matches with French teams in November 1928, influential official and CONI chairman, Lando Ferretti, baptized Italian rugby with Fascist rhetoric in the columns of Italy's most important newspaper *Corriere della Sera*.[12]

If we look at the fascinating scrums and the acrobatic jumps of the 'rugby men' we can see very clearly that the new Anglo-

Saxon game has the characteristics both of *feninda* and of *harpastum* and that rugby requires and produces such extreme virile physical effort that it may often justify the accusations of violence made against it.[13]

Even for the Fascists, searching through history to find the Roman roots of football, it was impossible to avoid the influence of ancient Greek culture on games and sports. As the Fascist version of history quickly pointed out, however, the Romans conquered the Greeks and absorbed and improved on Greek civilization. The Roman games of *feninda* and *harpastum* both had characteristics seen in rugby.[14] The English had been responsible for spreading the modern version of these games whose origins were, in this version of history, clearly rooted in ancient Rome. Fascists argued that the British had ruined the purity of these Roman games in the Middle Ages.[15] The English game of rugby had taken these Roman pursuits to much more violent levels, thus ruining a purity attached to their ancient precursors. Nevertheless, Ferretti was confident that Italians could excel at rugby.[16] Two days later, in an article in the same newspaper, the well-known sporting journalist Emilio De Martino also noted that rugby was a dangerous game even for the most courageous and manly of Italian athletes because, as he saw it, anything was admissible in trying to stop your opponent.[17] No doubt the limited knowledge of the game among Italian novice players contributed to these assertions as players were not well-versed in the physical use of the body allowable under the rules. Certainly it is possible that players not educated in the techniques of the game accentuated the violence seen in Italian rugby at the time. These criticisms notwithstanding, the Fascists saw the potential of rugby as a propaganda tool for conditioning the masses to their aims. As we shall see, such conditioning was not only physical but also ideological.

In addition to the links with a Fascist-inspired masculinity, rugby received confirmation as a vigorous, manly game in the first rugby text translated into Italian. In the years after 1928 several foreign coaches, most of whom were French, were imported to help to improve the standard of the Italian game.[18] At this time there was no official Italian rugby manual for players to consult. Efforts to overcome this were made by Aldo Cerchiari, who translated Charles Gondouin's famous introductory book on the game which was a part of the famous French *Bibliotheque Sportive* series that did for French sport what the Badminton Library series did for British sport. In his foreword to the translation of Gondouin's book, Cerchiari sets out to destroy the idea that rugby is a brutal and violent game, suggesting rather that it is no more violent nor dangerous than soccer. He goes further and defines rugby as the game that proves the athletic and moral potential of the individual. He suggests that rugby is, in fact, the most complete and rational of team games. For Cerchiari, rugby 'makes men'.[19] He added further comments of his own within the translation of Gondouin's text. He argues that the Italian aptitude for using the hands and feet in sport will favour the development of rugby and then he outlines some of the positive characteristics that he feels will also emerge from playing the game. These include: a willingness to work with others; a sense of co-operation; self-discipline; and the subjugation of the individual to the needs of the group. All these factors he thought would contribute to the renewal of ancient Roman traditions and return Italy to its rightful place as a world power.[20]

Cerchiari's construction of manliness in rugby was in tune with Fascist pronouncements on masculinity. He argues that the secret of powerful nations is in creating a spiritual unity among the masses who need to be educated and led intellectually and physically. Rugby is better than soccer as a tool of masculinist nationalism because the whole body is used in playing the game. Indeed, Fascist sporting ideology argued that the Italian people had a special aptitude for games involving the use of both hands and feet.[21]

Rugby gained impetus from these positive comments. In addition it received a further one from the arrival of foreign players with rugby experience as well as the playing of the first international match between an Italian team and Spain at Barcelona in 1929, which was won by Spain 9–0.[22] In the same year an Italian rugby championship began, won in its inaugural year by Ambrosiana Milano. Rugby's growth was threatened, however, by the arrival of a new ball game called *volata* that had first appeared in 1926. *Volata* combined rules from soccer and handball, giving it a stronger Italian pedigree that led to its official support from the regime.[23] *Volata*, unlike rugby, allowed players to pass the ball forward and was thus seen to be more natural in its flow, whereas the restriction to backward passing only saw rugby labelled as an 'unnatural' game.[24] *Volata* had eight players per side and used a round ball and a goal slightly smaller than that used in soccer. The new sport was immediately popular, with attendances recorded for some matches of up to 25,000 people, more than the total number of rugby players in the entire country.[25] So strong was the regime's support for the game that it actively suppressed the FIR in October 1929.[26] Rugby was attacked even though some clubs such as the Sporting Club Benito Mussolini conformed well to Fascist aims and ideology. Two possibilities have been advanced for rugby's suppression. One suggests that rugby was too closely linked to British culture and the other that there was a danger of professionalism in rugby particularly in the Lazio club.[27] Regardless of the precise reason, rugby clearly did not have the support of enough leading members of the Fascist hierarchy. The promoter of *volata* was Augusto Turati, secretary of the National Fascist Party (PNF).[28] Without a combination of Italian pedigree and influence 'in high places', rugby was unable to compete in the stakes for support of a hand-and-feet ball game in Italy at the time.[29] Soccer did not suffer the same fate as rugby, even though its modern roots were also British, because it was too popular. Pressure to promote soccer at the highest national levels was brought to bear on CONI that had 'passed on' the administration of soccer to the Italian Football Federation (FIGC) in March 1930.[30] In 1931 official support for rugby returned because its perceived role in preparing possible future soldiers was recognized.[31] Masculine contact could temper future soldiers and make them strong, courageous and fearless.[32] The vice-secretary of the PNF, Achille Starace, favoured rugby and offered his support for the game because he saw that rugby was a sport for fighting.[33] In 1931 Starace became the PNF's secretary. His continued support removed the suppression of rugby. Values of loyalty, self-control and fairness were subordinated to the exaltation of physical contact, the capacity for sacrifice, athleticism and group spirit. The masculine virtues that could be displayed in rugby performances were of much greater significance to the Fascists than the promotion of rugby and a rugby culture. Rugby's role in generating group cohesion, obedience, self-discipline and unity, in which the individual sacrifices personal needs to those of the community, was crucial. The Fascists believed that rugby provided one of the best arenas for military preparation where the logic of the totality becomes paramount.[34]

In 1932 a national rugby federation was re-established as the Federazione Italiana de Palla Ovale (FIPO). In the same year a university rugby championship was held in conjunction with those in other sports. In addition, rugby entered the military academies of Turin, Modena, Caserta and Livorno. In 1933 the term *palla ovale* was dropped and the formerly castigated English term 'rugby' was reinstated as FIPO became the FIR.[35] Although there was a return to the use of the name rugby, the Fascists went to great lengths to replace English terminology with Italian terms in efforts to maintain a semblance of an Italian pedigree surrounding the game.[36]

In 1934 Italy, seeking greater international prestige, supported France in the establishment of the Fédération Internationale de Rugby

Amateur (FIRA), obtaining the vice-chairmanship.[37] Relations
between Italy and France deteriorated and between 1938 and 1942
Italy played only against other members of the Axis alliance.[38] Milan
and Rome were the most successful teams in the Italian
Championships in the 1930s. Italy played international matches
against France (until 1938), Czechoslovakia, Germany and Spain, but
the dominance the regime hoped for was not realized.[39] Despite
temporary official sanctions against rugby and the lack of international
success, Fascist support in the 1930s enabled rugby to reach 106
officially-affiliated clubs and up to 7,000 other rugby teams by 1937.[40]

Rugby in Italy after World War II

After the war rugby had difficulties in detaching itself from being
labelled as the 'Fascist game'.[41] British troops spread the game along
the east coast of Italy, an area where it had not been played in any
significant way. By contrast, American troops in the western parts of
Italy spread baseball in that area.[42] These zones of influence have
continued. Rugby developed in areas where soccer was less popular
and where clubs had been established in the 1930s, but also in new
areas such as Catania in southern Sicily, L'Aquila in the Abruzzi
region of central Italy, and Rovigo and Treviso in the north-east.
Rugby is especially popular in towns without a team in the Serie A
competition in soccer. Most players have continued to come from a
university background.[43] The Italian Federation had a difficult time in
promoting rugby at grassroots level. Although CONI called for the
introduction of rugby into schools, few heeded this until the 1950s,
which made it difficult for rugby to gain a foothold among the young
and thus suffered by comparison with other sports. Nevertheless, there
were some notable exceptions. In the small town of San Donà di Piave
a rugby club was established in 1956 that was highly successful,
displaying a pattern of accomplishments unthinkable in Italian soccer
where the leading teams have always come from the large cities.[44]
Rugby remained highly popular among its adherents, and in the areas
where it was strong it did not remain an exclusive preserve of the elite.
As in the south-west of France, rugby diffused throughout society and
gained a popular following among all men, and particularly those
living in rural areas. The values of friendship, loyalty, self-discipline
and profound respect for the opponent found a new impetus in the
countryside, especially in those areas well isolated from larger urban
centres. At the elite level it was the rugby teams from mid-sized,
wealthy, regional towns that were the most successful and placed the
greatest stock in rugby. For example, Treviso, the home of Benetton,

has long been a dominant club.

Once rugby had shed its Fascist image all three major Italian amateur sports organizations, the leftist *Unione Italiana Sport Popolare* (UISP), the Catholic *Movimento Popolare* (MP) and the rightest *Fiamma*, organized rugby among the sports they promoted.[45] As a result of growth promoted by British input, the support of the major amateur organizations and the development of rugby in small, but well-financed towns, the larger centres that had dominated rugby before the war lost their ascendancy during the 1950s. These newer centres did not have strong soccer teams so great local attention was given to rugby whereas in cities such as Milan and Turin the success of their leading soccer teams limited the focus on rugby. In analysing the winners of the 22 tournaments between 1950 and 1971, Parma, whose soccer team never reached the Serie A, won three titles in rugby. Moreover, three towns whose football teams never reached either of the top two divisions, Rovigo, Treviso and L'Aquila, won seven, one and two titles, respectively. Napoli, whose soccer team only came to prominence later during Diego Maradona's era, won two titles. The exception to this is Padova, whose soccer team stayed in the Serie A for a number of years without major success, but whose rugby club, Fiamme Oro, won seven rugby titles.[46] Though there has been little detailed research into this phenomenon, a sociological study in the early 1980s examined the role of rugby in L'Aquila. The researchers found that virtually everyone in the town had some involvement with the game, as a player, working with the club or as a supporter. Rugby bound the community together and became a symbol for the town. Rugby is indeed linked closely with everyday life and popular culture in L'Aquila.[47] Despite the involvement of the whole community, men benefit from rugby more than do women. Success in rugby often leads to success in other spheres of life, providing the men who play for the local team with the social capital to succeed in other walks of life in the town. Indeed, men who are directly involved with the rugby club (players, officials, trainers and managers) are able to cash in on their prowess to move up the social ladder.[48] A similar situation operates in Rovigo known as 'a town on the scrum'.[49] With additional scrum connotations, in San Donà di Piave the rugby team is popularly known as *Razza Piave* in reference to the experience of local soldiers in a famous World War I battle where the Italians stopped Austrian troops on the border of the Piave River.[50] It is often suggested by the local inhabitants that the spirit of each of these towns is embodied in their 15 men on the field.

A number of changes took place in Italian rugby between 1955 and the 1970s. These included the return of Italy to international competition, greater organization of the game, improved training methods and increased fitness among players. Italy returned to playing internationally in 1955 when they played London Counties at the home of English rugby, Twickenham.[51] Italians also began to play outside their country, particularly in France where the Italian players Lanfranchi and Zani were stars of the French championship, playing for Grenoble and Agen, respectively.[52] By the end of the 1960s Italian rugby had a solid infrastructure and many looked to raise Italy's international standing. Many players had often not appeared to be very fit in the past, focusing more on the enjoyment of the game, with some being known as 'cupboard men'. In the 1960s, however, there was a move towards greater athleticism and fitness among players, while improved training methods entered the game. Thus a new athleticism emerged that had not been seen in rugby since the Fascist era when players were selected on the basis of strength, speed and agility. Players in the 1950s and the 1960s were not utilized as exemplars of clean, ordered sportsmen as had been the case in the Fascist period, where 'muscular Fascist sportsmen' were displayed as examples of how real men should look.

The domination of Italian rugby by a small number of teams led to a split in rugby in the 1960s. The military club of *Fiamme Oro* from Padova won four consecutive titles from 1958 to 1961. *Fiamme Oro* was renowned for recruiting the best army players from all over Italy to create a 'super team' of players.[53] In protest against such a hoarding of talent by *Fiamme Oro* and other top clubs, many clubs deserted rugby union and founded a rugby league federation.[54] In response to this problem the FIR sought to open up the competition for top players by allowing clubs to engage an unlimited number of foreign players, particularly encouraging clubs to attract *oriundi*,[55] overseas players with Italian ancestry, many of whom lived in Argentina or France. This followed the pattern of attracting players who had been employed by soccer clubs in the past. Of course, *oriundi* were more attractive than other foreigners as they could qualify to play for the national team.[56] Smaller clubs were still not satisfied with this new arrangement as they could not compete for the services of leading international players and argued that this was an implicit attack on the development of Italian talent.[57] Clearly this was a move toward professionalism, since to attract players from other countries it would be necessary to provide them with some form of inducement. As a result the FIR reduced the number of foreign players allowed on each team to only one for the 1980–81 championship.[58] Indeed, foreign players brought in by Italian teams became at least semi-professionals contracted to clubs, thereby breaking with the long-held international amateur traditions of the game. A number of great players, particularly from the southern hemisphere, such as Ian Kirkpatrick from New Zealand and later David Campese from Australia and Naas Botha from South Africa, came to play in Italy in the off-season. Others also moved from northern hemisphere nations later in their careers to play in Italy. Protests were lodged with the FIRA against this open violation of the amateur code. No penalty, however, was imposed on Italian clubs.[59] In 1973 in a South African tournament Italian players got their chance to face one of the dominant rugby nations for the first time. The success of South Africa could be seen in its provincial rugby structure, a level of organization that had not existed in Italy. As a result, in October 1973 Italian rugby organized a set of regional, select teams consisting of both Italian and foreign players mirroring to some extent the South African system. Those from northern clubs were grouped in a team named the Zebras. Soon after a team from the north-east was assembled and became known as the *Dogi*, the institutional name of the medieval heads of state of the Venetian Republic. Other regional teams were *Triveneto*, from Veneto, Fruili and Trentino, and the *Lupi* (Wolves) from central and southern Italy.[60]

In addition to the development of regional teams, renewed efforts at national level appeared as the FIR sought to bridge the gap between Italy and France in rugby. In 1975 the FIR engaged a national coach, Roy Bish from Wales, with the prime aim of launching Italy into the elite of the world's rugby-playing nations.[61] Italy eventually emerged alongside Romania as the best continental European rugby nation other than France. As Italian rugby became more professionalized in practice, sponsorships increased. As early as the 1960s, however, Faema, a coffee company, sponsored Treviso. At that time, though, rugby did not have enough visibility for the sponsorship to continue and Faema moved into sponsoring cycling by the early 1970s. In that decade other sponsors entered into relationships with rugby clubs, such as the ice cream company Sanson and the metal company Metalcrom. Their sponsorship of the leading clubs Rovigo and Treviso contributed to success on the field.[62] Napoli, by contrast, faded from the elite clubs as its soccer team rose to prominence and lured possible sponsors away from other sports. Brescia rose to prominence in the 1970s, winning the championship in 1975. In the 1980s Brescia was sponsored by the media mogul Silvio Berlusconi, who became very active in sports sponsorship in the Milan area, promoting soccer, rugby and ice hockey. Berlusconi's involvement placed sports sponsorship on a new level whereby rugby did not necessarily have to compete directly with soccer for sponsors' funds. As such, we cannot simply dismiss the entry of media barons such as Berlusconi or Murdoch as detrimental to the interests and profile of rugby union. Berlusconi's support enabled Brescia to pursue leading international stars such as David Campese, who began playing in Italy in 1984. Companies such as Finninvest and Benetton also attracted leading foreign players to their teams. Benetton engaged the New Zealander and perennial All Black John Kirwan for their Treviso club. While in Rovigo, the 'spiritual home' of Italian rugby where the national team plays at least one test match each year, the South African star fullback Naas Botha played for much of his career. At this time most leading clubs also began to employ coaches from abroad. The commercial logic behind the hiring of elite international players raised the profile and standard of Italian rugby, meeting the needs of sponsors, clubs and fans. In addition, the arrival of these players helped rugby to gain a greater media profile, which, although not that of soccer, substantially raised interest in the game, although other sports such as basketball, volleyball and ice hockey went further than rugby in the importing of international sporting talent.[63] The move towards professionalism in Italian rugby was not unproblematic, and some clubs such as L'Aquila and Padova refused to employ foreign players on professional-style contracts, preferring to remain strictly amateur and to uphold what they perceived as the sacred traditions of the game. Nevertheless, the end result of international influences on Italian rugby was the raising of standards in the game. Italian rugby became more recognized internationally and in 1981 Stefano Bettarello became the first Italian selected to play for the Barbarians. Later that year the FIR organized a major international congress on rugby in Rome with delegates coming from Australia, England, France, Ireland, New Zealand, Scotland and Wales. All facets of rugby were examined from the scientific and the coaching points of view.[64]

During the 1980s the FIR committed large resources to the modernization of rugby grounds and the building of new stadiums, since before then rugby teams were relegated to fields not needed or used by soccer clubs, many of these being in poor condition. In 1987–88 a play-off system was introduced into the top Italian league which further heightened interest in the domestic competition. Italy played in the inaugural Rugby World Cup in 1987 and throughout the late 1980s and the 1990s has played increasing numbers of test matches against the leading rugby nations. International recognition of these changes and the generally improved standard of Italian rugby came during the 1990s. In 1990 Italy was admitted to membership of the International Rugby Board (IRB) receiving two votes, and in the late 1990s, requested entry into the Five Nations Championship that will be realized in the new millennium.[65]

Physicality, Religion and Gender in Italian Rugby

The FIR have promoted rugby as having a particular educational value based on a broad, general philosophy of sport.[66] This philosophy is rooted in muscular Christian[67] concepts and has a direct grounding in the teachings of the Roman Catholic Church. Underlying this philosophy is the ethic of personalism where the balance between the needs of the individual to grow and live harmoniously are balanced with those of the social whole. Sporting education specifically is expected to balance these two elements through the utilization of the talents and energies of an individual with the more general needs of a team or social collective and context within which the individual acts.[68] In detaching rugby from its Fascist connections, where the needs of the group were emphasized even to the exclusion of individual development, the new Catholic muscularity stressed individual growth and improvement, noting that such things went hand-in-hand with learning to be part of a group. Indeed, for proponents of the new muscularity, individual development could be enhanced when one learned to be an individual but also when such development could be linked to that of a group.[69] Within this contemporary teaching of rugby, values such as respect for the opponent, loyalty, friendship and self-control were all stressed and encouraged through appropriate coaching and training. Contact with an opponent was, and still is, expected to be strong and virile but never brutal nor offensive. For the FIR rugby still makes men but not just any man, for this new philosophy is something to aspire to, something not easily achievable, but rather one that takes a particular form and requires immense dedication. Although this code surrounding rugby has not been specifically linked to men only, it is clear that the FIR took it for granted that its audience was male.[70]

Indeed, the FIR's animosity towards women was evidenced in their initial position on women's rugby as Italian women began to play. In the 1970s Italian feminism gained strength and, as a result, a number of laws were passed stressing equal status for women in society.[71] Women began to participate in many activities hitherto confined to men. In 1978 women began to form rugby clubs mainly in the north, although one club, Catania, arose in the south. Women's tournaments were held, although the FIR refused to recognize or support this development. In fact, it communicated strict regulations that were designed to limit women's rugby, threatening sanctions against any men who actively assisted women in their pursuit of the game by acting as officials or referees. This discriminatory policy forced many women to reject rugby union and form rugby league teams. Under the aegis of the UISP, a sporting organization more sensitive to the needs of sporting women, a women's rugby league was established in 1984, although the first championship had to be clandestine.[72] Some clubs failed to survive due to lack of financial and other support, although some managed to flourish. Indeed, a national Italian team participated in the inaugural Women's European Cup in 1988 and in the first Women's Rugby World Cup in Wales in 1991.[73] It was only three months before the World Cup on 15 January 1991 that the FIR finally officially recognized and legitimized the women's game. The FIR edited a book in 1992 entitled *Il rugby femminile* in which it over-turned its previous condemnation of women and its belief that rugby was a uniquely masculine activity. Rather it designed this publication to examine rugby, physicality and women's bodies.[74] Before that time the only manual available that mentioned women was a French one, published in 1984, again demonstrating the cultural borrowing from France present in Italian rugby. The FIR's new position on women was not universally accepted by all its officials.[75] A number continued to believe that the only place for women in rugby was to *'fare la calza'* ('make the socks'), although this viewpoint is declining. Ironically, perhaps, other women also malign women that take to this 'rough' sport.[76] Despite such hostility, FIR support has led to a general position that suggests that the virtues present in rugby may apply to women as well as men.

Women's rugby is strongest in the same regions as men's rugby, with teams in the traditional powerhouse towns of Rovigo, Treviso, Milano and L'Aquila. Benetton also sponsors a women's team in Treviso. Even though official support has appeared, many women's teams have kept their original names that were deliberately provocative towards the male rugby establishment. Thus women's teams have names such as *Le Streghe* (the Witches) of Rozzano (near Milan) or *Le Rose* (the Roses) of Rovigo, or *Rugby Rhosa* of Rho, which mocks the use of 'rosa' as a stereotypical female colour.[77]

The Future
Italian rugby is likely to continue to raise its profile both at home and internationally in the new millennium. Participation in the Five Nations championship in 2000 follows its competing for the 1999 Rugby World Cup, a competition in which the Italian team has already shown that it can perform well. To what extent the game is likely to

capture the imagination and attract the interest of increasing numbers of young school-aged Italians remains to be seen. *Calcio* is still the most popular, best supported and best funded game in Italy and seems unlikely to be superseded by rugby in the Italian footballing imagination in the near future. Rugby's links with Fascism will certainly recede as the generations of Italians who lived in that era pass on and this can only help in the further development of the game. As is the case in all rugby-playing nations, increased opportunities for women will also help to swell the numbers involved in playing as well as increasing the breadth and depth of interest in the game.

By comparison with many of the other major rugby-playing nations, Italy lacks an infrastructure to support the game at the highest levels. Most noticeably absent is a well-developed system of school-based rugby on which the major southern hemisphere rugby powers of Australia, New Zealand and South Africa, and the four 'home' nations of England, Ireland, Scotland and Wales each depend for the next generation of recruits to the game. And while rugby is played quite widely in Italian universities, it is the clubs which are looked to for recruits for the game. While the clubs have obviously been quite successful in promoting the game, their success seems to have been more evident in rural settings or in towns rather than in the larger conurbations or where *calcio* is particularly strong. It seems likely that this trend will continue.

The lack of school-based rugby has not harmed the development of Italian rugby as seriously as might have been expected. In fact, because of this it has been necessary to find other methods of raising standards so that the game could flourish. One of these has been to 'buy in' talent from outside, either in the form of *oriundi* or by offering strong financial inducements to overseas players who, at the end of their careers, having been looking to 'cash in' on their reputation and international success. The lack of a strong 'amateur' ethos in Italian rugby, the willingness of the FIR to allow overseas players to be able to 'play for pay', and the willingness of sponsors such as Benetton and Berlusconi to pay for playing and coaching talent has meant that Italy became one of the first nations to benefit from the commodification and globalization of rugby and the migration of rugby talent based on financial as much as playing opportunities. It remains to be seen whether Italian rugby can continue to do well in the new professional era when, at the elite level, payment for play is the rule rather than the exception.

NOTES

1. Channel One National News, 1 April 1997; comments from interview with Isabella Doria, Regional Committee Member (Lombardia) Italian Rugby Federation (FIR) by Gherardo Bonini, 7 April 1997.
2. Aldo Invernichi, 'Rugby', in Eugenio Enrile (ed.), *Encyclopedia dello Sport* (Rome, 1997), pp. 977–1017. Invernichi labels France as Italy's nemisis, its 'rivale impossibile'.
3. For a complete review of the history of Italian rugby see Pierlugi Fadda and Luciano Ravagnani, *Rugby: storia dalle origini ad oggi* (Milan, 1992), pp. 207–92.
4. Fadda and Ravagnani, *Rugby*, p. 207.
5. *Almanacco della Gazzetta dello Sport IX* (Milan, 1993), pp. 260–1.
6. Stefano Pivato, *L'era dello Sport* (Guinti, 1994), p. 97.
7. *Almanacco della Gazzetta*, p. 260.
8. Fadda and Ravagnani, *Rugby*, p. 211.
9. Ibid., p. 210.
10. Pivato, *L'era dello Sport*, p. 110.
11. Ibid.
12. Lando Ferretti, *Corriere della Sera*, 1 November 1927. The desire of Old Rugbeians to lay claim to 'their game' and endow Rugby School's football with both the ability to display 'a fine disregard for the rules' of the time, while also becoming the guardians of muscular manliness, offers an interesting parallel to the Fascist construction of history and the history of rugby in Italy.
13. The original comments were as follows: *Ebbene se si pensa alle 'melées' emozionanti ed ai salti acrobatici dei 'rugbymen', si ha la sensazione precisa che il nuovo gioco di marca anglo-sassone accoglie in sé le caratteristiche così della feninda come dell'arpasto, e dà vita ad un esercizio fisico tanto virile da giustificare talvolta l'accusa di estrema violenza.*
14. A recent work regarding ancient games analyses these ludic exercises. See Stefania Bossoletti, *La sezione 'Peri Paideoin' nell'Onomastikon* (Firenze, 1991).
15. Pivato, *L'era dello Sport*, p. 110.
16. L. Ferretti, *Corriere della Serra*.
17. Emilio De Martino, *Corriere della Sera*, 3 November 1927.
18. Fadda and Ravagnani, *Rugby*, p. 213.
19. Aldo Cerchiari, *Prefazio a Charles Gondouin, Il Rugby* (Milan, 1928), p. 7.
20. Cerchiari, *Prefazio*, p. 27.
21. Pivato, *L'era dello Sport*, p. 110.
22. See *Corriere della Sera*, 10, 12 March 1929.
23. Pivato, *L'era dello Sport*, p. 110.
24. See *Corriere della Sera*, 5 March 1929.
25. Ibid.
26. Giovanni Scuderi and Aldo Invernici, *Sport e Personalità. Valore educativo dello Sport. Il gioco di rugby* (FIR/CONI) (Rome, 3rd edn, 1990), p. 239.
27. Fadda and Ravagnani, *Rugby*, p. 212.
28. Ibid.
29. Pivato, *L'era dello Sport*, p. 110.
30. Scuderi and Invernici, *Sport*, p. 239.
31. Ibid.
32. Fadda and Ravagnani, *Rugby*, p. 216.
33. Ibid.

34. Cerchiari, *Prefazione*, p. 7.
35. Fadda and Ravagnani, *Rugby*, p. 212.
36. An ironic and critical appraisal of this nationalistic attitude is recalled in Armando Boscolo Anzoletti, *Il Rugby* (Milan, 1951), p. 13.
37. Fadda and Ravagnani, *Rugby*, pp. 94–5.
38. Ibid., pp. 214–15.
39. Ibid., passim.
40. Renato Bianda, Guiseppe Leone, Gianni Rossi and Adolfo Urso, *Atleti in Camicia Nera. Lo Sport nell'Italia di Mussolini* (Rome, 1983), p. 106.
41. This point was stressed strongly by Isabella Doria in her interview of 7 April 1997.
42. My thanks to Professor Pierre Lanfranchi of De Montfort University, Leicester for providing this information.
43. Fadda and Ravagnani, *Rugby*, pp. 217–18.
44. Gianni Colosetti and Nicola Bizzarro, *Rugby razza Piave. Fatti, resultati ed immagini di 25 anni di rugby a San Donà di Piave* (1984).
45. Felice Fabrizio, 'Storia dello sport in Italia', in E. Guaraldi (ed.), *Dalle società ginanstiche all'associazionismo di massa* (Firenze, 1977), pp. 267–80.
46. Fadda and Ravagnani, *Rugby*, p. 255.
47. Rosella Isidori Frasca and Vincenzo Camerini, 'Domenico é rugby a L'Aquila', in *Annali dell'Instituto Superore d'Educazione Fisica dell'Aquila*, Vol.2 (1983), Supplemento, pp. 69–75.
48. Ibid.
49. As described by L. Ravagnani, *Una città in mischia* (1987), passim.
50. See Colosetti and Bizzarro, *Rugby* for a full description of this event.
51. Fadda and Ravagnani, *Rugby*, pp. 222–3.
52. Ibid., p. 220.
53. Ibid., pp. 224–5.
54. Ibid., Società Ginnastica Torinese had tried just after World War II to promote rugby league but without success. See Anzoletti, *Il Rugby*, p. 151.
55. *Oriundo* is a word found frequently in Italian sporting language, indicating the national extraction of an Italian born in another country. Thus someone described as *oriundo francese* was born in France with parents or ancestors who were Italian, thereby allowing him to claim Italian citizenship.
56. As an example, Marcello Fiasconaro, a South African *oriundo* for Italian athletics and world record holder for the 800m in 1973, played rugby for *Concordia Roma* in 1977. There are a number of books on this issue in Italian soccer. See, for example, Antonio Ghirelli, *Stori del calcio in Italia* (Milan, 1974) and Gian Paolo Ormezzano, *Storia del calcio* (Milan, 1990).
57. See *Gazzetta dello Sport*, 13 September 1972.
58. Fadda and Ravagnani, *Rugby*, p. 238.
59. Ibid, p. 236.
60. Ibid., pp. 234–5.
61. Ibid.
62. *Faema* were disappointed with their investment in rugby and chose to switch their support to a professional cycling team headed by the Tour de France winner Eddie Merckx.
63. For a broader discussion of this topic see John Bale and Joe Maguire (eds), *The Global Sports Arena: Athletic Talent Migration in an Interdependent World* (London, 1994).
64. The proceedings of the conference were published in *1° Convegno Internazionale sul gioco del rugby, Roma 2/6 Novembre 1981, FIRA/FIR* (Rome, 1982).

65. Italy will compete in the Five Nations championship beginning in 2000.
66. See Invernici, 'Rugby', p. 118.
67. See L. Stefanini, 'Personalismo' in *Enciclopedia Filosofica*, Vol.6 (Rome, 1979), pp. 450–67 and in particular the sub-chapter on educational personalism. The two terms 'value' and 'personality' are overtly stated in the title and form the substance of this section. Included is the Prayer of the Rugby Men in which one prays to Jesus and his Holy Mother to protect the rugby men.
68. See Scuderi and Invernici, *Sport*, pp. 34–78.
69. Ibid.
70. See ibid., in which references to *virili* meaning 'menlike' are common.
71. In 1975, for example, a new Family Code became law.
72. See work by Andrea Fabbri and Marco Fogli, in Albero Nocenti (ed.), *Il rugby femminile in Italia* (Ferrara, 1992), p.11.
73. Ibid.
74. See A. Nocenti (ed.), *Il rugby femminile in Italia* (Ferrara, 1992) which was produced for the FIR.
75. Interview with Isabella Doria, 7 April 1997.
76. Ibid.
77. For a complete listing of these clubs see the official website (http://www.ichange.com.au/atitaly.htm#WomensClubs) of the Italian Federation of Rugby.

6

High School Rugby and the Construction of Masculinity in Japan

Richard Light

Introduction

In the last minutes of play in the final of the Japanese high schools national championships, Fushimi High School have produced an inspired come-back to score four quick tries in succession and are attacking Kugayama High School's line. They are given a penalty in front of the posts, but they are eight points behind and take a quick tap kick that catches the opposition offside to earn another penalty. Again they take a quick tap kick and spread the ball to the left only to be met by a solid defensive wall. They quickly recycle the ball and go to the right, desperately trying to keep the ball alive, but the winger is tackled short of the line. The ball comes back to the left to expose an overlap and the full back dives to score in the far left-hand corner. The sea of red supporters explodes and the television cameras zoom in on their ecstatic faces and then pan to the expressions of anguish among the blue supporters as they all anxiously eye the large clock over the scoreboard. The kicker lines up the conversion, approaches and strikes. The ball climbs then veers to the left and falls short. The full-time siren sounds. Kugayama have won the championship and their players embrace in delight and relief as the losers collapse about the ground in tears.

The 77th national high school rugby championships held in 1997–98 continued a tradition first established in 1918, one which has been interrupted only in the later years of the Pacific War. For the 45,000 senior high school rugby players in Japan the chance to take part in the festival of high school rugby at Hanazono would be the pinnacle of their rugby life; to be a member of *yuushou* (the championship-winning) team is the stuff of schoolboy dreams. Rugby is played throughout the entire year with most teams playing in several regional or metropolitan tournaments; but the national championships at Hanazono are the culmination of a year's playing and training for the teams that qualify to participate in a celebration of youth, culture and exemplary manliness. From over 1,200 high schools fielding teams in Japan 52 qualify through regional championships to compete on the sacred grounds of the Kintetsu Rugby Stadium in Hanazono, Osaka. School sport in Japan is played all year round and all the major team sports culminate in national championships which attract considerable attention from the general public. Schoolboy rugby is played in the shadows of professional sports, and particularly baseball, for most of the year but for two weeks every December and January it steps on to centre stage, along with high school soccer, to enjoy saturation media attention as teams from all over Japan do battle.

Although rugby is a lower profile sport than baseball, the characterization of the high school baseball championships as a national festival for the celebration of dominant cultural ideals and the spiritual and moral health of the nation's youth[1] is equally applicable to the rugby championships. The games played over two weeks between schoolboy rugby teams function both to celebrate the embodiment of dominant Japanese culture and to reproduce a culture-specific hegemonic masculinity. The way games are played, the training and the preparation for them and the rituals surrounding them act to embody a particular form of masculinity which shapes the practice of rugby in Japan. Further to this, the ways in which events at Hanazono are selectively represented by the media combine to construct and reproduce a particular hegemonic form of masculinity.

This chapter examines the nature and construction of a particular form of such masculinity as constructed through corporeal and discursive practices at the 1997–98 high school rugby championships. It identifies a dominant form of masculinity which is characterized by resilient Victorian/Edwardian ideals of manliness yet which is also distinctively Japanese and examines the ways in which such a form of masculinity is constructed. In recognizing the historically dynamic nature of hegemonic masculinity it also traces the changes in social conditions in Japan over the past century during which the constant tension between the ideology underpinning Western sporting practices and a native cultural hegemony have shaped the practice of rugby in educational institutions and sustained notions of what it is to be a man.

The Institutional Context of Rugby in Japan
Having established a professional league in 1936, baseball was the lone version of professional sport until the introduction of soccer's 'J League' in 1993. From the introduction of Western team games in the late nineteenth century, sport in Japan has functioned as a means of inculcating preferred social and cultural values, and as a form of social education. The ideal of the games ethic and the notion of games as an arena for the development of moral character which accompanied the

introduction and expansion of team games in the late nineteenth and the early twentieth century has continued to shape the practice of all sport in Japan from that time onwards. Although a professional baseball league was established in 1936, the marketing of professional soccer as a commodity from 1993 represents the first sign of the emergence of sport as entertainment in Japan and is a product of changing economic conditions and the influence of globalization in sport. There is also a national rugby competition for companies which has been attracting growing interest over the last 20 years. Ostensibly a non-professional competition between teams comprising company employees, it has been boosted by an influx of high-profile foreign players in recent years. Increasing engagement with the world rugby community has seen the strength of company rugby increase to the point where the annual game between the company and the university champions has become so one-sided that it was abandoned in 1997. In 1998 the team to play the champion company team was decided through games between the top university sides and the stronger company teams to ensure a more even contest. Although the company competition is functionally professional and imported players are attracted by generous contracts, the Japanese Rugby Union continues to articulate it as amateur and steadfastly opposes any professional-ization of the game.

From the first game played by a Japanese team in 1901[2] to the end of the Pacific War in 1945, rugby developed solely within institutions of education where it was profoundly shaped by an implicit perception of it as a vehicle for the promotion and reinforcement of dominant cultural values and social behaviours. Despite the development of company rugby since the end of the war, the rugby played at schools and universities continues to attract more public and media attention. The biggest crowd of the year is always at the annual match held between the traditional university rivals Waseda and Meiji. Held within days of the Oxford v. Cambridge match, attendance at the ground of 60,000 surpasses the attendance at the company finals or any games between the national team and international touring sides. Significantly, the interest shown in the Waseda–Meiji game and the national high school championships extends beyond those who follow rugby during the year to the general public who know little about it in particular yet recognize the cultural symbolism attached to the contests. The attention paid to the national championships for high school sport indicates the significance of school sport as a form of socialization in Japan and the significance of school rugby as a site for the embodiment of dominant culture and the construction of hegemonic masculinity.

The Social Construction of Masculinity

Research on masculinity and rugby has shown that, despite its geographical and cultural diffusion throughout the former British settler colonies, rugby has continued to be profoundly shaped by Victorian ideals of manliness in Australia, New Zealand and South Africa.[3] This chapter identifies a hegemonic form of masculinity evident at the 1997–98 Japanese high school rugby championships, which, although constituted by appropriated Victorian ideals of manliness, is differentiated from Western forms by the militaristic values of manliness derived from the feudal *samurai* classes. Introduced at the turn of the century, rugby has developed in Japan during periods of enormous social and economic change within a context of constant tension between the adoption of imported Western values from the late nineteenth century and the promotion of hegemonic feudal, ruling-class values. Connell argues that masculinities are culturally specific and develop dynamically and historically over time, and that the social construction of gender must be understood as both a product of history and a producer of history.[4] In order to better identify and understand the particular nature of the hegemonic masculinity which characterizes Japanese rugby at Hanazono it is useful to account for it as the product of larger historical and social changes in this century. Rugby, and other Western team sports, as practised within the education system, played a central role in the development of national identity and homogeneous cultural values during the shift from a feudal to an industrialized, capitalist society in the nineteenth century. More specifically, rugby has played a significant role in the development of a cultural hegemony that has provided continuity and social order and has maintained positions of power and influence in times of profound social change. Within such processes the practice of rugby has been shaped by a hegemonic, exemplary masculinity produced by the dynamic tensions between imported Victorian/Edwardian manliness and native notions of manliness derived from the *samurai* classes.

Recent sociological research has also illuminated the importance of institutional settings in the construction of masculinity in sport. Gruneau and Whitson[5] have shown how business and political interests construct the hyper-aggressive masculinity that characterizes Canadian hockey and Messner[6] emphasizes that, when boys begin playing sport, the development of their masculine identity is significantly shaped by their entry into the organized institution of sport. The construction of masculinity through young men's participation in sport is intimately shaped by the institutions within which it takes place and they are typically marked by hierarchical, competitive structures which interact with larger political and economic forces. From the turn of the century until the increase in the popularity and profile of company rugby over the past 25 years, rugby has developed within the confines of educational institutions. Played in universities and secondary schools for almost a hundred years, rugby has acted as a vehicle for the bodily inculcation of particular social and cultural values.

Victorian Manliness and Japanese Cultural Hegemony

Following the end of over two centuries of isolation, the Meiji Revolution saw the dismantling of the feudal system as Japan rushed to modernize and close the gap between itself and Western, industrialized nations. The 1870s were characterized by a thirst for anything Western with the wholesale adoption of Western social, economic and political institutional models. But by the last decades of the nineteenth century this had been tempered by a growing rejection of Western liberal values by conservative forces which saw these as a threat to the social fibre of Japan. The ideal of *Wakon Yosai*, the active acceptance of Western technology and institutional organization alongside the preservation of Japanese values, shaped the adoption of Western political, economic, military and educational systems. A period of growing national confidence was marked by military success in the Sino-Japanese War from 1894 to 1895 and later the Russo-Japanese War (1904–5). Introduced during this period, rugby and other Western team sports played within universities and schools functioned as media for the development of a modern national identity. First introduced by expatriate Americans in 1872, baseball in particular played a central role in the development of national identity as the nation grew in confidence, encouraged by expanding industrial and military might.[7] Although it had been played by foreigners at the port cities of Yokohama and Kobe from the mid-nineteenth century, rugby was not played by a Japanese team until the turn of the century. The Englishman E.B. Clark was born and received his early education in Yokohama, but studied at Cambridge University where he learned to play rugby. He returned to Japan to teach English at Keio University where, with Ginnosuke Tanaka, also a Cambridge graduate, he began teaching rugby in 1899. In 1901 a team from Keio University became the first Japanese one to play rugby in a game against a 'foreigners' team' from Yokohama. Keio lost their first game 35–5 against the expatriates, but within five years tasted victory. As players from Keio graduated, rugby began to spread and was increasingly taken up by other universities and schools.

The transformation of Japan from a feudal to a modern society was achieved in a remarkably short time during which the ruling oligarchy had to find different modes of control to deal with the accompanying social upheavals and the problems of maintaining social order. As a central element in the modernization of Japan a mass education system, introduced in 1872, was aimed at both the creation of a skilled and productive work force and the promotion of a sense of national identity, cultural homogeneity and social order. This involved the promotion of the values of the ruling *samurai* classes as the culture of the Japanese people. The holders of power in Meiji Japan showed faith in the use of tradition as a counter to social unrest and revolution and, as Williams contends, tradition can be a radically selective process used to validate and reinforce relationships of power.[8] The family and state ideology taught in schools were articulated as 'traditional' but were selected adaptations of tradition. The family ethic taught in schools was actually the Confucian ethic of the ruling classes and not the tradition of the dominated classes, the majority of Japanese. By 1890 schools had incorporated this ethic into the Education Rescript and the curriculum for schools while promoting the values of the *samurai* as the values of all Japanese. The Japanese populace had been prone to express grievances through violence before the Meiji Revolution[9] and controlling it was an urgent task confronting the government. One of its major strategies for control was the fostering of an ideology conducive to the maintenance of social order through the state education system. After the turn of the century, the government sought to further emphasize social control through the promotion of the emperor as the head of state and values of loyalty, obedience and obligation to him in an imperial ideology propagated through the press and the educational system.

Japan's frantic rush to establish itself as a modern, industrial and military power was largely initiated by a realization of its vulnerability to Western colonial intentions. In the mid-nineteenth century Japan's military vulnerability to external threats was made evident when, in 1854, forces under the command of Admiral Perry pried open the ports of Shimoda and Hakodate to American trade and this was soon followed by similar agreements with other powerful Western nations. European and American settlements soon flourished in port cities around Japan where the British and Americans brought with them their games ideologies and indulged in the manly pastimes of sport at social and recreational clubs, some of which still function today. The annual rugby match between the Yokohama Foreigners Club and the Kobe Recreation and Athletics Club is still the keenly contested highlight of the two clubs' rugby seasons. World-wide British colonial expansion and its military might was widely attributed to the moral strength imparted into its leaders through the playing of games, and by the late nineteenth century the vigour of team sports had come to function as a symbol of national strength and health in England. Roden contends that the absence of sport in foreign lands came to be interpreted as a sign of cultural, racial and moral inferiority to the British and that this shaped Western views of the Japanese in the mid-nineteenth century as effeminate, under-exercised and morally inferior.[10]

The manly pursuits of foreigners playing sport contrasted with the sedentary Japanese students and many of the foreign teachers employed at universities voiced their concern with the apparent poor health and lack of virility among their students. Gymnastics had been encouraged in schools by the Department of Education as early as 1872 and the National Institute of Gymnastics was established in 1879. By 1885 gymnastics was compulsory in all schools. Universities, however, were exempt from compulsory gymnastics and, in response to Western criticism of under-exercised and physically weak students, the teaching of sport as part of the education of the social elite was preferred. Following the introduction of baseball in 1872 and soccer a year later, other forms of Western sport were gradually introduced into the universities over the next few decades. It was not until the 1890s, however, that sport began to spread throughout the universities as national confidence grew and rugby was introduced at Keio University.

Baseball had become the main team sport played in Japanese universities by the early nineteenth century and rugby was first introduced as a means of keeping students active during the winter months while they were not playing it.[11] Adopted sports benefited from a rise in nationalism following Japan's victory in the Sino-Japanese War which stimulated the growth of games at universities. The rise in the popularity of games during a period of growing national confidence and a search for a modern national identity also saw attempts to locate the driving games ideology and Western ideals of manliness within traditional, *samurai* culture.[12] This was in keeping with policies guided by the ideal of *Wakon Yosai* and saw the values of the feudal *samurai* class grafted on to the Victorian ideals of manliness. The martial arts of judo and kendo, derived from *samurai* techniques of warfare, clearly embodied the values of the *samurai* and explicitly articulated the ideals of *bushido* but they were the practices of the feudal elite and were individual in nature, featuring one-on-one contests. Their solitary nature precluded them from functioning to inculcate the collectivist ideals of 'traditional' culture promoted as a means of maintaining social order. The nature of team games and the analogy between the playing field and the battlefield articulated in Britain made Western team sports such as rugby attractive for the promotion of national identity[13] and masculinity shaped by appropriated notions of manliness and driven by the *bushido* code. Although Western team sports originated in foreign settings they underwent significant cultural transformation in a process by which they came to function as vehicles for the promotion of discrete Japanese national identity and operated as sites for the construction of an increasingly militaristic masculinity.

Martial Arts and Sport

Despite a fascination with all things foreign early in the 1870s, the appropriation of Western technology and institutional organizational models was increasingly guided by the 'traditional' values of Japan's ruling class. The expansion of team sports in universities and then into schools around the turn of the century saw ideals of Victorian manliness intermeshed with the military values of the *samurai* classes as central elements in the development of national identity and the dissemination of cultural hegemony. Under these conditions rugby enjoyed a period of growth throughout the school system marked by the first national championships in 1918 and the founding of a national body in 1926.[14] In the early stages of the Meiji Restoration the wearing of swords in public was banned and the martial arts of the *samurai, bujitsu,* waned, having no apparent place in the development of a modern society. With emerging national sentiment at the close of the century the transformation of the feudal arts, generically known as *bujitsu,* experienced a revival led by the reconstruction of *jujitsu* into the modern sport-like form of judo by Kano Jigoro. The modern forms of the martial arts were reconstructed into sporting forms as influenced by the adoption of Western sport, yet maintained a strong sense of tradition through their connection to the pre-Meiji *samurai.* Inoue contends that *budo* contributed strongly to the maintenance of a national cultural identity and the continuation of traditional values in times of great social change.[15]

The liberal 1920s saw a rapid expansion in schools and universities playing rugby and the establishment of a national ruling body, the Japan Rugby Football Union, in 1926. Rugby flourished during this period with major university rugby matches commonly attracting crowds of over 20,000. During this period of growth several universities' rugby teams undertook overseas tours and hosted visits by foreign teams in the early 1930s with an Australian students' team touring in 1934. Growing nationalist sentiment from the late 1920s, however, initiated changes in the practice of rugby and other team sports. The values of the *samurai* classes promoted through *budo* increasingly came to guide the practice of rugby and other team sports as martial arts training was incorporated into the national curriculum and was promoted as symbolizing the 'traditional Japanese spirit'. By the 1930s the rise in militarism saw the practice of Western sports heavily influenced by the militaristic and nationalistic values of *budo* as martial arts grew in popularity and Western sports declined. Despite the collective nature of team sports, their Western origins and values of individualism and liberalism, they were seen to promote threatened nationalist sentiment in schools and Inoue contends that they underwent processes of 'Japanization'.[16] The 'traditional' martial arts were used as a model for the practice of sport in schools to better embody Japanese spiritual values and to infuse Western sport with 'Japanese spirit'. As Japan headed towards war in the late 1930s, Western sports suffered a decline in popularity and were radically transformed to promote what were seen as the unique qualities of the Japanese and a nationalistic militarism. English terms were dropped in favour of Japanese and rugby was known as the 'fighting game'. Rugby in pre-war schools and universities in particular was characterized by the promotion of extreme militaristic masculinity and severe hierarchical disciplinary practices often resulting in death.

Culture, Rugby and *Seishin*

As with the host of American baseball players who spend time playing in Japan, the majority of rugby players who accept the lucrative offers to play in Japan are confronted with an immensely different approach to training and playing the game they know so well. The wealth of popular press writings by baseball players in Japan such as Robert Whiting's popular book *You've Got to Have Wa* is testament to the extent to which baseball has been culturally transformed into the national game of Japan.[17] Articles published in Western rugby magazines by players based in Japan also illuminate the vast differences between playing and training in Japan and in the West. Considering the significant cultural differences between Japan and rugby-playing countries such as Australia and New Zealand, this is not surprising. Despite the effects of globalization and the increasing world-wide commodification of rugby, there are features of play that distinguish one nation's rugby from another and that may arguably be attributed to different cultural contexts and versions of hegemonic masculinity. Even though France plays regularly against Ireland, Wales, Scotland and England in the Five Nations tournament, there is no doubting that they play a style of rugby quite distinct from any of the British or Irish sides. As the former Wallabies forwards coach Bob Templeton points out, the common cultural traits of the French, Italian, Spanish and Argentinian are embodied in a particular way of playing, which he describes as 'extremely flamboyant'.[18]

There are identifiable features in the dominant approaches to playing and to training in Japanese rugby which differentiate it from those in Western countries. Foreigners who have played rugby in Japan, particularly at university level, are invariably shocked at the differences in training and the emphasis on daily, long, hard and debilitating training regimes. Australian school and club teams typically train two to three times a week during winter for 1½ to 2 hours a session. Many of the schools fielding rugby teams do not aspire to success at the national level and take a relaxed approach to training, with rugby functioning as a means of getting together and sharing the joys of being in a club. However, for those competing at elite levels training typically involves hard sessions six days a week for 11 to 12 months of the year, with little variation in activity or intensity. Training is underpinned by the assumption that more is better, that effort produces results and that training harder and longer is the answer to losing games. In Japanese schools there is a similar emphasis on effort in academic endeavour. Teachers make little use of IQ tests and the idea of working to one's ability, often heard in Western schools, is foreign in a school culture where success is linked to effort and failure is seen as evidence of not working hard enough. There is a clear assumption of achieving victory in rugby games as the direct result of effort, sacrifice and single-minded commitment in which there is a clear correlation between 'hard training' and winning. The ideals which shape training also characterize the way the game is played with the emphasis on the moral qualities of courage, commitment, personal sacrifice, effort and perseverance manifested in aggressive contact and the maintenance of high-speed play. Like the American baseball players who have written popular books on what they see as bizarre extremes of training in Japanese baseball, foreign rugby players are also shocked at the daily grind of training in Japan and the emphasis on 'guts' rugby.

When Japanese training practices and game styles are analysed the features which most distinguish them from Western practices can be identified as the products of a culture specific ideal of manliness which is guided by *seishin* ideology. While the concept of *seishin ryoku* (*seishin* power) is not always explicitly articulated, it is something that is subjectively experienced rather than being objectively understood and tends to operate implicitly. Coaches mention *seishin* and several players at the national high school championships singled out the development of *seishin* as the most important aspect of their personal development through rugby. Some coaches, who were usually more conservative in their approach to rugby, clearly articulated values and personal qualities associated with *seishin* such as *ganbaru* (do your absolute best), *isshokenmei* (give everything), *konjo* (guts/courage) and *gaman* (endurance, perseverance). These are qualities admired and expected in all sportsmen in Japan and, arguably, to a large extent, from boys playing rugby in many Western schools. The qualities admired and expected in Japanese school rugby players have much in common with those expected from boys in middle-class schools in Australia, but the methods used to develop them differ considerably. While much of the masculinity that can be identified in Japanese rugby is derived from the very same ideals of manliness which shape rugby around the world, the manifestation of *seishin* and its associated ideals most clearly differentiate it from other forms.

Seishin is a key cultural concept which was central to the ideology of the *samurai* classes and the code of *bushido*. It is tied into a particular view of human existence as a unity of mind, body and soul that differs markedly from the Western, Cartesian-derived dualism of mind and body. Moeran describes *seishin* as a general reference to the inner being, spiritual fortitude and self-discipline developed through particular physical training.[19] During the period of militarism leading up to the Pacific War the concept of *seishin ryoku* (spiritual power) was appropriated and employed by the military to promote faith in the unlimited potency of spiritual concentration. Although most Japanese were aware that the material might of the USA far surpassed that of Japan, this was countered by the promotion of faith in spiritual power as evident in the nationalistic glorification of *Yamato damashii* (the spiritual power of the Japanese race).[20] The traditional discourse of *seishin* ideology promoted by the pre-war military extolled a belief in the power of the human spirit, when fully cultivated through appropriate physical training, to overcome material opposition, but such faith was significantly diminished following the country's defeat in the Pacific War.

Through its association with pre-war militarism, education that promoted *seishin* was officially frowned upon after the war.[21] The occupation forces identified *seishin* ideology as a central element of the extreme military masculinity promoted in pre-war schools and set out to eradicate it from the curriculum. The US Department of State's revision of the Japanese Education System document, written in 1947, forbad the teaching of military subjects, the wearing of military-style uniforms and the teaching of 'classical' sports such as *kendo* that 'encouraged martial spirit'.[22] It also stipulated that, 'Physical training should no longer be associated with the *Seishin Kyoiku*' (*seishin* education).[23] Acting under the advice of the Education Commission, the State Department, for the guidance of the Supreme Commander for Allied Powers (SCAP), set out to rebuild the Japanese education system along the lines of the American model. To encourage the fostering of democratic ideals in schools, the authorities set up the club system within which a variety of extra-curricular activities were to be offered. Sport was to be practised within the club system where students were to be given enough autonomy to encourage independence and initiative. Had the occupying forces known more about the extreme versions of militaristic masculinity which developed in pre-war sports clubs they may have taken a different approach as, ironically, the sports clubs of universities and schools provided fertile sites for the re-emergence of *seishin kyoiku*. Severe training regimes, hazing and strictly enforced student hierarchies became common characteristics of post-war clubs with rugby clubs being among the most severe.[24]

Many Japanese and foreign scholars see 1945 as a turning point in Japanese society and Inoue argues that the relationship between sport and *budo* was reversed in post-war Japan whereby the practice of *budo* became 'sportized'.[25] There is no doubt that the practice of martial arts, initially banned after the war, and sport were quite different in post- and pre-war Japan; but while the structure of sporting practice may have changed, the implicit ideology underpinning it remained. As part of the occupation forces' attempts to root out militarism and the values associated with it, the General Headquarters of SCAP prohibited the practice of *budo*. Martial arts were banned in schools and Western sport was promoted in the quest to democratize Japan. With the resumption of judo in 1948 the martial arts were gradually reintroduced but in forms that were intentionally structured along the lines of Western sport. An examination and analysis of rugby as practised in contemporary schools and universities, however, indicates that they continue to be profoundly shaped by the ideals of the feudal military classes and bear much similarity to the practice of *budo* and its original form as *bujitsu*.

The cultivation of *seishin* has traditionally been achieved through particular physical training and the development of inner strength.

Behaviour concerned with the restraint of personal desires through specific corporal training is clearly evident in the practice of the martial arts such as karate, kendo and judo. The practice of traditional martial arts cultivates spiritual strength through stressing the perfect union of body and spirit as a necessity for successful physical performance. The particular methods of physically cultivating *seishin* are commonly derived from the practice of religious discipline which involves simple, repetitious, monotonous and physically-demanding tasks. At religious ceremonies incantations are constantly repeated and, in the practice of Zen meditation, practitioners must sit motionless for long periods and endure the pain of sitting absolutely still on their heels in *seisa* with a perfectly straight back lest they be struck sharply with a wooden bat by the senior monks. The way that rugby teams in Japanese schools train bears much similarity to the martial arts and is driven by the same *seishin* ideology.

School Rugby

With a strong sense of hierarchy maintained in most school rugby clubs, juniors are often treated harshly as a means of 'sorting out the men from the boys', with the more traditional clubs explicitly setting out to cut down the number of first-year members to a tough core of players who have the moral qualities perceived as necessary to be of use to the team. First-year players typically endure particularly severe and unrewarding training. In some of the more conservative schools the first years may not be permitted to train with the ball and are restricted to running and callisthenics for the duration of the year. They may also be required to perform menial tasks, such as raking the dirt field, washing the seniors' jerseys as well as pumping up the rugby balls before training and deflating them after training each day. Two weeks before the national championships one of the members of a well-known team said that as a first year he and the others were often made to do physical punishment such as push-ups if the seniors felt that they were not fully focused on their rugby. He referred to it as *katsu,* which is the term to describe the practice of senior monks hitting younger ones during meditation if they move or seem to be off-task. When compared to the more liberal practices of soccer, rugby functions as a conservative sport in Japan where the emphasis is on the development of character and good manners. For players who are members of the stronger and more competitive clubs there is a strong emphasis on 'hard training' that involves suffering physical and emotional hardship over years of membership. In the often severe training regimes that characterize training in the 'powerhouse', vocational schools, elite-level rugby players are subjected to year after year of hardship which is seen to develop good manners, courage, commitment, tolerance and perseverance. These are qualities required for the employment into which many of these players will enter after graduating from school. Membership of a strong school rugby club can act as a sound reference for employment for school-leavers and can gain them entry to university and then into work where the same conservative ideals of manliness are generally valued.

The constant repetition of basic movements in the martial arts, and in most sport, is thought both to test and to foster the ability to develop inner strength.[26] The purity of spirit which is required in the more refined arts, the less overtly physical cultural practices such as the tea ceremony (*sadou*), flower arrangement (*ikebana*) and calligraphy (*shodo*), is also developed through bodily discipline. Bourdieu contends that culture exists within the body, in the habitus, and is embodied through daily social and cultural practice.[27] While culture is manifested in the material products of practice, such as works of pottery, paintings and arrangements of flowers, these are the products of embodied culture, the result of particular ways of using the body. Within each of these practices the student develops *seishin* through bodily experiences which test the individual's ability, physically and emotionally, to endure, and require little intellectual input. Class consciousness is weak in Japan but there is no doubt that access to resources is uneven and that there is inequality of opportunity.[28] Rugby is played at schools ranging from the lowest academic level vocational schools to the most elite and exclusive private schools. But although there is variation in practice across class lines, the general training practices of school rugby in Japan tend to conform to this model. Analyses of game styles at Hanazono also indicated that they were significantly shaped by *seishin* ideology.

The Construction of Masculinity at Hanazono, 1997–98

Dominant approaches to training in high school rugby clubs bear much similarity to those of *budo* and close examination reveals a clear link between rugby training and the militaristic, *samurai* ideals of manliness. Training is typically characterized by an emphasis on sustained physical effort, personal sacrifice and suffering. The majority of high school rugby players competing at Hanazono were in their final year of high school and trained for six, sometimes seven, days a week, for almost 12 months of the year. Even though there are 'rugby clubs' operating in primary schools, entry into junior high school offers the first chance for players to be involved in a 'serious' rugby club. Most of the elite-level players in high school rugby begin playing at junior high school, but for the majority of Japan's secondary school rugby players their introduction to the game does not begin until their first year at senior high school. In 1996 there were approximately 1,500 senior high schools fielding teams, but only around 300 junior high schools offered the opportunity to play. Elite-level players spend six years committed to rugby, training almost daily, year in year out, in clubs where the demands on their time and energy are seen to test and cultivate the moral qualities of perseverance and resolve, their *gaman*. For the majority of traditionally strong school rugby clubs, training regimes typically comprise learning and drilling patterns of play which contribute to strategies which are predictable. Games resemble a war of attrition where victory goes to the stronger. Training is usually characterized by simple movements and drills which are repeated to the point of physical and emotional stress. Strong teams learn to suffer and endure in regimes which create tension between the inner being and the outer body; where the human spirit must overcome the weakness of the flesh.

The ubiquitous 'run pass' is almost universally used in high school training. Training is always conducted in large groups and most squads at the 1997–98 tournament comprised 40 to 60 players who all trained together. 'Run pass' is usually performed in small groups and, as the name suggests, involves running up and down the field passing the ball laterally. Sometimes the passing may vary but essentially the groups run at top pace passing the ball, up and down the length of the field. The more traditional teams may do this for over an hour. The groups must keep up the pace of execution and no one must fall behind or give in to fatigue. The training involves little skill and little intellectual input but it requires stamina and the ability to keep going. For these players, when the same pattern or basic movement is repeated at length and the body begins to tire, the spirit must be strong enough to take over. Such training is essentially anti-intellectual in that it requires little cognitive engagement and is aimed at the development of internal qualities that those in the West might call 'character' or mental toughness developed through corporal means. It is a quasi-religious struggle for control over the body, an internal struggle between the inner, social being and the body.

For a drill aimed at improving passing and catching it is inefficient, with each player often handling the ball only once for each 100m of running with little scope for, or expectation of, individual decision-making. However, the duration and pace of the activity make it physically demanding. This is a universally popular exercise with high school rugby teams and typifies much of the training that teams undertake. It involves the repetition of simple movements which become automatic to a point where the physical demands placed on the body test and develop physical stamina and, more significantly, strength of will and perseverance. The repetitive and physically-demanding nature of these exercises facilitates execution as an unconscious action and the body takes over from the mind. This constitutes a process of embodiment in which culture, ideology and a specific masculinity are imbedded into the physical habitus, beyond the reach of the conscious mind and where the body accepts what the mind might otherwise reject.[29]

The practice of the martial arts is also characterized by constant repetition in training, aimed at building the same fighting spirit (*konjo*) admired in rugby. This approach to training aspires to the attainment of a state of 'mind' called *mushin* which, loosely translated, means 'no mind'. It is a state in which there is no conscious thought which can interfere with the embodied reactions of the practitioner and has always been central to the *samurai's* single-minded commitment and his acceptance of death. This state of 'mind' is reached through constant repetition of techniques and of responses to attacks until they become second nature. *Mushin* is a Zen concept which has guided not only the *samurai* arts of warfare but also the code of behaviour, *bushido*. The training of the *samurai* in swordsmanship and other arts of war was focused on the development of a state of spiritual and corporal harmony, a state of 'no-mindedness', which allowed him to act with clarity and detachment.[30] Suzuki's description of *mushin* illuminates a distrust of the intellect and a faith in embodied learning in the practice of the martial arts which also characterizes much of school rugby training. He discusses it as part of the last stage of Buddhist discipline in the quest for enlightenment:

> intellectual calculations are lost sight of and a state of no mindedness prevails. When the ultimate perfection is attained, the body and limbs perform by themselves what is assigned to them to do with no interference from the mind. [The technical skill is so autonomized it is completely divorced from conscious efforts.][31]

Zen philosophy formed a central element of the *samurai* ethic and the attainment of *mushin* through diligent and constant training was seen to lead to the complete harmony of mind, body and soul. In striving to empty the mind of conscious thought during training the *samurai* attempted to reach a state which is a:

> state of mind [that] gives itself up unreservedly to an unknown 'power' that comes to one from nowhere and yet seems strong enough to possess the whole field of consciousness and make it work for the unknown. Hereby he becomes a kind of automaton, so to speak, as far as his own consciousness is concerned.[32]

Training for teams at Hanazono 1997–98 varied in levels of aggression and contact but were all characterized by extended repetition and the refinement of playing patterns where set attacking plays such as backline 'sign plays' and backrow 'side attacks' from the scrum were drilled and drilled. All sessions usually finished off with unopposed team runs performed at top speed, sweeping up and down the field for up to an hour in each session where, again, pressure was placed on the individual to keep up and not give in to fatigue, pain or discomfort. There is a particular version of manliness at work here which emphasizes achievement and competency solely through physical effort as a manifestation of moral qualities, while rejecting competency or achievement resulting from intellectual input or cleverness.

Game Style and Training at Hanazono

Schools in Japan in which sport forms the primary focus of the curriculum tend to be those which cater for the less academically-inclined students. Contrary to popular misconceptions in the West, not all students aspire to enter university and find employment as a white-collar 'salariman'. Only 12 per cent of the population are university graduates and only 12 per cent work in large companies.[33] For those set on the academic path the demands of the university entrance examinations, the *jigoku jukken* (exam hell) normally preclude participation in sport. Membership in the school rugby club normally means training and playing six days a week, 12 months a year for the entire three years of high school. Such demands on time and energy usually require students to make a choice between sport or study. Consequently the strong rugby playing schools tend to be lower academic level public, or vocational, schools. There are exceptions and at the 1997–98 championships there were half a dozen academically elite schools competing, with one of them winning an exciting final to take the championship for the first time in 11 years.

The majority of schools in which rugby forms a central element of the curriculum draw on students from lower socio-economic backgrounds where the practice of rugby functions as a form of social education and where it often offers the only chance for the disadvantaged to gain access to the cultural capital of a university degree. While there is evidence in the corporal and discursive practices of school rugby to indicate class-specific approaches to training and playing, there was no explicit articulation of class and, with a few exceptions, the games at Hanazono in 1997–98 over the two weeks of competition displayed similarly characteristic approaches to play. In the final an academically elite private high school from Tokyo was pitted against a vocational school from the Kyoto area.

The vocational school, *Fushimi Kogyo Koko* (Fushimi Technical High School), is widely known in Japan. The founder of the rugby club was first appointed there as a teacher over 20 years ago when the school was overrun by 'delinquents'. As a former All-Japan player he introduced rugby as a disciplinary practice through which he was able to transform the school and establish the game as the focus of the school's identity, assuming a role which is not dissimilar to that which rugby played in some nineteenth-century English public schools. Mr Yamaguchi's success inspired a long-running and popular television series based on his story and contributed to a period of growing popularity for rugby. Through the complex system of sports admissions rugby now provides the sole means of achieving a university education for boys at this school. Yamaguchi is a charismatic and colourful figure who is well known around Japan. He believes in continuous, hard training as the best means of educating boys and maintaining social cohesion among Japan's troubled youth. Although he is no longer the official director of the club but is employed on the Kyoto City Board of Education, he is still deeply involved with it and oversaw its 1997–98 campaign.

His team's opposition in the final came from an academically elite school in which all students qualify for university and come from upper-middle-class backgrounds where rugby was only one of six major sports. Here the players were also required to meet demanding academic requirements. Despite the marked differences between the two schools, when viewed in comparison with game styles in Western schools such as those of Australia, the Japanese schools showed similar, distinguishing characteristics. There was some evidence of variation in game play from team to team, but it is beyond the scope of this chapter to examine them. The surge in foreign players competing in the company leagues has seen significant changes in training and game play at this level, but such changes have yet to affect, in any very significant manner, the practice of rugby at university and high school level. For the purposes of analysis, the games are discussed in terms of the distinguishing aspects of play which can be connected with a culture-specific form of hegemonic masculinity. The majority of games at Hanazono were played at high speed with an emphasis on keeping the ball alive and moving at all costs. Japanese teams invariably display great stamina which results from their training. Stamina can be seen as a tangible measure of effort and a measure of spiritual strength which can be used to assert a form of physical superiority in games by maintaining a consistently high pace of play to outlast the opposition.

In line with the ideal of keeping the opposition under pressure, teams ran to form scrums and line outs and often took the option of a quick tap kick when kicking for touch might have been a better option. Kicking for touch allows the team to make territorial gains and maintain possession by having the throw at the line out. Yet many teams choose both to keep the pace of play as fast as possible and to assert a physical superiority over the opposition. During one of the quarter-finals a team favoured to win its game found themselves trailing by two points with five minutes to go. They launched a series of attacks which placed them 5m short of the opponents' line. They then received a penalty kick about 10m inside the sideline but chose to take the quick tap and attack. They were camped on their opponents' line and launched one frontal forward charge after another, all to no avail. During the last few minutes they received another penalty but, again, chose to attack the line. Despite three scrums where they won possession they continued repeatedly to have their forwards charge into the opposition. This approach was employed by one of the half-dozen academically elite schools competing which made the tactics chosen more surprising. At the sound of full time they all collapsed on the ground in tears and the crowd applauded loudly. The newspapers reported the game positively as a test of character and determination in which the losing side courageously battered the wall of defence in a display of commitment and determination.

Despite the opportunity to kick a penalty goal and win the game the losing side appeared determined to demonstrate superior power by crossing the line. While the ideals of courage, personal sacrifice and 'putting your body on the line' for the team can be linked with Victorian ideals of manliness, as can the anti-intellectual nature of practice, the influence of a uniquely Japanese masculinity is also evident. *Seishin* thought views physical power as the manifestation and expression of spiritual strength and, while it is often seen as a measure of spiritual strength, physical achievement which relies on cleverness or trickery alone, no matter how spectacular it may be, is not viewed as spiritual strength.[34] While clever plays and outstanding skills may win games and draw applause from the crowd, it is the clash of man on man in tests of physical strength which is seen as an indicator of both manliness and cultural health. It is the forward charging up field dragging defenders with him, the big tackles that stop a runner dead, and the desperate and relentless counterattacks that draw the biggest applause from the crowd and act as markers of collective masculinity. A win which is not earned through sacrifice, effort and commitment is one which would not be valued.

The former Scottish international Jim Greenwood identifies the patterned structure of Japanese rugby that makes it predictable and contributes to the playing of games as battles of attrition where the symbolic spoils of victory go to the strongest and fittest.[35] He contends that there is a deep-rooted distrust of innovation and of being different. Under these circumstances the team that earns victory is seen as the one which has trained the hardest and longest. Victory in such battles of attrition as acted out at Hanazono 1997–98 are earned by teams which display the characteristics of hegemonic masculinity and outlast, out power and overcome the opposition in displays of superior physical strength as a manifestation of spiritual strength. Although the captain of the losing team in the quarter-final may have thought about taking the shot at a penalty goal to win, the importance of victory alone was exceeded by the need to win in the expected manner. His team were known for their aggressive and 'gutsy' forward play and the expectations of the team's supporters, the other students, staff, parents and old boys, to win in a way which exhibited the character of the team may well have overridden the victory-at-any-cost approach.

Fair Play

One of the most striking features of Japanese rugby in general is the absence of foul play and violence outside the rules. The courage, commitment and willingness of players to lay their bodies on the line are well known by Australian players who have opposed touring sides. Disregard for personal welfare in the heat of battle is an expected quality of all Japanese players. Violent use of the body is admired, expected and a marker of manliness but only if it is legitimized by the rules. Any form of violence committed outside the rules and ethos of the game is frowned upon by team mates, spectators and coaches alike. The line between violence which is acceptable, and expected, and that which is unacceptable is clear and distinct. The ethos of fair play is alive and well in Japan. In his response to a question on fighting, a player who played in the final at Hanazono (a prop forward who played in the All Japan high schools national team,) said:

> Getting a few whacks in rugby is part of the game and even if it's outside the rules I can put up with it. Of course I might want to hit back and I might occasionally step on someone in a ruck but I'm not that sort of player. You have to control yourself on the field, the best way to get them back is to play better and take them out in hard tackles. Basically I think that 'fair play' [in English] is very important and is the special feature of rugby, it's the true meaning of the game.

His response reflects the ideal of fair play and restraint which is evident at most levels of rugby in Japan. Hegemonic masculinity in Japanese rugby demands aggression and total personal commitment for the sake of the team, but there are equally strong expectations of playing within the rules. Courage, sacrifice, loyalty and commitment are equally admired in Australian or New Zealand rugby but, at any level of rugby in Australia and New Zealand, fighting and 'marginal' play often act as markers of masculine status. For many, the highlights of the 1996 Bledisloe Cup match at Suncorp Stadium, according to the *Australian Rugby Review*, was 60 minutes of Wallaby dominance, 'helped by Michael Brial's defiant stand up stoush with All Black centre Frank Bunce'.[36] In Japanese rugby, although there is the occasional fight, it is seen as a sign of personal weakness, as an indication that the individual lacks the control over his emotions expected of him. The ideal of manliness in Japanese rugby demands *konjo* and singlemindedness (*omoikitte, seijitsu, isshokenmei*) but is offset by concerns with restraint and self-control. The expectations of sacrifice, commitment, aggression and effort are balanced by the cultural value placed on team/group spirit and restraint as demanded by behavioural ideals of self-*enryo* (discipline) and *gaman* (tolerance, perseverance). Martial arts exponents are expected to show courage and strength in the *dojo* (place of training) but the consequences of striking somebody in anger on the street would be dire for any highly-ranked practitioner of karate or any other traditional martial art. This is acutely evident in the stringent expectations of correct behaviour for *sumotori* (*sumo* 'wrestlers') and the consequences for even the most minor transgression of their strict code of conduct.

Greenwood describes Japan as a bastion of the amateur spirit where there is a strong emphasis on gentlemanly conduct on the field. He argues that the practice of rugby in Japan is characterized by the public-school notion of games as shapers of character and the sports field as an arena within which to express it. He argues that it is the faith held in rugby as a builder of character that drives the Japanese to 'cheerfully' expend extraordinary time and effort on rugby, year in, year out, through the heat of summer and the cold of winter.[37] The form of masculinity that characterizes rugby in schools bears much similarity to the original Victorian ideals of manliness but it also displays distinctively Japanese notions of manliness originating from the feudal, ruling classes. The form of masculinity evident at Hanazono 1997–98 is the product of social changes over the past century which have been characterized by a constant tension between conservative native culture and Western values. The relationship between native and Western values in Japanese society is dynamic and in a state of constant change and is likely to see changes in the practice of rugby in schools and movements in the type of masculinity that shapes it.

NOTES

1. B. Moeran, 'Individual, Group and *Seishin*: Japan's internal cultural debate', in T. Lebra and W. Lebra (eds), *Japanese Culture and Behaviour* (Honolulu, 1986).
2. Y. Ikeguchi, *Kindai no Ragubi Hyaku Nen Kan* [A Hundred Years of Modern Rugby] (Tokyo, 1981).
3. J. Nauright and Timothy J.L. Chandler (eds), *Making Men: Rugby and Masculine Identity* (London, 1996).
4. R. Connell, *Masculinities* (Sydney, 1995).
5. R. Gruneau and D. Whitson, *Hockey Night in Canada* (Toronto, 1993).
6. M. Messner, 'When Bodies Are Weapons: Masculinity and Violence in Sport', *International Review for the Sociology of Sport*, Vol.25, No.3 (1990), pp. 203–17.
7. D. Roden, 'Baseball and the Quest for National Dignity in Meiji Japan', *American Historical Review*, Vol.85, No.1 (February 1980), pp. 511–34.
8. R. Williams, *Marxism and Literature* (London, 1977).
9. W. Beasley, *The Rise of Modern Japan* (Tokyo, 1990).
10. Roden, 'Baseball and the Quest for National Dignity'.
11. Y. Ikeguchi, *Kindai no Ragubi Hyaku nen Kan*.
12. Roden, 'Baseball and the Quest for National Dignity'.
13. Ibid.
14. I. Abe, Y. Kiyohara and K. Nakajima, 'Sport and Physical Education under Fascistization in Japan', *Bulletin of Health and Sports Sciences*, Vol.13 (1990), pp. 25–46.
15. S. Inoue, 'Sports and the Martial Arts in the Making of Modern Japan', paper presented to the International Conference for the Sociology of Sport, Japan Society for the Sociology of Sport, Kyoto, 27–29 March 1997.
16. Ibid.
17. R. Whiting, *You've Got to Have Wa* (New York, 1990).
18. Quoted in S. Waddington, 'Old World Beckons', *Courier Mail* (Brisbane, Australia), 8 October 1997.

19. Moeran, 'Individual, Group and *Seishin*'.
20. T. Lebra, *Japanese Social Organization* (Honolulu, 1976).
21. T. Rohlen, *Japanese High Schools* (Berkeley, 1983).
22. US Department of State: Revision of the Japanese Educational System, Doc. 40, Item 10, 1947. Cited in H. Passin, *Society and Education in Japan* (Tokyo, 1987), p. 290.
23. Ibid.
24. Rohlen, *Japanese High Schools*.
25. K. Van Wolferen, *The Enigma of Japanese Power* (Tokyo, 1993); and Inoue, 'Sports and Martial Arts'.
26. Lebra, *Japanese Social Organization*.
27. P. Bourdieu, *Distinction: A Social Critique of the Judgement of Taste* (London, 1984).
28. Y. Sugimoto, *An Introduction to Japanese Society* (Cambridge, 1997).
29. P. Bourdieu, *In Other Words: Essays Towards a Reflexive Sociology* (Cambridge, 1990), p. 29.
30. I. Nitobe (compiled and edited by Charles Lucas from original work, 1899), *Bushido: the Warrior's Code* (Burbank, CA, 1976).
31. D. Suzuki, *Zen and Japanese Culture* (Tokyo, 1988).
32. Ibid.
33. Sugimoto, *An Introduction to Japanese Society*.
34. T. Rohlen, 'Spiritual Education in a Japanese Bank', in Lebra and Lebra (eds), *Japanese Culture and Behaviour*.
35. J. Greenwood, *Think Rugby: A Guide to Purposeful Team Play* (London, 1986).
36. M. Brooks, 'The Year in Review', *Australian Rugby Review,* Vol.1, No.9 (1996), p. 22.
37. Greenwood, *Think Rugby, passim*.

7

Crossing the Line: Women Playing Rugby Union

Alison Carle and John Nauright

Introduction

We have seen how rugby developed in colonial contexts and as it moved from its British core to other countries. So far in both this book and in *Making Men* we have examined only male rugby players and their rugby cultures. Since the 1970s, however, women have taken to the playing of rugby union in ever larger numbers. Significant numbers of women now play the game in the British Isles, elsewhere in Europe, North America and Australasia. Women have had a long history of participation in modern sporting activities although they have faced countless barriers to sporting competition, particularly in any 'contact' sports.[1] As we move into the twenty-first century, many more doors are opening for the sporting woman and games previously thought to 'belong' to men, are becoming attractive options for women. One sport that is enjoying increasing popularity among women is rugby union. Although liberal feminists may be delighted at the apparent breakdown of the masculine exclusivity that has been imposed on rugby in the past, a thorough investigation of the format of the game as it applies to women highlights a sporting field that reinforces and echoes historical, masculine-orientated stereotypes. This case study examines women's rugby culture through an analysis of an Australian rugby club and the culture that surrounds its women's team, as well as questioning the culture that emerges around the playing of such a hyper-masculine sport. This will be done in an attempt to understand why women are playing rugby football when they face strong societal opposition based on historical, social and physical perceptions about the relationship of women to contact sports.

In contemporary society sport is seen not only as a physical struggle between competitors, but also as a phenomenon that has the potential to define those who play and support such activities. Sport is particularly significant in socializing young men into the performance of masculinity. Feminists view this social categorization that distinguishes females from males as a major problem that continually creates inequality between the sexes.[2] These patterns do much to perpetuate the existing discrimination and exploitation of women, so that some have described sport as the last true bastion of male domination.[3] These differences are constantly reinforced with the continuing exploitation and discrimination, existing in most popular sports, so that 'the determination of males to preserve sport as a male activity and privilege has affected every stage of the development of sport for women'.[4]

One of the main views shared by feminists is that women have the right to control their bodies and make choices in their own interests, independently of those promoted by men or the state.[5] It therefore seems ironic that, until recently, the majority of feminist researchers have ignored female sporting bodies, 'nor have they always seen the relevance of physicality or empowerment through physical activity, to feminist politics'.[6] In arguing for the placing of the body at the centre of feminist analysis and politics, Elizabeth Grosz states that the body has been the site of female oppression in society:

> Instead of granting women an autonomous and active form of corporeal specificity, at best women's bodies are judged in terms of a 'natural inequality,' as if there was a standard or measure for the value of bodies independent of sex. In other words, women's corporeal specificity is used to explain and justify the different social positions and cognitive abilities of the two sexes. By implication, women's bodies are presumed to be incapable of men's achievements, being weaker, more prone to irregularities, intrusions, and unpredictability.[7]

Although women athletes have the opportunity to experience the same aspects of sport that men do (such as the pursuit of a common goal, camaraderie and belonging), the unsettled relationship that exists between gender and sport 'provides a very different context for the experience of community in women's sport'.[8] Women face the problem of constructing communities in sport that conform to overriding conventions dictated by wider societal constructs that, on the whole, serve to minimize and trivialize their exertions. The recent increase in female athleticism represents a genuine challenge by women to gain equality, self-definition and control of their own bodies, to such a degree that it challenges male domination.[9]

This case study of female rugby players answers Ann Hall's call for more 'studies in which women athletes are asked to reflect on the significance of the body and physicality to their experience of sport'.[10]

Despite the relative lack of material analysing women's experiences as players of contact sports, one study that examined women's basketball, shows how female athletes use the physicality and emotionality of their game as a way of learning about their self-identities though their lived experiences both on and off the court.[11] Nancy Theberge's recent ethnographic study of a Canadian women's ice hockey team supports Rail's findings for basketball, in illustrating the contested terrain of gender, through the examination of ice hockey, Canada's 'flag carrier of masculinity'.[12] The distinct conclusions drawn in these cases illustrate the potential such interactive studies have for broadening our comprehension of the relations between gender and contemporary sport. With a dearth of archival material and secondary literature, it was necessary for us to conduct interviews and utilize ethnographic methods to uncover the experiences of women rugby players and the problems and prospects women face in 'crossing the line' that formerly excluded them from contact sports such as rugby.

Rugby union became a game played, controlled, promoted and watched by males. Rugby as a historical cultural practice has long reinforced the general notion of men in sport as an overclass that has resulted in men's greater access to opportunities, rewards and power.[13] Few, if any, sports, have provided the cultural capital for success in wider society than rugby union and membership of the rugby fraternity. Male rugby has been underpinned by female domestic service and the male rugby culture built on the denigration of women and homosexuals, thus reinforcing a masculinity centred on bodily contact and performance, but one legitimated through the marginalization of the Other. The relationship between masculinity and rugby was passed generationally between fathers and sons and rugby participation became synonymous with learning to be a man in the public schools of England and the private schools of the British Empire. Even though the characteristics of climate, immigration, demography and geography led the 'sport-obsessed', colonial Australians to adapt rugby football to some extent, these underlying themes of total masculine domination were transferred to the private, and some state, schools in Australia.[14]

Twentieth-century Western boys, therefore, entered a society with preconceived stereotypical ideals supported by the creed of rugby (or other football codes) and masculinist social values continued to be nurtured by sports such as rugby union and its surrounding administration and culture. Most women have been excluded from football from the outset, as John Bale states, 'the preference for a football as a toy for boys, but not girls, reflects a form of sex-appropriate behaviour that has led to women being excluded from playing rugby since infancy'.[15] For most of the century, and still for most women, their roles in rugby have been restricted to the domestic servicing of men through the washing of rugby clothing, supplying food for club dinners and taking sons and partners to rugby matches, among other activities. Women were to be present purely in supportive roles. Shona Thompson (1988) describes the domestic positioning of women in rugby union well:

> The domestic labour of the women has always served rugby. One is able to cite an endless list of chores traditionally done by women for the benefit of the men and boys who play rugby. It would include providing meals, catering for visiting teams, shopping for, laundering, mending and ironing team uniforms, transporting sons to practices and games, waiting on the sideline, attending to injured bodies and egos.[16]

Many New Zealand women used the 1981 South African rugby tour of their country to protest against the rugby culture and the way it promoted masculine and misogynist ideals. A group called Women Against Rugby (WAR) was formed and they withdrew from the domestic servicing of rugby during the tour. Although this was over-shadowed by the other political attacks also associated with the tour, it was the first real step toward breaking down male exclusivity in rugby union in a country where the game was deemed to be a major national sport for men.[17] By the 1980s in the United States and Canada women had already started playing rugby in large numbers, where the men's national sports are identified as baseball, basketball, American football and ice hockey. In places where rugby was a major national football code for men, women's rugby was slower to emerge.

Despite the presence of strident criticism and public beliefs in gender-specific activities, many women continued to strive for a wider range of sporting opportunities throughout the twentieth century. In 1921 over 200 women met to establish a women's rugby league competition in Sydney, Australia. Women's matches continued into the 1930s with over 2,500 spectators witnessing a charity match in 1930 in aid of Sydney's unemployed women.[18] Rugby league competition soon disappeared as male authorities colluded to keep women off male rugby league grounds. A women's competition in rugby league re-emerged along with rugby union competitions in Australia only in the late 1980s and 1990s, though without support from male rugby league organizations.

In the USA and Canada women began to play rugby in large numbers by the 1980s and in 1983 the Women's Rugby Football Union (WRFU) started in England with only 12 member clubs. In the following decade membership swelled to over 2,000 playing members affiliated with 120 clubs. Scotland, Ireland and Wales soon followed, setting up their first international teams. This increase in female athleticism represented what Messner terms generally as 'a genuine quest by women for equality, control of their own bodies, and self-definition, and as such represents a challenge to the ideological basis of male domination'.[19]

Although these structural developments suggest that the hostility to women's rugby may be on the wane, more subtle analysis suggests a more complex picture. The most obvious and influential illustration of these factors can be determined through the media where the coverage of women's rugby has been generally mixed and limited. *Rugby World*, the rugby magazine with the widest international circulation, normally devotes only one page to women's rugby, and a similar pattern is repeated in other publications or popular newspapers. This under-representation of 'rugby women' in the media is similar to the general pattern for all women's sport.

The particular way in which sport is covered also hints at the reluctant toleration of rugby as an option for women, rather than its broad acceptance. The media constantly portray women's rugby as a novelty event, and, likewise, the women who play are represented through 'fluff' pieces or photographs that show them in highly sexual and feminine poses, or the opposite extreme as 'ugly' or brutish types who are not 'real women'. Such representations are politically motivated, and despite the apparent realism and objectivity of photographs, rarely do they portray neutral images.[20] The way that the media show that, despite women's athleticism, they still manage to retain a woman-like quality illustrates these promoted sexual differences.[21] In the late 1990s, for example, the New Zealand media has made much of the fact that Melodie Robinson, one of the national rugby team players, is a former Miss Canterbury and thus a 'real' woman (even though she plays rugby union better than most men). An extreme example of the representation of women rugby players appeared in 1995 in a feature article with accompanying pictures in the Australian sporting monthly magazine *Inside Sport*; although this depicted women rugby players as dirty, unattractive and masculine on one page, at the same time it attempted to legitimize some players' positioning as 'real women' by including glamorous, highly-sexualized photographs of them off the field. The article thus framed the story along the lines of 'What are nice girls like you doing playing a sport like this?' or 'Can you believe these are rugby players when you see them all dressed up?' This discussion highlights a contradiction that underlies coverage of women's sport, and especially of women's rugby, although we shall see that these conceptions are present at club level as well. While the media continue such contradictory coverage of women players and their game, rather than portraying them as rugby players, coverage will undermine women's efforts, further trivializing them and their competitions.

Women thus face 'symbolic annihilation', as the advancement of stereotypes such as 'women who play rugby are butch/lesbian/men' and thus not 'real' women, overshadows the skill and the competitiveness of the women's game. Such a process works hand-in-hand with a trivialization/marginalization framework that compares women's rugby performances direct to those of men. The combination of these factors 'support[s] and reproduce[s] the masculine values and practices of competitive sport'.[22] It is in this context that we sought to understand better how and why women come to play such a hyper-masculinized sport and what they feel about the game. We sought to comprehend wider perceptions of women playing rugby and how they related to the practices of rugby that have been so inscribed as definers of masculinity as things that 'make men'. In order to do this we focused on one women's team in Brisbane and their experiences within a larger male-dominated club.[23] All the team members were interviewed in 1998 and some in 1997. Interviews were also held with the team's coach, club officials and some male club members. A survey of male attitudes towards women players was also undertaken. In addition, one of us (AC) participated in training, went to team meetings and observed matches and post-match and other social functions throughout 1998.

Background
Men's rugby first became established in Brisbane in the 1880s. By 1887, just five years after the first recorded rugby match in the town, there were 36 registered clubs.[24] The club we investigated began in 1911 and has a history of success with nearly 200 players having been selected to represent Queensland, though in the 1990s the club has not been as successful. By contrast, a women's rugby competition only began in 1993 in Queensland and the women's team at the club has won the majority of premierships in the women's competition. Queensland women who wanted to play held meetings in 1992 with existing male rugby clubs and secured support from several so that a

competition could begin. The women's competition plays under the Australian under-19 rules that apply to all categories of rugby other than the men's first grade. The only real differences are in scrummaging rules and match length. Under these rules once the ball enters the scrum it is not allowed to move more than 1.5m. The length of halves in the women's game is 35 minutes compared with 40 for men. Otherwise the game is the same. Most of the women players have considerable sporting experience, some having represented the state or nation in other sports before taking up rugby union. The age of players at the club extends from 18 to 35, although most are in their early twenties. Most of the players went to private schools where sporting opportunities were limited to those deemed appropriate for women such as netball, hockey, swimming, athletics and rowing.

So what attracted the women to play rugby union when many of them played other sports at a high level? Some began when friends asked them to try, many for its novelty value. One player stated clearly that she wanted to be able to play any sport that boys could play:

> The first I heard about it was when they started … the team down at the club, and a friend of mine from school … said, 'Let's go down and play', because we had always gone down and watched the guys play. We just thought it would be really cool [and] we could show that we were just as tough as the boys… .

A minority of the players had experience playing rugby league at state high schools and many had played touch rugby, the latter being one of the fastest growing social sports in Australasia.

Bodies on the Line: Rugby, Teamwork and Friendship

Unlike most other sports, in rugby union an individual cannot succeed for more than a couple of seconds without significant support from the rest of the team. In men's rugby the type of teamwork needed has long been imbued with larger educational properties. To play rugby well as part of a team and to take the physical punishment without complaint was thought to prepare middle- and upper-class men for challenges in adult life.[25] As Light shows in this volume, in Japan the manly concepts that surround rugby fused with Japanese codes of manly behaviour and emerged in the practice in rugby of individual sacrifice to the point of physical and emotional exhaustion among players. For these Australian women the links between physicality and bodily sacrifice for the team and team-mates is a significant part of the game which binds players together as a team and as friends. Carly highlighted her love of rugby by saying:

I honestly believe there is no other sport that is as physically and mentally demanding. It is fitness, it is strength. It is power and it is thinking the whole time. There are some sports which are actually predictable … With rugby there are so many things that are out of your control. *You could be the best player in the country but if you haven't got somebody else when you get tackled to come and support you, there is absolutely no point* [emphasis added].

This necessity led the women to form close friendships off the field and to spend much of their socializing time together. Kirsty suggested that the reasons come from the intense physicality in rugby:

I think that you get to make friends that you don't ever make in any other sport. I've played netball at higher levels and stuff like that and you don't make such good friends at netball. There's not the social and camaraderie that you get with rugby and I think part of that is that when you are out on the field *you are kind of putting your body in the hands of someone else.* You're saying, *'Right, I'm going to go down over that ball and I expect you to protect me and I know you can do that.'* I think a real trust forms and I think that's part of the reason friendships are so intense and good [emphases added].

From the general comments of all players it may be deduced that the rough nature of rugby and the teamwork required creates a social bonding that is stronger than in other sports. The intense nature of friendships and loyalty may also be enhanced due to the marginal nature of rugby as an acceptable female sport within wider society. Palmer in a similar study of a women's rugby club in New Zealand argued that women form close relationships as part of identification with rugby as something that sets them off from other sub-cultures.[26] In addition, while there are eight men's teams at the club, there is only one women's team, thus the women are in a minority within the rugby club as well as beyond it.

A Women's Rugby Culture?
A specific social environment surrounds the club. Without exception, the women we studied all believe that this is a major contributing factor to their enjoyment of rugby. The set-up of the clubhouse includes a function room, storage and physiotherapy centre, a dance floor and, of course, a bar. The clubhouse overlooks the number one oval and regular functions are held after every home game, while

gatherings throughout the year are also organized for both the men and the women players at pubs and clubs. Although drinking was not compulsory, and a couple of the women do not drink for health and religious reasons, the majority of these social occasions placed a large emphasis on alcohol consumption. Unofficial 'awards' of alcohol were given to the players in recognition of their efforts on the field; and at the formal presentation dinner, male prize winners for all of the teams were given jugs of beer while the women's Best and Fairest player was given a glass. The player then had to drink it as quickly as possible, as was the norm with most drinking occasions. This in itself is significant since it reinforces the existing stereotypes that women cannot take the same amounts of drink as men and heavy beer drinking is not really ladylike. Many men believe that women are supposed to be physiologically unable to 'handle their piss'.[27]

Men have defined most aspects of the rugby subculture and their actions provide a 'yardstick' by which women's behaviour and then potential acceptance is often measured. Desire for acceptance often leads the women to adopt behaviour that in other circumstances would not be seen as appropriate or welcome. Examining women's rugby in the United States, where women have not had to come under the specific authority of male clubs, Wheatley argues that women's behaviours serve to separate and distinguish their cultural form and are carried out through several traditions and practices that are neither determined nor defined by men. She states:

> The women's version of rugby disrupts the male, heterosexual hegemony of the rugby subculture by exposing female physical capability in a typically male enclave, while openly expressing a distinct identity and lifestyle through its social proclivities. The women's rugby style challenges patriarchal ideology in sport and leisure and social and sexual relations.[28]

In Australian and New Zealand clubs, however, it is clear that women players have adopted behaviour that conformed to dominant 'manly' traditions surrounding rugby. A desire to be viewed as 'one of the [rugby] boys' and, therefore, to cement their standing within the club itself has led women players to adopt cultural attributes that emulate men in the club.

At the club Tuesday night became recognized as the time where the 'gossip' of the past weekend's exploits was broadcast to the team, and special attention was given to the weekend drinking exploits of certain players. Those who were not known as heavy drinkers were often ribbed for their poor 'performance', as were those who initiated or participated in casual romantic relationships with any of the club's male players during the season. Although all the women insisted that there was no pressure on any particular player to drink, they also acknowledged that the structure of the social events certainly encouraged it. One said:

> I play it because I really like the people I play with. I really enjoy the club … I really enjoy the club situation. Through the club I have met so many people in the other Grades and you always know that if you rock up to the club, there will always be people you can chat and have a beer with. It's just a really nice atmosphere. [Continued] I've got friends from footy and I find the time I spend with them is drinking time. It's not peer pressure, it is just because we all like to drink. I suppose it is part of the culture.

Another replied:

> Occasionally I'll go out and not drink, that will be a rare thing, it may only happen once or twice a year, but that wouldn't be a problem. I'd be the driver and sort of keep an eye on everyone and make sure everyone sticks together and that sort of thing. I don't think that not drinking is a problem, but it is definitely the exception.

The majority of interaction between the male and the female teams occurred in a drinking environment, and it was at these functions that the women felt that they were the most accepted. One of the women said: 'The vast majority of it [drinking] would be after a game, [we'd] have a few beers. If it is someone's birthday you invite the entire team to the party. If we socialize with the men it is definitely in a pub environment or a function.' This interaction was later qualified by the women's coach who felt that the reason the women got on in the club was because they conformed to what the men expected of them in that environment:

> The women came in and the first year they were here they made such a difference to this club, you wouldn't believe. This club was the most antisocial, mixing club I have ever been in in my life. If you had a pie night you would be lucky to get six people there. We didn't have functions and if we did then nobody turned

up, except for the annual dinner, which is usually booked out. The first year they put on very cheap meals on Tuesdays and Thursday nights and the girls came, and it was a different atmosphere from the start. The guys came and talked to girls and girls talked to guys which was great. It was quite a marked difference in the atmosphere. Now they have been accepted here more so, and better than any other club. Probably because they are a little more feminine than for some of the girls in the other clubs... I think while they maintain this level, they'll be accepted.

It is clear from this evidence that women players are accepted in the club as long as they try to look feminine while conforming to dominant behaviours within the rugby culture. The women players are thus faced with having to perform the rugby culture while performing 'femininity'. Indeed, despite outward appearances of acceptance, an undercurrent of male hostility was also present.

Reactions from both Past and Present Male Rugby Players

As women are entering traditionally masculine arenas and sanctuaries at an accelerated rate the 'changing relations between the sexes lead men to stake out and fiercely protect clearly demarcated masculine space'.[29] Sport, and more specifically combative sports such as rugby union, are seen to be the last, true, male preserves, and as such, the women, who are now threatening the traditions and masculine exclusivity of rugby, are symbolically degraded, mocked or vilified.[30] This degradation is acknowledged by most of the women players. Boutilier and SanGiovanni cite three main reasons why men resist women's entry into sport. First, the underlying desire to keep sport as a masculine agency that serves to prescribe the specific roles men will undertake in their adult life. Secondly, to maintain the current ranking of sex roles, and finally, to 'preserve an exclusively male realm that allows for expressiveness and intimacy – qualities that are typically absent from what is generally viewed as appropriate behaviour for men'.[31] These factors are epitomized by the organization surrounding rugby union clubs in general, and is individually highlighted through the marginalization of women rugby players, both from the outside public and from within the club. Theberge proposes that one way this marginalization occurs is through the male domination of the administration and organization of sporting clubs.[32] This club is no different, although it has one female manager and a female physiotherapist (as well as a male one). Only two of the 13-member club board are women. Additionally, despite the women's team having being incorporated for five years there are no female coaches. Club personnel argue that there are no qualified female coaches, although one of the women's team members has coached overseas. One board member, who has been on the board for more than a decade, also said that it was generally accepted that it would be a long time before women would be qualified enough to be able to coach rugby teams. He was present when the proposition to affiliate a women's team was presented to the board and said:

> We accepted the fact that women's rugby should come in, but it wasn't our committee that decided to start up a women's rugby team. On the other side of the world everybody plays women's rugby. If they [the University women] wanted to play they should be able to play. It would have been different if Australia was the first country to play it. There was still opposition from lots of people like ... 'Rugby's a man's game and this is men's stuff', [and] even now the women are there [at the club] but they are not noticed.

With this in mind, perhaps the most marked responses to the women rugby players were highlighted through the women's perceptions of what the male rugby players of the club thought of them, when these were compared with the men's true reactions. All the women players felt that the men were incredibly supportive of their efforts both on and off the field. One stated, 'Hands down they are the most supportive club. From word of mouth from other girls from other clubs... a lot of them are just flat out getting training grounds.' And another said, '*En masse* we are very lucky, we are the luckiest team in Australia. We have the best assimilation between the men and women, there is no doubt.... We are so lucky. I honestly believe the boys view us in a very positive light.'

The disparity between the women's and the men's beliefs is more clearly illustrated in comments collected in a confidential, written survey from male University players, both from First Grade and Colts' teams. Although all the women players saw the men as being supportive of their achievements, quite different reactions appeared when male players' perceptions were recorded. Although the men responded in a generally supportive way, as was expected by the women, it was done in such a manner that showed little respect for their game. The men felt that the only reason they were around to watch the women's team play was because the women played after First Grade and they were at the club drinking with their team-mates.

In addition to the fact that most support was apparent only due to the timing of matches, male players also harboured some negativity towards women players. One male club member said, 'Girls in footy gear, covered in dirt, bashing the shit out of each other is not my idea of attractiveness. I think it is more the social interaction after the games that leads to any kind of friendships. My support is pretty much limited to "well done" if they win and "bad luck" if they lose.' Generally the men responded in a patronizing or denigrating tone when referring to the women's game. 'As a spectacle I think very little of it. It is unfair to compare them to the guys ... Girls rugby just can't compete in a game revolving around strength and speed, they can't be expected to.' Another responded, 'Personally I have only found novelty value out of the whole concept of "chicks" rugby.' Two of the respondents made directly hostile remarks towards their female counterparts: 'Every now and then I come across one with just a little too much testosterone for a so-called woman. This is a big turn-off... They aren't designed to play rugby and if they want to play with footys they should stick to touch football.' The other agreed by saying, 'Rugby is a man's sport. As long as they realize this and don't try to match us, things will be all right.'

When questioned again about these types of reaction from male club players, the women players remained adamant that they were the lucky ones, who were being allowed to play the game. One said, 'We need to learn from these boys, they have been playing for 200 years and we've been playing for five. We are so lucky.' Any overt, negative reactions were accepted on an individual level or attributed to the fact that the boys were acting well within their rights as male members of the club. One example of this type of reaction occurred at the end-of-year club dinner where the Master of Ceremonies actually had to ask the crowd (made up of predominantly male players) to respect the recognition the 'girls' were being given by one of their senior players. The women attributed this behaviour to the fact that the boys were too 'drunk and just being boys'. This reaction was defended by some of the male players as being a reaction to the particular individual presenting, rather than as a lack of respect to the women's team on a whole.

These responses illustrate two things. First, the fact the women believe that they are getting a good deal, even though they are discriminated against, emphasizes how they serve to reproduce patriarchal assumptions that are present in hyper-masculinized environments such as the rugby club. Second, the way they excuse male behaviour also reinforces the gender order and escalates the existing male dominance. Even though some players may react in this manner because they are intimidated about speaking out against the sometimes negative environment, through observation it was determined that the majority of women players just did not realize that they might be entitled to something better.

Likewise, the majority of the women believed the rugby administration to be incredibly supportive of the women's team. Louise stated:

> Admin are great. We get the same rights as everyone else in the club which is excellent and I know a lot of other clubs have had trouble with the admin and they weren't accepted by the club as a rule ... I think that's one good thing about [our club], that there's no problem like that.

However she qualified this by going on to say:

> We always get the worst training oval. Last year we trained on 5C which is the little strip between the main oval and second oval. We didn't even have our own oval to train on, which was fine, you know. It was more than adequate for us and we got used to it. [This year] we've been put on to the second oval but we've sort of snuck on to the first oval, I don't know how. It's good. It is so much better, but I mean that's fair enough I suppose. First and Second Grade are their [the club's] priority.

This type of response illustrates the obvious conundrum facing the female players, where, aside from the more obvious negative reactions from the male players, much more subversive marginalization also seems to go either unnoticed or is, in fact, accepted as being appropriate. This is perfectly illustrated in Louise's summation of the training fields. As she mentioned, originally the women did not even have an oval to train on and they had to run on a strip of grass that ran between the two main ovals. Five years after a women's team was incorporated at the club and four premierships later, the women were finally given a position on an oval, which they share with two other men's teams. Again, this did not seem to bother any of the women, and, in fact, most of them felt that they were 'lucky' because they had been given any ground at all.

Another factor that illustrates the subversive marginalization of the women may be seen at Tuesday night training where an impromptu meeting is held for all University Club members. Various messages, congratulations, selection and playing results, as well as items of interest and finance, are broadcast there to the players. On only a few occasions were the women addressed specifically, even though they were the most successful team in the club, the only team to make it to a grand final; while individually 15 players made the Queensland squad and four the Australian national team that reached the semi-finals of the 1998 World Cup. Likewise the language that was used by the 'announcers' excluded the women by its very nature, when the speakers constantly referred to the group as 'guys', 'fellas' or 'gentlemen', and rarely corrected themselves. Then when they did correct themselves, it was an exaggerated effort, on occasion condescending. Comments such as 'Gentlemen, and of course the lovely ladies...' illustrated this attitude; however, again it was usually ignored by the female players. One said that she did not mind being addressed in this way as it made her feel 'like one of the guys and more accepted'.

This type of marginalization was not restricted to this club and is spread throughout the whole Brisbane women's competition. The women's teams were constantly given inadequate playing times, often the last match of the weekend after the men's first grade, to the point of games often being too dangerous to play due to poor lighting conditions or the roughness and poor quality of the fields. Many women complained of the poor state of the facilities they faced. As each of the clubs was individually responsible for the allocation of grounds and match times, however, there was little opportunity for change to be initiated. Some clubs failed to supply referees, resulting in non-qualified people taking control of the game, and at some venues the women were not supplied with changing rooms and had to strip down in the in-goal area in front of the spectators. Aside from a few grumblings from a couple of the more experienced players, nothing was said about factors within the group and only through direct questioning were these issues addressed by the players. One replied:

> I guess we can always claim our ground and say we're training here if we are training on an oval, and I don't think any of the girls have any qualms about walking into a changing room and saying 'We need to get changed in here' ... And you know we are always given sheds at [our club] but at some of the other clubs you just have to walk in and say, 'Come on we need the sheds.' We've done that before; we just need to stand up for ourselves. I'm sure the blokes from the other grades would just walk in on another team if they were getting changed. We are really quite lucky.

The only real bonus for women's rugby in Brisbane is that many matches are played after the top men's teams so that the number of spectators who see them play is much greater than might otherwise be the case. Many who watch come away impressed with the skill levels among the women players, although this acceptance is often reluctant or qualified with other comments about women playing such a 'masculine' game.

A Pack of 'Women': Public Perceptions and Player Reactions

Due to the inevitable controversy that surrounds the participation of women in any sport which has socially, historically and culturally been defined as 'masculine', reactions to women's participation in rugby vary widely. Throughout our investigation we determined that the players all thought that outsiders generally approved of their playing; however, variations became apparent after observing and questioning different groups from parents and other male relatives, to older club members and spectators to male players. The women believed that they were supported and that their rugby was seen to be a good thing in the eyes of their peers, work-mates, some of their parents and particularly within the (male) club. Reactions from the general public ranged from amusement, to direct interest about the format of the women's game, to out-and-out disgust, and, only for a minority, general approval. Such diversified responses were typical of the players 'out of rugby' friends or work-mates who are defined by a greater number of demographic and social values.

When the players' parents were asked what they thought of their daughters playing rugby, almost without exception the initial response was negative. After examining the replies we determined that there are two main reasons for this. First, negativity was attributed to the fear of injury either in a game or during training. Stacey felt that both her parents did not actively support her playing rugby for this reason: 'My mother who plays tennis and all that sort of stuff, is not keen, she is still not keen. Well, I guess she's not totally against it, she comes and watches a game when they are in town, but she's scared of injury.' Likewise, Louise felt that most of her mother's opposition to the game stemmed from her concern about injury:

> Mum said, 'No, you are not allowed to play', she was really against it. She was afraid of me getting hurt and all that sort of stuff... When I first went down to [rugby] I didn't tell her that I was playing because I knew she would not like it.

Louise also has a brother who played rugby throughout school and college, but neither her mother nor her father expressed the same concerns for his safety. Injury fears stemmed mainly from other female family members, although most of them eventually became more supportive either after they had seen a game or had come to the realization that the physical contact was relative. One player, in fact, attributes her mother's initial negative response to a knee-jerk reaction, shaped by years of stereotypical conditioning.

The second type of negative reaction from parents conformed more specifically to the stereotypes associated with the game, that it was unsuitable for women since it is too rough, a 'man's' game or even unladylike. Although this type of reaction was evidenced by Stacey's mother, it was most common from fathers or other family members who had played rugby previously. One player felt that both her ex-rugby-playing father and her brother were against the idea of her playing the sport for these reasons. She said:

> [It is] wrong, wrong, wrong. My dad has played rugby all of his life and he said, 'This is not a girl's game, this is not for girls'…
> My brother, although he respects the ability of the sportswomen, he knows they are very fit, very strong and very healthy, but he just doesn't think women should be in a contact sport.

Another said:

> [My brother] doesn't like me doing it because women shouldn't play rugby. They are not physically built for it… I don't actually think he has seen me play…. My flatmate is really against it. He admits it is fine that I play, but he seriously thinks that we shouldn't play because we are not physiologically built for it.

And finally Kirsty said: 'Well Dad said, "Oh my God, I have finally got a boy"!'

These responses are typical of the stereotypes promoted by the public schools in the nineteenth century and subsequently by hegemonic masculine attitudes surrounding violent contact sport. These types of value still exist and are reinforced in the private, Greater Public Schools (GPS) in Brisbane. Masculine values are supported in two main ways throughout these educational institutions. First, the current relationship between the 'brother' and 'sister' private schools fosters separatist attitudes towards rugby union. As rugby is still seen to be the most manly and prestigious sport for the boys at these schools, much emphasis is placed on playing in the first XV and wearing the school's jersey with pride. Games are held on Saturday afternoons, with the girls of the 'sister' schools often in attendance. Many of the women acknowledged that it was seen to be the socially acceptable thing to do and admitted that they were aware that their main role was one of support, rather than to show a genuine interest in the game. One player stated, 'The boys played it at – Grammar and I watched that just because it was a big social event.' This type of response also extended to the co-ed private schools where rugby is again actively promoted as the distinguished sport for boys, while netball is the most celebrated and illustrious one for girls. This structure is reinforced through the social activities that surround both games as well as certain events that incorporate the two 'flag-carrier' teams. At one of these schools, a netball competition between the A Grade schoolgirl team and the First XV rugby side was an annual event, with parents and administration drawing on its appeal to raise funds and socialize. A rugby match between the two sides, however, would never be considered. These examples illustrate how schools still serve to echo and reinforce popular ideals and in turn reinforce the lower status of women's sport in society.

The second way in which masculinist beliefs are protected and fostered in Australian schools is through compliance with education administration. Although the club players came from both state and private schools, many believed the sport, social and cultural structure of the GPS schools would result in their being less likely to adopt any sort of physical game for women as a school sport in the future. Although many of those who attended single-sex GPS schools thought rugby was accepted by their peers and classmates, they all agreed that the more 'conservative' administration would never adopt such an 'unladylike sport'. One club player, who is still at school, started campaigning for the inclusion of women's rugby as a sport at the GPS school. Although she established what the Queensland Rugby Union thought was an appropriate and viable format for a school competition, after taking her proposal to the headmistress, she was initially turned down, on the grounds of specific issues of supervision, safety and time allocation. She then adapted her plan to deal with these issues but was turned down again with no apparent reason being given. There is a long way to go before women rugby union players are accepted widely and young girls are given the similar opportunities to play as boys.

Conclusion

Despite hostile attitudes from many quarters, rugby is one of the fastest growing sports for women internationally. It is attractive due to the physical contact, the teamwork and loyalties that are part of it. As this study demonstrates, women who take up rugby union face a number of obstacles, from hostile family members, to poor training and match conditions. When players were asked they were quick to point out problems but felt that the positives far outweighed the negatives. Women continually referred to their genuine love for rugby and the social interaction surrounding the game. Many said that they 'lived for rugby', which provided them with the chance to enjoy a physical contact sport where they could test their bodies. This group of women playing a 'man's game' suggests that they are directly challenging the hegemonic structure that surrounds and defines contemporary sporting cultures, particularly in rugby union. Although previous studies of women in 'masculine' sports have framed their analyses in terms of resistance to male-dominated sporting structures and cultures, it is clear that the situation for women involved in the playing of these sports is more complex and cannot be reduced to resistant cultural practices. The players, although apparently stretching the boundaries of feminine-appropriate behaviour, conform to male expectations of how they should 'perform' their roles in rugby on and off the field. Much more comparative work needs to be done on women in rugby union, but it is at least clear from the studies done thus far that women who play rugby relate to the game and its attendant cultural practices in a similar fashion to men.

NOTES

A version of this paper appears in *Football Studies*, Vol.2, No.1 (1999).

1. There are now many sources discussing this issue. For an example see Jennifer Hargreaves, *Sporting Females* (London, 1994).
2. For example, see Susan Birrell and Nancy Theberge, 'Ideological Control of Women in Sport', in Margaret Costa and Susan Guthrie (eds), *Women and Sport: Interdisciplinary Perspectives* (New York, 1994).
3. Jim McKay, *Managing Gender: Affirmative Action and Organizational Power in Australian, Canadian and New Zealand Sport* (Albany, 1997).
4. Leonie Randall, 'Women and Sport in Australia', *Current Affairs Bulletin*, August 1993, p. 20.
5. Robert Connell, 'The State, Gender and Sexual Politics', *Theory and Society*, Vol.19, pp. 507–44; M. Ann Hall, *Feminism and Sporting Bodies: Essays on Theory and Practice* (Champaign, IL, 1996).
6. Hall, *Feminism and Sporting Bodies*, p. 50.
7. Elizabeth Grosz, *Volatile Bodies: Towards a Corporeal Feminism* (Sydney, 1994), p. 14.
8. Nancy Theberge, 'Gender, Sport and the Construction of Community: a Case Study from Women's Ice Hockey', *Sociology of Sport Journal*, Vol.12, No.4 (1995), p. 390.

9. For example, see Michael Messner, 'Sport and Male Domination: the Female Athlete as Contested Ideological Terrain', *Sociology of Sport Journal*, Vol.5, No.3 (1988), pp. 197–211; Mariah Burton Nelson, *The Stronger Women Get, the More Men Love Football: Sexism and the American Culture of Sports* (New York, 1994).

10. Hall, *Feminism and Sporting Bodies*, p. 64.

11. Genevieve Rail, 'Physical Contact in Women's Basketball: a First Interpretation', *International Review for the Sociology of Sport*, Vol.25, No.4 (1990), pp. 269–84; and 'Physical Contact in Women's Basketball: a Phenomenological Construction and Contextualization', *International Review for the Sociology of Sport*, Vol.27, No.1 (1992), pp. 1–22.

12. Theberge, 'Gender, Sport and the Construction of Community'.

13. See Margaret Carlisle Duncan and Cynthia Hasbrook, 'Denial of Power in Televised Women's Sports', *Sociology of Sport Journal*, Vol.5, No.1 (1988), pp. 1–21.

14. Murray Phillips, 'Football, Class and War: the Rugby Codes in New South Wales, 1907–1918', in John Nauright and Timothy J.L. Chandler (eds), *Making Men: Rugby and Masculine Identity* (London, 1996), pp. 158–80.

15. John Bale, 'Women's Football in England: a Socio-Geographic Perspective', *Physical Education Review*, Vol.3, No.2 (1980), p. 137.

16. Shona Thompson, 'Challenging the Hegemony: New Zealand Women's Opposition to Rugby and the Reproduction of a Capitalist Patriarchy', *International Review for the Sociology of Sport*, Vol.23, No.3 (1988), p. 206.

17. For more on this, see ibid., pp. 204–12; and John Nauright and David Black, '"Hitting Them Where it Hurts": Springbok–All Black Rugby, Masculine National Identity and Counter-Hegemonic Struggle, 1959–1992', in Nauright and Chandler, *Making Men*, pp. 181–204.

18. See Marion Stell, *Half the Race: a History of Australian Women in Sport* (Sydney, 1991).

19. Messner, 'Sports and Male Domination', p. 197.

20. For a discussion of this process see Margaret Carlisle Duncan, 'Sports Photographs and Sexual Difference: Images of Women and Men in the 1984 and 1988 Olympic Games', *Sociology of Sport Journal*, Vol.7, No.1 (1990), pp. 22–43.

21. Birrell and Theberge, ' Ideological Control of Women in Sport'.

22. R. Pirinen, 'Catching up With Men?: Finnish Newspaper Coverage of Women's Entry into Traditionally Male Sports', *International Review for the Sociology of Sport*, Vol.32, No.3 (1997), pp. 239–49.

23. Interviews were conducted during the 1997 and the 1998 season by Alison Carle, who also attended training and club and team functions. The names of the participants have been changed. Original data are held by the researchers at the University of Queensland.

24. For a discussion of the early history of rugby in Queensland see Peter Horton, 'Rugby Union Football and Its Role in the Socio-Cultural Development of Queensland, 1882–1891', *International Journal of the History of Sport*, Vol.9, No.1 (1992), pp. 119–31.

25. Chandler has researched this aspect of rugby in some detail, for example, see Timothy J.L. Chandler, 'The Structuring of Manliness and the Development of Rugby Football at the Public Schools and Oxbridge, 1830–1880', in Nauright and Chandler, *Making Men*, pp. 13–31.

26. Farah Palmer, 'An Ethnographical Study of the Women's Rugby Subculture in New Zealand: Challenging and Contributing to Societal Norms of Femininity',

B.Phed. Honours Thesis, University of Otago, Dunedin, New Zealand, 1995.

27. Roy Masters, 'The Joy Ruck Club', *The Independent Monthly*, June 1996, pp. 44–5.

28. Elizabeth Wheatley, 'Subcultural Subversions: Comparing Discourses on Sexuality in Men's and Women's Rugby Songs', in Susan Birrell and Cheryl Cole (eds), *Women, Sport, and Culture* (Champaign, 1994), p. 207.

29. Birrell and Cole, *Women, Sport, and Culture*, p. 160.

30. Eric Dunning, 'Sport as a Male Preserve: Notes on the Social Acceptance of Masculine Identity and Its Transformations', in Birrell and Cole, *Women, Sport, and Culture*, pp. 163–79.

31. M.A. Boutilier and L. SanGiovanni, *The Sporting Woman* (Champaign, 1983), pp. 100–1.

32. Nancy Theberge, 'Towards a Feminist Alternative to Sport as a Male Preserve', in Birrell and Cole, *Women, Sport, and Culture*, pp. 181–92.

8

The Global Union: Globalization and the Rugby World Cup

Brett Hutchins and Murray Phillips

Twenty years ago, the idea of a rugby World Cup would have seemed like the product of a fevered imagination. Playing rugby at the top in the mid-seventies meant playing for your country, every now and again being carded for the British Lions and, if you were lucky, being picked. Clubs in Ireland did not play clubs in Scotland or, for that matter, Wales or England, except on rare occasions. Likewise, the Scottish clubs kept themselves to themselves. Only a smattering of English clubs, and only those in the West Country, had regular fixtures with the Welsh. There were no leagues at all. We were, at least in England, happy in the tradition of the game. Coaching was still a dirty word; training was largely unscientific and progress something that happened in America.[1]

These are the recollections of Derek Wyatt who, as a former coach, selector and England representative, was involved in northern hemisphere rugby two decades ago. Following the 1995 Rugby World Cup held in South Africa, Marcel Martin, the chairman of the organizing body, perceives the game in a radically different way:

By concentrating on... [a] terrestrial, free-to-air TV strategy and supplementing it with some pan-continental cable-satellite coverage RWC was able to deliver an audience of nearly 2.7 billion in 124 countries which confirmed the RWC as the fourth largest TV event in the world after Soccer World Cup, the Olympics and [World] Track and Field Championships.[2]

These citations encapsulate two competing versions of rugby union: an international amateur sporting competition contrasted with a professional, global, sporting commodity. The World Cup is a prime example of the shift from rugby cultures based on sporting values and practices that once supported, sustained and reinforced amateurism, to those that have established a new ascendant hegemonic order in which professionalism and commercialism dominate.[3] In this context the World Cup is both part of a larger sports entertainment industry, employing global marketing and media strategies, and also an example of several highly commodified, global, sporting competitions as recognized by Marcel Martin. Rugby is now part of a 'global flow' that 'concerns cultural commodities that move within a market framework'.[4] The concept of globalization is used in this chapter to understand how rugby has entered this global flow.

Globalization is a term that has slipped into popular usage and also one that generates considerable debate in academic circles. In academe globalization is a contested term that has emerged from an amalgam of contrasting and fragmented literature.[5] Within this globalization processes take on a discursive character that sees the features of these processes shift, often markedly, from one institutional context to the next. For example, it is far from likely that notions of globalization have uniform features in Western and non-Western societies, first-world and third-world countries, or in football codes as disparate as Australian Rules Football and international rugby union.[6] The lack of uniformity and continuity in globalization analyses leads to an argument that the evidential basis of globalization – what is actually 'going on' – is lacking.[7] The purpose of this chapter is to present and analyse 'real' evidence of globalization through the 1987, the 1991 and the 1995 rugby union World Cup tournament. Source material is mainly drawn from Australia and New Zealand with much of this literature and many of these data having a particular local and national emphasis. It is argued, however, that the events and reports highlighted are deeply enmeshed in globalized economic, media and sporting processes.[8]

It is unsurprising that the achieving of consensus on a definition of globalization has proved elusive given the diffuse range of work from which it has emerged. There are, however, common strands: some form of spatial and temporal compression of, and growth in the interdependence of, world-wide relations.[9] For our purposes globalization is conceived of as the intersection of innumerable power relationships played out in, through and between the local, national and the global, across the interdependent terrains of culture, social life, politics, economics and the media.[10] While economics and the media are the chosen focus here, it is not possible to isolate these from other social relations. The media and economics are, after all, inescapably subject to social and cultural coding.[11] Nevertheless, our main concerns are the role of multinational media and television broadcasters, sponsors, advertisers and rugby union's controlling bodies, as they seek to utilize the World Cup as a cultural product to open up and maintain international rugby markets and audiences.

1987: a Commercialized and Commodified Amateur World Cup

The inauguration of the World Cup indicated that rugby administrators had officially recognized, albeit reluctantly in some sections of the International Rugby Board (IRB), that the code was part of a global sports media, entertainment and commodity market. Adhering to the market demand of maximizing audiences, 1987 was selected as the year for the first Cup so as not to clash with other meta-sporting media events, the 1988 Seoul Olympics and the 1990 Italy Soccer World Cup.[12] Further to this, rugby set out to integrate into a reconfiguring of global media and communication processes. Burgeoning global communications market trade had grown from US$350 million[13] in 1980 to US$1,600 billion and growing by 1986[14]; while world-wide the numbers of television receivers rose from 192 million in 1965 to 710 million in 1986.[15] These developments within global communications technology facilitated rugby's drive for international audiences.

Rugby's development during 1987 and beyond also underlines the instrumental link between globalization processes and the 'spread and intensification of commercialization'.[16] The staging of the World Cup in Australia and New Zealand was the most expensive, commercialized, *amateur* sporting event ever arranged up to that point.[17] Television, sponsors, advertisers, merchandizers and spectators underwrote a tournament that had estimated expenses of US$2.3 million and reported a profit of A$3.4 million.[18] Increasing commercialization fuelled ideological tension. On the one hand, the IRB's adherence to amateur practice ensured that players could not be paid direct for competing in the 1987 World Cup, thereby supposedly providing 'a powerful medium to demonstrate the strength of this [amateur] conviction' in the face of professionalism and commercialism in wider sporting practice.[19] On the other hand, the IRB actively solicited money from commercial entities such as television networks, corporate sponsors and advertisers who contributed to making the 1987 World Cup a moderate financial success.

Giving rise to such an ideologically fraught sporting event is the spread of commercialization within the wider political economy of sport. According to Tasker and Wyatt, the decision to stage the 16-team 1987 World Cup had been the rugby establishment's indirect response to the (only just) failed 1983 launch of a 'rebel' professional World Championship Rugby competition, a concept resembling Kerry

Packer's successful setting up of World Series Cricket in 1978–89.[20] Compromise and negotiation of professional and business practices within rugby also occurred on a number of other fronts. Australian administrators were openly admitting the need to market their sport aggressively in order to compete in the domestic and the international marketplace.[21] The IRB agreed to lift allowances for international players in the lead up to the Cup so as to see that 'they are not financially disadvantaged for the inordinate amount of time they are these days required to devote to international competition'.[22] Rumours continued to abound over 'boot money' and 'shamateurism' in the sport.[23] Furthermore, controversy arose during the Cup following reports that New Zealand players would be banned from the tournament for accepting money to appear in television advertisements for commercial products, thereby contravening rugby's amateur regulations. Rather than ban the players, however, the IRB declared the advertisements a 'grey area'.[24] Ultimately, by officially sanctioning the World Cup, the IRB had contributed to the rolling-back of the already contested amateur status of rugby union world-wide. Grundlingh stresses the impact of the gradual ascension of a 'corporate cultural capitalism'[25] in the sport:

> rugby union, though officially an amateur game, committed itself to a world where agents and advertisers turn fame into fortunes. Once this occurred, the game, the players, and its administration could never be the same again.[26]

From a financial and organizational viewpoint, the 1987 event proved a qualified success. Expected profits were reduced by the event organizers, West Nally, going bankrupt following their alleged mismanagement and the October 1987 world stockmarket crash.[27] Despite this, the Cup produced rugby's first ever million-dollar gate, was exposed to approximately 300 million television viewers internationally, and registered excellent television ratings especially for the host nation.[28] The co-host of the tournament, the Australian Rugby Union (ARU), certainly saw value and further potential in the World Cup concept, declaring it an 'immense success' and appreciating the enormity of the 'marketing possibilities' it presented.[29] ARU income for 1987 outstripped that of the previous year by almost A$1 million and the year following by over A$700,000. Indeed, a commercial 'gateway' appears to have opened for the ARU with television fee and sponsorship income showing unabated growth into the 1990s.[30]

Any success experienced by rugby through the World Cup concept was reliant on the successful packaging of long-held rival nationalisms inherent to international rugby competition within a single tournament. These nationalisms were used to market and sell the legitimacy of the rugby contests to global audiences.[31] The money and audiences attracted in 1987 ensured the future of the World Cup. As an editorial in the New Zealand *Auckland Star* declared:

> ... it is clear already that organizers, despite widespread public apprehension, were justified totally in their confidence in an event that is bringing a new and important dimension to international sport.[32]

1991: Television and Global Acceleration
Rugby affirmed its place on the global sporting and media stage during the 1991 World Cup held in the United Kingdom, Ireland and France. It reached a television audience estimated at 1.75 billion in 103 countries and produced a surplus of £11.7 million.[33] Such a marked audience increase compared to that in 1987 can be attributed to a number of interrelated factors, including improved organization and promotion and greater knowledge of the event world-wide. Equally important, the burgeoning audience stemmed from technological development within the global television industry. The emergence and growth of satellite programme distribution during the mid-to-late 1980s and 1990s signalled a shift from a medium that addressed largely national and sub-national communities, to one that had the capability of addressing trans- and cross-national communities.[34] This shift was assisted by a major growth in international communications infrastructure during the previous two decades, so much so that only the poorest African and Asian countries were without national television services by the 1990s.[35] A sporting media event such as the 1991 World Cup was well positioned to draw upon the improved distribution capabilities of such technology and the wider access to viewers within a global media community.

The organizers of the 1991 World Cup set out in pursuit of television's reach. Television Sport Leisure Ltd. (TSL), a London-based, independent, television production and sales company, were appointed to sell the broadcasting rights internationally and went on to produce approximately 59 per cent (£11.7 million) of the total commercial revenue for the event.[36] Regular broadcasts (of perhaps questionable quantity and quality) reached the world's largest, untapped, commercial, television market, China.[37] It should be noted, however, that in the face of such abundant television revenue, the ideological tension between commercial business practice and amateur sporting practice continued. Some players expressed dissatisfaction with the lack of financial rewards they received from what was a highly commercialized and profitable tournament. Among those unhappy were the Australian winger David Campese, who threatened legal action for the unauthorized use of an unflattering image of him to sell a commercial product, and the French players who demanded more money for the promotional work expected of them.[38]

The growing global commodity market surrounding the 1991 World Cup extended into sponsorship and advertising. The increasing role of advertising in the globalization of the world economy put the Cup organizers in a felicitous situation. A key benefit was that the United Kingdom ranks third in the world for advertising spending on a per capita basis.[39] This figure, combined with the fact that the number of hours of television watched globally tripled between 1979 and 1991,[40] ensured advertisers and sponsors who eagerly sought to gain access to a transnational client-base through this global media event. The 1991 Cup organizers appointed one of the world's largest advertising agencies, the British-based Saatchi & Saatchi, to handle sponsorship arrangements.[41] They, in turn, extracted £3.7 million (or 18.5 per cent of the total turnover) from sponsors.[42] From transnational television to transnational sponsorship and advertising, rugby had entered an integrated, global, commercial, media market. As the Australian *Sydney Morning Herald* reported, rugby had never before 'been analysed so deeply or found itself so immersed in the chase for the elusive dollar as this World Cup'.[43] The Cup represented a sea change in the presentation, commodification and consumption of international rugby.

The accelerating intersections between globalization processes and rugby competition also filtered down to other levels of the sport. For example, at the national level in Australia commercialization of the sport intensified. The ARU's international television rights were successfully handled by Communication Services International (CSI)[44] and, for the first time, domestic television coverage rights were purchased by a commercial network instead of by the Australian public broadcaster, the ABC. As their 1991 Annual Report indicated, the ARU was fully cognisant of the media/sport/capital nexus lying at the heart of commercial sport. By signing with a commercial television network the ARU hoped to bring about more promotional opportunities and augment sponsorship opportunities for the code nationally.[45] The importance of the Australian victory in the 1991

World Cup in precipitating such a move and its role in producing a record ARU television fees and sponsorship income of A\$1,203,016 cannot be underestimated.[46] The World Cup had raised rugby's popularity and profitability on a global stage and, in turn, across the Australian national and regional terrain. The ARU acknowledged the importance of the Cup:

> The next three-year preparation for the 1995 World Cup will require more costly funding if the Wallabies in that year are to adequately defend their World Cup title. All countries have now recognized the World Cup as the ultimate Rugby prize and most have the resources available and will be prepared to financially expend to the limit in a bid to win the coveted crown.[47]

Given the immense importance placed on the World Cup by national rugby unions globally, it appeared inevitable that the next tournament would take on an even greater significance in world sport.

1995: Global Expansion and Further Profit
The 1995 World Cup in South Africa made further inroads for rugby into the global sporting entertainment market. It is estimated that the tournament reached almost 2.7 billion people in 124 countries to confirm its position as the fourth most-watched sporting event in the world.[48] The expanding television audience for the Cup was, in part, due to further transformation within global communications technology. Television rights for the Cup were sold to 15 licensees internationally. Providing substantial additional media distribution above and beyond these licensees were 'service delivery platforms' controlled by multinational media conglomerates. These 'platforms' have been expanding regionally and hold the potential for a complete global reach.[49] During the 1995 World Cup they included 'Eurosport', which reached 30 countries, 'Star TV' which broadcast into 50 national television markets in the Middle East, Asia and Far East, 'Horizon' in French Africa, and 'M-Net' in English-speaking, southern African countries.[50]

The approach to the administration of the World Cup in South Africa increasingly resembled that of large-scale business in the wider, global, corporate environment. The statement of the chairman of the Rugby World Cup Marcel Martin emphasizing 'marketing', 'packaging', 'buyers' and 'marketplace', highlights the shift towards the commodification of rugby:

The success of the commercial programme of a sporting event is determined by both the quality of the rights available and the ability of the event organizer and their marketing agents in packaging and selling those rights in the international market place... Rugby can sell itself, however it needs capable, professional marketers, who could package it smartly, make it available to the potential buyers and get the best price for it. It is important to know the marketing departments of the big companies interested in buying this type of event.[51]

For the 1995 Cup multinational companies included Toyota, Coca-Cola, Visa, Heineken and Rank Xerox. Other agents contributing to this explicitly corporatist approach included the appointment of the 'biggest noise in sports commerce', the International Management Group (IMG), as joint commercial advisers to the Cup.[52] The appointment was triggered by accusations of questionable commercial management from sections of the rugby community after the 1991 event. No such accusations can be made of the 1995 Cup, which produced a reported profit of A\$60 million.[53] The only notable barriers to commercial success in South Africa appear to have been the host nation's lack of a tourism infrastructure, high crime rates and the difficulties in finding an insurance company for the event.[54] Judging by Cup profits, both hurdles appear to have been negotiated.

As alluded to earlier, a key element of globalization is the rise, proliferation and role of multinational media corporations.[55] It is the global media that have laid the foundations for global capitalism.[56] A defining feature of the global media is the tendency towards the centralization of control. International rugby is immersed in this process. Just before the 1995 Cup, South Africa New Zealand Australia Rugby Inc. (SANZAR) was formed, with this new organization developing 'the Perfect Rugby Product' – the southern hemisphere Tri-Nations Series and Super 12 Competition.[57] In a deal worth US\$555 million over ten years, exclusive television rights to these high-profile games were purchased by the fifth largest media corporation in the world, Rupert Murdoch's News Corporation (News Corp).[58] Significantly, Murdoch views sport world-wide as 'the single most important' means to develop News Corps' global, digital, television system.[59] According to Fitzsimons's excellent account,[60] the formation of SANZAR had been motivated by the threat of another Murdoch-owned, cross-continental football competition, Super League, which threatened to poach many of rugby union's top internationals. On top of this threat, came the real possibility that a (ultimately failed) 'rebel' organization, World Rugby Corporation (WRC), could steal almost all the establishment's top players.[61] The end result was that Murdoch prevailed through his securing the SANZAR deal, to the considerable benefit of his pay-television interests in the southern hemisphere. News Corp achieved greater a centralization of media control over both rugby codes in Australia, New Zealand and South Africa. Due to rugby's world-wide scope, Murdoch's pay-television empire is well situated to take advantage of an anticipated increase of from 26 to 38 per cent between 1995 and 2000 of global households with either cable or satellite television.[62] The important historical footnote to all these events was the August 1995 IRB announcement that open professionalism was to be officially sanctioned in the sport.[63] Corporate, commercial and professional practice had finally claimed official sanction within rugby union internationally.

At the national level the commercial ramifications and importance of the World Cup for home unions remained constant. For the ARU, the poor Australian performance in 1995, making only the quarter-finals, combined with the expenses of defending the establishment against Super League and the WRC, resulted in a trading loss of A$800,000.[64] As the chairman of the ARU Leo Williams noted:

> The early part of this was concerned with the abortive 'Mission Repeat' programme in which nothing in the way of time, personnel or money was spared in giving the Wallabies total support in their quest to defend the World Cup title. The results were bitterly disappointing.[65]

Such disappointing on-field and balance-sheet results, however, did not in any way weaken the ARU's determination to have a 'much larger mass entertainment presence in Australia'.[66] Across the Tasman, the relative achievement of New Zealand at the 1995 World Cup, as runners-up to South Africa, and their continuing, excellent record at the international level, helped to generate unprecedented revenue. A five- year sponsorship deal with Adidas, worth in excess of NZ$70 million, was signed in 1997. As the richest international rugby sponsorship ever, a key intent of the agreement was to promote the All Black jumper as a globally-recognized uniform in the same manner as the Italian and the Brazilian soccer strip.[67] That this jumper could viably serve as a commercially-profitable, global symbol of sporting prestige may be partly attributed to the transnational media exposure and marketing arising from the World Cup. Through the global media, the World Cup event has driven the maturation process of a self-perpetuating, 'profit- driven social order'[68] in international rugby, and consequently seen the most successful national rugby unions looking and thinking transnationally for promotional and marketing avenues.

Conclusion: the Future

The extent and the pace of change in rugby union has been remarkable. Over the last three decades rugby has been transformed from an inwardly-focused game played at local, provincial and national levels, as described by Wyatt in the quotation opening this chapter, to a quadrennial, globalized, sporting spectacle played by professional athletes from a growing number of nations. While the demise of amateurism may have been predictable, as this ideology was anachronistic in the context of contemporary commodified sport, the changes that have accompanied professionalism are striking. Athletic migration, which has been a characteristic feature of professional sports for many years, is now prevalent in rugby union as players move between clubs, provinces, nations and even football codes as the cultural divide with rugby league is traversed.[69] For over a century it was heresy to play league and the banished players were rarely welcomed back into the fold. Contemporary footballers now make decisions about which code, with whom, and on what continent they are to play, based on similar criteria to those used by professionals in other sports. It is astonishing that, at least in the southern hemisphere, a multinational company, News Corp, has been able to secure the television rights to international rugby in Australia, New Zealand and South Africa for a decade and, as a result, reconfigure the sport for elite players, administrators and fans. Testament to the influence of News Corp in rugby union and rugby league is speculation about a merging of the codes which would dismantle over 100 years of antagonistic, competing and contrasting football cultures.[70] The commodification of rugby has, in a relatively short period, in comparison with other football codes, seen the sport embrace sponsorship, marketing and merchandizing to the extent that virtually all features of the playing surface, player uniforms, support staff, coaches and stadiums stand as symbols of corporate capitalism. John O'Neill of the ARU captures this aspect of the game: 'rugby as a community sport and as a social movement is linked inextricably with rugby as a business. Each depends on the other in this professional age.'[71]

Comprehension of the changes that have unfolded comes from examining rugby and the common features of commercial sport in a rapidly globalizing world. First, increased commercialization goes hand-in-hand with globalization, so that we should not be surprised that the World Cup is a highly commercialized event. Secondly, global sporting events such as the Olympic Games, Soccer World Cup, and the International Track and Field Championships have all attracted interest from a mixture of local, national and multinational companies. The Rugby World Cup, as underlined by the 1995 tournament in South Africa, has also served as a target for sponsors willing to capitalize on rugby's audience potential. Increasing commercialism exacerbated the existing tension within the ideology of amateurism: how could you have a sport saturated with corporate capitalism and whose administrators made many decisions based around principles of economic rationality, asking its players to deny this reality with respect to their services? Thirdly, technological developments within the global television industry have worked in favour of sporting events looking to increase their profiles. The initiation and development of the World Cup coincided with the development in satellite programme distribution that has enabled the media to address trans- and cross-national communities. There have also been accompanying transformations in global communications with the formation of 'service delivery platforms' controlled by multinational media conglomerates. These transformations underpin Marcel Martin's belief, expressed in the opening of this chapter, that free to air, cable and satellite television delivered the 1995 Cup to almost 2.7 billion people in 124 countries. Three decades ago this level of global media coverage in any sport was impossible.

Given all these transformations and the processes set in motion, there is little doubt that the sport will continue to change. Many questions are posed. How will the rugby community respond to further commodified and commercialized versions of rugby union? As top-level rugby moves on through the 1999 World Cup in Wales and the 2003 tournament in New Zealand and Australia is it possible that there will be resistance to globalizing processes? Will those who lament the demise of the 'rugby amateur' abandon the global professional version of the code? Will those followers who value the intrinsic components of rugby be alienated by recent changes to rules which have shifted the emphasis from 'play' to 'display'? Can corporate forces engineer a merging of rugby union and league? Will World Cup administrators recognize the growing band of female players whose equivalent tournament does not share in any of the media coverage or commercial sponsorship, or is the globalization of rugby serving to disadvantage women's rugby?[72] Can the World Cup offer genuine opportunities to non-traditional rugby countries or will the game remain a celebration of former British colonies and their masculine prowess even if in commodified form? The answers to these questions are difficult to predict, but what is clear is that globalization processes within rugby and the media have had, and will continue to have, an indelible effect on the sport. Unless there is a significant restructuring of the administration of rugby on an international scale the continuing dominance of commodified and commercialized administrative and management practices in rugby union is inevitable. Not only has the commodification of rugby worked to reshape international rugby in the late 1990s, but the changes have infiltrated all levels of rugby union.

NOTES

Our thanks to Malcolm MacLean and Janine Mikosza for their advice and suggestions on drafts of this chapter.

1. D. Wyatt, *Rugby Disunion: the Making of Three World Cups* (London, 1995), p. 17.
2. M. Martin, 'Kickoff: Making Money for the Game', *Rugby World*, Issue 24 (December 1995), p. 28.
3. J. McKay, G. Lawrence, T. Miller and D. Rowe, 'Globalization and Australian Sport', *Sport Science Review*, Vol.2, No.1 (1993), p. 18.
4. B. Houlihan, *Sport and International Politics* (London, 1994), pp.174–5.
5. These theories include dependency and development research, world-systems theory, international relations theory, epochal historicization, civilizational analysis, cultural imperialism, cultural hegemony, colonialism and post-colonial theory, and more recently, the modernization and Americanization arguments. For discussion of these theories see: M. Albrow, *The Global Age: State and Society Beyond Modernity* (Stanford, CA, 1997), pp.7–27, 101–5; J. Bale and J. Maguire (eds), *The Global Sports Arena: Athletic Talent Migration in an Interdependent World* (London, 1994), pp.12–16; A. Biersack, 'Local Knowledge, Local History: Geertz and Beyond', in L. Hunt (ed..), *The New Cultural History* (London, 1989), pp. 82–4; S. Cunningham and E. Jacka, *Australian Television and International Mediascapes* (Melbourne, 1996), pp. 3–24; P. Donnelly, 'The Local and the Global: Globalization in the Sociology of Sport', *Journal of Sport and Social Issues*, Vol.20, No.3 (1996), pp. 239–57; G. Jarvie and J. Maguire, *Sport and Leisure in Social Thought* (London, 1994), pp.146–60, 230–63; R. Gruneau, 'The Critique of Sport in Modernity: Theorising Power, Culture and the Politics of the Body', in E. Dunning, J. Maguire and R. Pearton (eds), *The Sports Process: a Comparative and Developmental Approach* (Champaign, IL, 1993), pp. 85–109; Houlihan, *Sport and International Politics*, pp. 173–201; J. Maguire, 'Globalisation, Sport Development and the Media/Sport Production Complex', *Sport Science Review*, Vol.2, No.1 (1993), pp.29–47; J. Mandalios, 'Historical Sociology', in B. Turner (ed.), *Blackwell Companion to Social Theory* (London, 1996), pp. 278–302; T. O'Regan, *Australian Television Culture* (St. Leonards, NSW, 1993), pp. 98–9; R. Robertson, *Globalization: Social Theory and Global Culture* (London, 1992), pp.10–15; R. Robertson, 'Glocalization: Time-Space and Homogeneity and Heterogeneity', in M. Featherstone, S. Lash and R.

Robertson (eds), *Global Modernities* (London, 1995), pp. 37–40; C. Rojek, *Decentring Leisure: Rethinking Leisure Theory* (London, 1995), pp. 92–6; and D. Rowe, G. Lawrence, T. Miller and J. McKay, 'Global Sport? Core Concern and Peripheral Vision', *Media, Culture and Society*, Vol.16, No.4 (1994), p.673.

6. (Western and non-Western countries) Mandalios, 'Historical Sociology', pp. 281–6; (First and third world) J. Bennett, 'Hunger and the Politics of World Food Supply', in A. Giddens (ed.), *Human Societies: a Reader* (Oxford, 1992), pp. 285–9; A. Hoogvelt, 'The New International Division of Labour', in Giddens (ed.), *Human Societies*, pp. 281–5; and (Australian Football), S. Alomes, 'Australian Football: the International Game? The Danish Australian Football League and the Internationalisation of Australian Football, 1989–1996', *Sporting Traditions*, Vol.13, No.2, pp. 3–17.

7. S. Cunningham and E. Jacka, *Australian Television and International Mediascapes*, p. 9 and R. Robertson, 'Glocalization', pp. 26, 28.

8. D. Rowe, 'The Global Love-Match: Sport and Television', *Media, Culture and Society*, Vol.18, No.4 (1996), p. 565.

9. Though far from universally accepted, more frequently quoted definitions of globalization are those of Roland Robertson and Anthony Giddens. Robertson refers to globalization as 'the compression of the world and the intensification of consciousness of the world as a whole'. Giddens refers to globalization as 'the intensification of world-wide social relations which link distant localities in such a way that local happenings are shaped by events occurring many miles away and vice versa'. R. Robertson, *Globalization: Social Theory and Global Culture*, p. 8 and A. Giddens, *The Consequences of Modernity* (Stanford, 1990), p. 64.

10. For discussion of power relations in globalization analysis: M. Featherstone and S. Lash, 'Globalization, Modernity and the Spatialisation of Social Theory: an Introduction', in M. Featherstone, S. Lash and R. Robertson (eds), *Global Modernities* (London, 1995), p. 3; S. Lash and J. Urry, *Economies of Signs and Space* (London, 1994), pp. 281–2, and Rojek, *Decentring Leisure*, p. 94.

11. Robertson, *Globalization: Social Theory and Global Culture*, p. 4, and Robertson, 'Glocalization', p. 31.

12. Wyatt, *Rugby Disunion*, p. 27. The year 1989 was also ruled out to avoid a clash with the British Lions tour of Australia.

13 We use figures in this chapter in American (US), Australian (A) and New Zealand (NZ) dollars as well as British pounds. At the time of writing the Australian dollar was worth about 62 US cents and 38 pence but it has fluctuated from as low as 55 US cents to as high as 78 cents in the 1990s. The New Zealand dollar is worth about 90 per cent of the Australian dollar.

14. E.S. Herman and R.W. McChesney, *The Global Media: the New Missionaries of Global Capitalism* (London, 1997), p. 38.

15. A. Sreberny-Mohammadi, 'The Global and the Local in International Communications', in J. Curran and M. Gurevitch (eds), *Mass Media and Society* (London, 1991), p. 122.

16. Herman and McChesney, *The Global Media*, p. 8.

17. The idea of a rugby union World Cup had been floated as far back as the 1950s. This was followed in the 1960s by the former international referee Harold Tolhurst's proposing a 28-day 'world' tournament in Australia involving the British Isles, France, Australia, New Zealand and South Africa. See N. Tasker, 'The World Cup: a Concept Born of Necessity', in N. Tasker (ed.), *Rugby World Cup 87: ABC Guide* (Crows Nest, NSW, 1987), p. 4 and Wyatt, *Rugby Disunion*, p. 25.

18. (Expenses) N. Shehadie, 'World Cup Papers: Part II', *International Rugby*

Review, March/April 1995, p. 12, and (Profit) S. Zavos, 'In Defence of the Cup', World Cup Liftout, *Sydney Morning Herald*, 23 May 1995, p. 4 (A$ = c. US$0.70).

19. N. Shehadie, 'Foreword', in P. Jarrat, *The Wallabies Versus the World* (Sydney, 1987), p. 2.

20. Tasker, 'The World Cup: a Concept Born of Necessity', p. 4; and Wyatt, *Rugby Disunion*, pp.24–31. For details of the David Lord-instigated World Championship Rugby concept see P. Fitzsimons, *The Rugby War* (Sydney, 1996), pp. 7–8; N. Tasker, 'World Cup Fever', *The Bulletin*, 25 April 1995, pp. 93–4; Tasker, 'The World Cup: a Concept Born of Necessity', p. 4; and Wyatt, *Rugby Disunion*, p. 26. For discussion of World Series Cricket see G. Haigh, *The Cricket War* (Melbourne, 1993).

21. R. Turnbull, 'Foreword: a New Era and Change', in *Rugby 87: Official Publication of the New South Wales Rugby Union* (Sydney, 1987).

22. Ibid.

23. G. Campbell, 'Money in Rugby?', *Australian Rugby News*, 10 May 1991, pp. 3–5; A. Kervin, G. Campbell, K. Quinn and D. Retief, 'The Death of Amateurism', *Rugby World*, September 1995, pp. 27–8; I. Stafford, 'Time for Change', *Rugby World*, January 1995, pp. 13–14; and N. Tasker, 'The Wallabies v the Wannabes', *The Bulletin*, 30 May 1995, p. 42.

24. See 'Cup TV Ads Axed, Paper Claims', *Auckland Star*, 4 June 1987, p. 1; Editorial, 'Rugby Still Rattling in Its Shackles', *Auckland Star,* 4 June 1987, p. 8; and L Knight, 'TV Ads "Grey Area", Say Rugby Chiefs', *Sunday Star*, 7 June 1987, p. C1.

25. A term used by David Rowe in his book, *Popular Cultures: Rock Music, Sport and the Politics of Pleasure* (London, 1995), p. 24.

26. A. Grundlingh, 'The New Politics of Rugby', in A. Grundlingh, A. Odendaal and B. Spies, *Beyond the Tryline: Rugby and South African Society* (Johannesburg, 1995), p. 19.

27. Wyatt, *Rugby Disunion*, pp. 40–1; also see J. Kendall-Carpenter, 'Learning the Ropes', *International Rugby Review*, May/June 1995, p. 12.

28. (Gate) L. Knight, '$1m Cup Final', *Auckland Star*, 18 May 1987, p.14; (television internationally) I. Stafford, 'Money Matters', *Rugby World*, June 1995, p. 50; and (host nation) *Auckland Star*, 1 June 1987, p. 14.

29. 'Executive Director's Report', in Australian Rugby Union Football Ltd., *Annual Report* (Kingsford, Sydney, 1987), p. 12.

30. 'Income and Expenditure Statement', Australian Rugby Union Football Ltd., *Annual Report* (1987–90).

31. It appears paradoxical that the attempt to extend rugby's global audiences is played out through the evocation of rival nationalisms, especially given the prominence afforded to questions of diminished sovereignty of the nation-state within globalization analyses. See E. J. Hobsbawm, *Nations and Nationalism since 1870: Programme, Myth, Reality* (Cambridge, 1990), pp.1–13, 163–83; and Featherstone and Lash, 'Globalization, Modernity and the Spatialization of Social Theory', p. 2.

32. Editorial, 'Fears Founder', *Auckland Star*, 25 May 1987, p. 8.

33. Stafford, 'Money Matters', p. 50. Audiences for the 1991 World Cup have been estimated at as high as 2 billion. See R. Thomas, 'Rugby's Marvellous Month', in I. Robertson (ed.), *Official Book of the Rugby World Cup 1991* (Sydney, 1991), p. 179 and 'Top Six are Cream of the Crop', *Sydney Morning Herald*, 5 November 1991, p. 39.

34. Cunningham and Jacka, *Australian Television and International Mediascapes*,

pp. 8–9; S. Cunningham, 'Television', in S. Cunningham and G. Turner (eds), *The Media in Australia: Industries, Texts, Audiences* (St Leonard's, NSW, 1993), p. 28; Herman and McChesney, *The Global Media*, p. 45; and T. O'Regan, *Australian Television Culture*, pp. 25–31.

35. Sreberny-Mohammadi, 'The Global and Local in International Communications', p. 122.
36. (TSL) Kendall-Carpenter, 'Learning the Ropes', p. 12; Wyatt, *Rugby Disunion*, p. 58; and (revenue) Stafford, 'Money Matters', p. 50.
37. Y. Preston, 'TV or not TV: Union-watching in China', *Sydney Morning Herald*, 31 October 1991, pp. 44, 46; and Thomas, 'Rugby's Marvellous Month', p. 173.
38. (Campese) G. Growden, 'Campese Ready to Sue over Insult', *Sydney Morning Herald*, 2 October 1991, p. 56; and (French players) G. Growden, 'French in Dispute over Franc Receipts', *Sydney Morning Herald*, 5 October 1991, p. 66. Campese was also named player of the 1991 World Cup for several outstanding performances.
39. Herman and McChesney, *The Global Media*, p. 58.
40. Ibid., p. 39.
41. See Kendall-Carpenter, 'Learning the Ropes', p. 12; and J. Sinclair, 'Advertising', in Cunningham and Turner, *The Media in Australia*, pp. 96–7.
42. Stafford, 'Money Matters', p. 50.
43. G. Growden, 'A New Era Kicks Off', *Sydney Morning Herald*, 3 October 1991, p. 40.
44. 'Report from the President', in Australian Rugby Union Football Ltd., *Annual Report* (1991), p. 4.
45. Ibid.
46. 'Income and Expenditure Statement', in Australian Rugby Union Football Ltd., *Annual Report* (1991), p. 20.
47. 'Report from the President', in Australian Rugby Union Football Ltd., *Annual Report* (1991), p. 4.
48. Martin, 'Kickoff', p. 28.
49. Cunningham and Jacka, *Australian Television and International Mediascapes*, p. 8.
50. 'Kickoff', *Rugby World*, Issue 21, May 1995, p. 15.
51. Martin, 'Kickoff', p. 28.
52. N. Cain, 'World Cup Bonanza Tipped to Hit $60m', *International Rugby Review*, October/November 1994, p. 6. For discussion of the effect of IMG on Australian sport see G. Wright, 'The Firm: How IMG Is Changing the Face of Australian Sport', *Sydney Morning Herald*, 16 November 1996, p. 58.
53. 'Profile: So Who Is Louis Luyt?', *Sydney Morning Herald*, 9 May 1998, p. 60.
54. (Infrastructure) Cain, 'World Cup Bonanza', p. 12; (crime rates) 'World Cup Diary', *Sydney Morning Herald*, 8 June 1995, p. 53; and (insurance company) Wyatt, *Rugby Disunion*, p. 101.
55. Sreberny-Mohammad, 'The Global and the Local in International Communications', p. 123.
56. Herman and McChesney, *The Global Media*, pp. 8, 13.
57. Fitzsimons, *The Rugby War*, p. 34, and; 'Chairman's Report', in Australian Rugby Union Football Ltd., *Annual Report* (1995), p. 6.
58. ($555 million) Fitzsimons, *The Rugby War*, p. 96; 'Rugby's Cut', *International Rugby Review*, July/August 1995, p. 9. (News Corporation) Herman and McChesney, *The Global Media*, p. 70. For information on News Corporation and discussion of the effect they have had on sport see: Herman and McChesney, *The Global Media*, pp. 70–7; J. McKay and D. Rowe, 'Field of Soaps: Rupert v. Kerry

as Masculine Melodrama', *Social Text*, Vol.15, No.1 (1997), pp. 69–86; and P. Sheehan, 'Game Plan', *The Age Green Guide*, 5 March 1998, pp. 1–3.

59. Herman and McChesney, *The Global Media*, p. 75.
60. Fitzsimons, *The Rugby War.*
61. (Super League) see M. Colman, *Super League: the Inside Story* (Sydney, 1996); Fitzsimons, *The Rugby War;* G. Growden, 'League Set to Plunder Western Samoa', *Sun-Herald*, 4 June 1995, p. 94; G. Growden, 'Murdoch Pays His Union Dues', *Sydney Morning Herald*, 24 June 1995, p. 70; P. Wilkins, 'Professionalism: the New Age Dawns', *International Rugby Review*, May/June 1995, pp. 3–5; R. Masters, 'Rugby Anxiety over Supping with News', *Sydney Morning Herald*, 26 June 1995, p. 37; and (WRC) see N. Cain, 'Player Power', *Rugby News*, September 1995, pp.10–15; P. Jenkins, 'The Bitter Battle to Control Rugby', *International Rugby Review*, September/October 1995, pp. 4–5; P. Jenkins, 'The Bluster Down Under', *Rugby News*, September 1995, p. 25; R. Palenski, 'Divided We Stand', *Rugby News*, September 1995, pp. 22–3; 'Rule Changes for Rugby Circus', *Sun-Herald*, 21 May 1995, p. 56; and S. Zavos, 'The Rugby Game Survives', *International Rugby Review*, September/October 1995, p. 16.
62. Herman and McChesney, *The Global Media*, p. 45.
63. 'The Report that Changed the Game', *Rugby World*, October 1995, pp. 13–16; and 'The Ruling', *International Rugby Review*, September/October 1995.
64. 'Managing Director and Chief Executive Officer's Report', in Australian Rugby Union Football Ltd., *Annual Report* (1995), p. 7.
65. 'Chairman's Report', in Australian Rugby Union Football Ltd., *Annual Report* (1995), p. 6.
66. ARU Board Presentation, *Australian Rugby: Creating a Future*, presented on 11 July 1996.
67. 'The Future is All Black after Huge Jersey Deal', *Sydney Morning Herald*, 21 October 1997, p. 44.
68. Herman and McChesney, *The Global Media*, p. 10.
69. Bale and Maguire, *The Global Sports Arena.*
70. M. Lynch and P. Lynch, 'World in Union or World in Super League', *International Rugby Review*, September/October 1995, p. 12; J. O'Regan, 'One Game?', *Rugby News*, September 1995, pp. 10–11; J. Reason, 'Thin End of the Wedge', *Rugby News*, March 1995, pp. 42–3; M. Reason, 'Through the Looking Glass', *Rugby News*, November 1995, pp. 24–5; and 'Towards a New Era', *Rugby World*, November 1995, pp. 20–2.
71. J. O'Neill, 'The Game's Future Is Bright if We All Work as a Team', *Sydney Morning Herald*, 22 September 1997, p. 30.
72. See A. Carle, 'Crossing the Line: Women Playing a "Man's" Game. An Ethnographic Study of a Women's Rugby Union Team in Brisbane', BA Honours Thesis, University of Queensland, 1998; and Ch.7 above.

9

Professionalism, Commercialism and the Rugby Club: The Case of Pontypridd RFC

P. David Howe

> The interaction of tradition and progress, of sport and society, of players and administrators, of spectators and the press is now acting as a yeast in club after club. It is the connection between international glory and domestic pride that gave Welsh rugby its beginning and will, through the fostering of amateur local rugby guarantee its continuity.[1]

When Smith and Williams made this statement in reference to Pontypridd Rugby Football Club in 1981 no one could have foreseen the difficulties the adoption of professionalism would generate. Money, often portrayed as the medium of professionalism, has long been an influence in both codes of rugby football. However, it was not a sudden influx of economic capital that led to the transformation of Rugby Union from an amateur game to a professional concern. The desire of the players to be rewarded financially as their devotion toward the game became more professional was fundamental in this development.[2] In fact, the transformation in attitudes of rugby players has been the catalyst for the shift toward a professional game. Such a transformation cannot occur in isolation and was contemporaneous with the shift from pastime to spectacle that the game has undergone since its invention. The lack of success of the game to embrace professionalism has resulted in the financial ruin of several of the larger clubs both in Wales and England.[3] This chapter will highlight key factors that led to the transformation from the final stages of amateurism to professionalism that has taken place at Pontypridd RFC since February 1994. What occurred from the time of the acknowledgment of professionalism and the official announcement of the International Rugby Board (IRB) in August 1995 has changed the structure of the game profoundly.[4]

Professionalism from my observations denotes the changing of the attitudes of club officials with regard to the players, who have the

ncially rewarded for their time commitment to training
are benefiting at their expense. Commercialism, on the
y be seen to be concerned with the transformation of
that these shifts in attitude can be financed. What is of
ce therefore is the influence of money from the Union,
sponsors, and how it has affected the players and their
supporting community.

It is my contention that changes in the game of Rugby Union have
not been so much a shift from amateurism to professionalism,[6] but a
transformation from a co-operative organization to a commercial
enterprise. Such a shift may be examined structurally on two levels –
at the level of the game's administration and within individual clubs[7] –
and by examining these structures the role of financial capital in the
game can be established. For most clubs the tools of commercialism
are focused to allow their organization to operate at cost. In other
words, profit margins are not the issue, but having the finances to pay
the bills is fundamental and therefore clubs such as Pontypridd RFC
may be seen as in a transitional stage at present between a co-operative
institution and a business enterprise. Larger clubs such as Cardiff RFC
have targeted business success as a goal and as a result have recently
become public limited companies (PLCs).[8] The question remains as to
whether it is possible for both types of club to survive in the volatile
environment that exists in contemporary modern Welsh rugby.

Hegemony and the Development of League Rugby

Since the early years of the game, power in the administration of the
affairs of the national squad as well as the general management of
clubs has rested with the Welsh Rugby Union (WRU). The Rugby
Football Union (RFU) was established in 1871 in order that former
pupils of Rugby School and other public schools who had adopted the
game could play matches of 'their' game throughout the country, and
therefore a degree of uniformity was imposed.[9] As the game became
more popular throughout the British Isles each region was encouraged
to establish its own administrative committees and thus the WRU was
born.[10] The WRU set down rules in accordance with the RFU and later
the IRB as to how the clubs should be organized to comply with the
amateur ethos on which the game was originally established. Each club
was given a vote on the general council of the WRU. Therefore the
WRU may be seen as very much a co-operative organization with each
club having a vote in electing union officials. Involvement on union
committees may be seen as an action performed by all the Welsh clubs.
In the 1990s, however, there has been a push from leading clubs

competing in the Premiership of the WRU to secure a greater say in how the game is administered. As the game has become open leading clubs have felt that they must have more control over their destiny. Money through corporate sponsors has begun to be made available to the WRU and the clubs (especially the top-flight ones) have felt that if sponsors relationship with the WRU was allowed to continue in the same manner then the clubs would not get what they deserve. Action has been taken to force the WRU to listen to the top clubs[11] as they have founded their own commercial committee, known as First Division Rugby Limited (FDRL).

The development of league rugby is of importance in that it may be seen to be the start of real commercialism in the sport. Rugby has been getting more competitive since the 1920s with the advent of unofficial league structures, which eventually led to the establishment of the merit table.[12] At this time the results over a season became important; however, before this winning was considered important only within the context of each match. Each club established its own fixture list and therefore it might not play the same opposition as the neighbouring community. While from the 1930s Pontypridd was involved in the Glamorgan League playing many local clubs, the merit table altered this focus toward a national level. What really initiated commercial interests was the re-establishment of the WRU Challenge Cup. The Cup was the first indication of national superiority for its winner, since without winning each match a club cannot progress to the next round. The WRU Challenge Cup was introduced in 1971,[13] and until this time there had been an attitude that participation in rugby made you fit, whereas since the advent of the Cup there has been a marked shift in ideology whereby you must be fit to play rugby.[14] It is here that the level of time commitment has greatly increased.

The re-establishment of the cup competition by the WRU has seen a shift in the emphasis on winning. While a point-scoring system was developed in the early days of the game, and therefore winning was of importance, the establishment of a knock-out competition that offered a cup meant that winning had begun to take on even greater significance. Success in such a competition also did a great deal to draw spectators to the grounds. In the current climate I would suggest that spectators become of fundamental importance, as they are transformed from having a role of simply observing matches to consuming the products that may be associated with the club or the union. As a result of increased access to consumers, local businessmen increasingly wished to contribute to their successful club. Their hope has been to gain exposure for their enterprise within the community. One of the Pontypridd supporters commented:

> While the ads in the programmes detract from the available space for stories and commentary on the club, when I am on the high street I will take my custom to the businesses that support our club.[15]

Increased exposure as a result of association with a club until recently was limited to advertising in the programme and around the club ground. The late 1980s saw the addition of sponsor's names to the club kit, much in the same manner as has been the practice in Association Football for some time. With the advent of 'official' league rugby in 1990–91 rugby continued to head toward an era of commercial enterprise rather than that of a co-operative club game. A major brewery, Heineken, was the league's sponsor until the end of the 1995–96 season. The gimmicks that have been used for the league's promotion (and therefore by association the products) are varied. When Pontypridd's Neil Jenkins became the first player to score 1,000 points in league competition, one can of lager was presented to him for every point he had scored. Heineken has since pulled out of Welsh domestic rugby and instead is sponsoring the European Rugby Cup. The WRU was unable to attract another league sponsor for the 1996–97 season, which is perhaps an indication that future commercial interest will be in Europe for the top clubs. Partly because of the loss of the league's main sponsor, FDRL began to monitor the business actions of the WRU and has played a role in negotiating all the major sponsorship contracts that might have an impact on club rugby in Wales. The struggle, between the WRU and FDRL, may be seen as a hegemonic battle for long-term control of the game. As the game continues to grow and the importance of European rugby takes centre stage, the role of FDRL in voicing the collective concerns of the elite clubs in Wales has been of paramount importance.

The problems that exist now in the restructuring of rugby in Wales are occurring in other nations;[16] however, it is perhaps more important in Wales as the game is a national obsession. The balance of power within rugby in Wales has yet to be completely determined but it is clear that FDRL is eager to be given its fair share of the money that the WRU receives from any television agreements. Commenting on the relationship between FDRL and the WRU, Pontypridd RFC team manager and the chairman of FDRL Eddie Jones said:

> I am a rugby man with a wealth of experience in the game. We [FDRL and WRU] are in this together and Welsh rugby will get nowhere unless we work together as one.[17]

With clubs such as Cardiff becoming publicly limited companies in their own right,[18] the end of the co-operative era in rugby is close at hand. As a result, in the future the power of the WRU may be limited to running the national squad.

The current environment is not so clear, however, with many clubs in the premiership in financial difficulty as a result of basing their budgets on money they hoped to receive. This placed the Union back in a strong position since several clubs have had to take out low-interest loans in order to survive.[19] Pontypridd RFC, except for being unable to further develop its clubhouse, is not in the same financial difficulty as these clubs since it has better managed its resources.[20] Because Pontypridd was strict with spending at the outset of the open game, many players began to look around for better deals from other clubs; however, most are now glad they stayed as some clubs have released players from their contracts to cut spending. The habitus of the club is one of the reasons players wanted to play for Pontypridd, but in the professional game whether this environment will continue to be a draw for talent remains uncertain.

Clearly the power that has existed within the WRU is a result of its control of the money that has come into the sport. By controlling the distribution of funds that have been secured through sponsorship as well as rights for television and gate receipts for international matches, the Union has been in a position to dictate how the game should be structured.[21] With the establishment of an open game the WRU's position as 'banker' for the game of rugby in Wales is coming under threat. The clubs feel that, due to the increased media exposure, which is in part a result of their more entertaining play, they should receive more of the money generated by the game. The financial teething problems of clubs are not unexpected since changes to the game have been rapid.

Television, Commercialism and a Restructured Game

Television may be seen as a vehicle of transformation in the game of rugby union. While broadcasts often feature contrasting heroic personalities, they are primarily designed to 'trap' the largest possible audience.[22] Before recent Five Nations clashes between Wales and England (1993–95), BBC Wales built the event up as a clash between the public school and Cambridge-educated Rob Andrew and the valleys lad Neil Jenkins, at opposing outside-half positions. Such publicity in the Principality led to the vilification of Andrew in Wales in spite of his obvious talent. Television benefits from this contrived struggle. Free advertising is also initiated by the printed media when previewing matches which may be attended by only a limited number of spectators. Such prematch analysis certainly swells television audiences and hence increases the benefits to sponsors and, in turn, will increase the price Welsh Rugby may hope to receive the next time its television contract is negotiated.[23]

As there has become an increased presence of the media at major events on the rugby calendar, including most premiership matches, winning a match has become so important that the game has begun to stagnate. Finishing high in the league table can mean promotion to the next division and therefore more exposure, which in turn should lead to more sponsorship. However, if the game is boring television networks and other media will soon become uninterested. If and when such a situation arises action needs to be taken. Because of the importance of attracting spectators the IRB a decade ago increased the value of a try to five points, believing that, by making it worth two points more than a penalty, teams would be encouraged to run the ball more frequently. This in turn would lead to a more attractive style of rugby, thus drawing more spectators and would bring more money to the club, and, ultimately, the Union.

Spectators did become drawn to the game; however, these rule changes became only a short-term solution as the necessity for a win, in both league and cup matches, and led to a new form of 'conservative' play, where the penalty became the primary method of scoring. Clubs in the Welsh premiership, which by 1994–95 were competing for a place in the European Club Championships, were determined to win at any cost. Therefore players began to break the rules deliberately by being off-side or 'killing-the-ball', preferring to give away a chance at a penalty goal rather than allow a try to be scored, as a result of their poor play.[24] Clubs with good goal kickers soon began to dominate as this unruly desire to stop a try often worked against the offenders when a successful penalty goal was kicked.

An attempt was made at the beginning of the 1995–96 season to return the game to its more spectator-friendly running style, by giving clubs in the Welsh leagues the chance to gain bonus points for positive play.[25] In this manner the game has been forced to become more fluid and thus more entertaining, increasing the amount of media coverage[26] and rekindling Welsh 'myths' of fluid rugby and outside-halves 'who were like gods'. However, this system has no effect on cup matches which means a team may play in a different manner for cup and league matches, therefore making the coach's job more difficult.[27]

With an increased focus on European rugby, whether the bonus point system will still be used during future seasons is unclear. Wales is the only nation that has adopted this measure in order to make the game more exciting. As a result the style of winning league matches has been transformed. With no incentives for flair (that is, bonus points for tries) in European competition such changes in domestic Welsh rugby may have a detrimental effect on the performance of the club sides against European rivals. The Pontypridd Director of Rugby Eddie Jones commented:

> As for bonus points, we are the only country competing in the Heineken Cup adopting them. It means our sides are going into the tournament under different rules. We need a decision on bonus points sooner rather than later…[28]

A bonus point system may make the game more spectator-friendly,[29] which in turn may increase the size of the viewing audience in the short term. The game of rugby must be marketed in such a way as to highlight its distinctive qualities. By attracting an audience of consumers in this manner their support would be long term. Therefore, by encouraging the audience to embrace the structure of the game rather than altering it to suit their tastes, the impact of professionalism would not be as testing on the Unions or the clubs. There is a distinctive habitus that is embodied in the game of rugby.[30] If this can be packaged then the selling of the game to consumers (vitally important in the professional era) will be more manageable for clubs.

Commercialism at Pontypridd RFC: Will Habitus Sell?

Throughout my time researching at Pontypridd RFC I was struck by the distinctive habitus of the club.[31] Since its establishment in 1876 it has come to be embraced by the community as the game of rugby went from being a simple pastime for its participants to a spectacle performed every week for the community. In this manner the club became more than just an organization that allowed for the playing of structured games; it was transformed into an institution that drew the attention of spectators and by doing so became a spectacle. This spectacle has become one of the symbols of Pontypridd and as a result an individual who plays for the club may be seen to be gambling with his body inasmuch as he would risk physical well-being for a good result. It is this act of bodily gambling[32] for a winning performance on behalf of the club that is at the core of the habitus defined by members of the squad at Pontypridd RFC.

In an era where financial rewards in the form of contracts now can be made to the players, it is of interest that one of the first club sponsors to advertise on the Pontypridd jersey was Rizla cigarette papers, back in the late 1980s. The association of the club with a sponsor that is also connected to bodily gambling[33] may be more than a coincidence. This manufacturer has a big factory in the Treforest industrial estate just south of the town and gave several players jobs while they were the club sponsors, feeling that the association with the club would improve their sales. Many people who smoke 'roll-up' cigarettes are often unfashionable and so too at the time were Pontypridd, so the association was well constructed. This is partly a result of sport being as risky as the use of tobacco, but the enjoyment that can be gained from both products makes the association plausible. There is also the influence of machismo in this association since tobacco smells 'male' (as does the sweat of a sportsman).

Changes have also occurred in the marketing of replica kit. Twenty years ago Pontypridd did not have a supporters' shop and only a few clubs were selling replica kit. Today things are different. While the turnover of the whole premiership of Welsh rugby is only a fraction of the £14 million taken in a recent season by Manchester United Football Club,[34] this is an avenue which has been expanded over the last decade. Replica kits have been sold heavily only for the last dozen years, since possession of a team jersey was once thought to be a right that had to be earned. Money-men involved in elite soccer and rugby began to realize that it was a good way to capitalize on their club's success. Sales of rugby jerseys have increased as teams have begun to wear polyester jerseys which can be made in a wider variety of styles to get away from the boring, conservative hoops, stripes or patchwork that have been the basis of most jersey designs since the game was invented. Pontypridd's jersey, which came out in the autumn of 1994, is a big success and is unique in that it was designed to be a large club crest, thus combining old and new styles. With the purchase of the team shirt the supporter is attempting to embody the 'heroism' that is associated with the players at the club, which may positively influence the supporters' physical self-image. In fact, street fashion now incorporates sports team uniforms and as a result the leisurewear industry has expanded to give the consumer more choice in what he can purchase.

Because rugby has become big business many companies are willing to give products to Pontypridd RFC for the use by the players

– as a form of advertising. Today more often than not the club will charge manufacturers for the use of their 'breathing–billboards' (the players). For example, commitment to fitness and the success of the club extend to the use of diet supplements and fluid replacement products as well as equipment, and the club has agreements with several firms to supply the required goods. While I was at Pontypridd this component of the marketing of the club was the responsibility of the players' representative on the club's committee. By controlling these areas of off-field enterprise the players are able to increase their value to the organization. Such involvement also takes the pressure off[35] members of the administrative committee since all these individuals at the club were unpaid volunteers (until the end of the 1997–98 season).

Strained domestic social relations in Pontypridd can be seen to be a by-product of the new professionalism of attitude which, in turn, is a result of the commercialism that is associated with modern rugby. The time involved in professional preparation for the sport puts a great strain on social relationships. This includes simple things such as attending all club training sessions, personal fitness training as well as monitoring dietary intake of both food and liquid. Such commitments may to some appear minor, but for the family, which misses leisure time with its husband or father, time becomes a valued commodity. For this reason, the desire and actions that are generated to increase the performance of players are what largely distinguishes devoted amateurs from participants. Players, therefore, have much more in common, in terms of levels of commitment, with professional sportsmen who make their entire living through sport.[36]

Defeating the opposition on match day is no longer sufficient in itself, since success every week is the key if a club is going to stay in its division. The WRU Cup competition still provides great drama and certainly a club generates great kudos from being successful in this competition; but a club's survival in the first division is more important than winning the Cup as it will reflect on the club's ability to attract sponsorship and quality players. As a result, team officials, through the players,[37] are more likely to risk their well-being for a win in the league than in a cup match. Pontypridd has a great history as an elite club; however, the inability of the side to win the cup (until 1996) is a black mark on its otherwise good reputation. By the end of the 1990s it had been in the finals three times and is the only club to have made it to two consecutive appearances (1995 and 1996). In spite of its cup success in 1996, the club was still relatively unfashionable. Although Pontypridd town is still not a fashionable place to live, even after the decline of its heavy industry, the club has always produced quality players who often have to go to other clubs, such as Cardiff or Swansea, to gain a place in the Welsh squad. It has been suggested that this is a result of two things: first, stereotypes about society in the valleys and the rough-and-tumble way that valleys sides have traditionally played rugby; and, secondly, that the club has failed to win the league.

One of the fundamental components of the habitus that makes Pontypridd RFC unique is that, regardless of who you are, you will not be tolerated if you are full of self-importance.[38] Neil Jenkins, for example, in spite of being a star on the Welsh squad for whom he has been the saviour more than once (in a time when Welsh rugby needs all its 'stars'), is modest about his success. The quality of letting others sing your praise is found throughout the Pontypridd squad. This attitude stems from a trait that is endemic in the culture of the Rhondda Valley. Because of the traditional, harsh physical environment both geographically and in the work place, popular reverence was not a frequent occurrence. This could be due to the camaraderie of the work environment, but when a hero does come along he has to be modest because the traditionally fragile existence of the community as a whole continually suggests that it may be someone else who is revered tomorrow. Those who feel they should be revered (and as a result become openly self-centred in their outlook towards others) are often not respected within the community. The only time that overt arrogance is acceptable is on the pitch. A remarkable transformation appears to occur in a number of the star players at Pontypridd. The Wales scrum-half Paul John is extremely brash when he is tending the scrum; however, off the pitch he is a very modest individual.

'Humility of individuals, but bravado of the squad'[39] is the way it might be described because, as a unit on match day, Pontypridd represents an excessively confident vehicle of sporting success. Such demeanour may play a part in attracting commercial investment to the club, although it is success on the pitch which is the ultimate focus of potential investors' interest. On-pitch performance is a barometer of how much exposure a club will receive in a given season. What the habitus of the club can do is help to attract specific investors who may share the same philosophy, although for them they may be initiated first in the boardroom. In this manner Pontypridd RFC was able to sign a sponsorship deal with Pro-Line, a company that makes the neoprene strapping used in the protection of the body during sporting activity.

Commercialization of the habitus may be seen to manifest itself in the way the clubhouse is structured. All the other clubs in the premiership appear to be less egalitarian in the physical structure of their facilities.[40] After matches, at other clubs, the players, the committee and the supporters all have separate bars in which to drink and socialize. Players do not appear to be encouraged to mix with the supporters. In this manner the players are given an elevated status, yet the end result is a reduction in the supporters' sense of community. In Pontypridd, however, although separate bars do exist the players first have a post-match meal and a drink. After this they gravitate to the clubhouse bar. All the players appeared throughout my study to enjoy fraternizing with the supporters. Even when Pontypridd travelled to the larger clubs the players would join 'their' supporters for a drink. The sense of community among the players is very strong and there is a clear realization that their rugby would not be as enjoyable nor for that matter as financially rewarding if it were not for the support of the community. By sharing post-match chatter the players are able to bring a small amount of joy into many supporters' lives, since for them there is nothing like rubbing shoulders with the stars.

In order to keep up with the new roller-coaster of commercialism in the game Pontypridd has initiated a programme to actively recruit sponsors to the club.[41] Businesses may be involved in a number of ways. At Sardis Road (the club's ground) advertising boards are the most expensive form of advertising available except for the main sponsorship of the club.[42] On a yearly basis these pitch advertisements start at £750 while programme advertising starts at £150 plus VAT for a quarter-page, to £350 plus VAT for a full-page yearly advertisement. The success of the club in the 1990s has meant that the match programme has expanded by four pages, which are full of advertising. Another way the club raises funds is through match sponsorship where sponsors get between 20 and 40 match tickets, access to a hospitality room and a mention over the public-address system several times during the game, as well as their company logo on the programme cover. The cost of this exposure is £500 per match. All these avenues for generating advertising revenues are increasingly important as the costs of running a successful club become greater with each season. One of the interesting changes is that from the 1995–96 season at the bottom of each page in the programme is a statement *'Please support our advertisers – Remember, they support us!'*. This is a definite indication of a club at least feeling that it is thoroughly embedded in the community's consciousness. Pontypridd is in the process of obtaining planning permission to build a new clubhouse and this will eventually generate even more capital as there will be more hospitality boxes for hire.

Star Employees
The major sponsor at Pontypridd while I was in residence was a locally-based firm Just Rental which has shops throughout Wales. This firm was the only one that advertised on each jersey that the players wear (as well as on the authentic replicas) and it established a full-blown advertising campaign around its employee and Welsh superstar Neil Jenkins. Other players are also employed by the company, as it is in the firm's interest to support a successful side. In fact it was rumoured that if Neil Jenkins were to leave Pontypridd it would be able to renegotiate its contract with the club. It is important then that the club maintains strong bonds with Jenkins both on and off the pitch. Interestingly the firm began by renting out coin-operated televisions which, due to the poverty in the area, is a method that a lot of people used to maintain an acceptable level of household entertainment. Of course, this method of viewing television is more expensive in the long run but for individuals with little or no capital it was the only alternative to a hire-purchase scheme. Rental also means that one can change the appliance as the technology advances. Therefore the company's livelihood is heavily dependent on the economic climate throughout the valley as well as on the performance of the club on the pitch, which, in turn, is directly linked to the number of live televised matches, for which the club is the focus.

Because of the changes taking place in the modern game it is of vital importance that clubs as a whole become more forward thinking. The reality of the modern game of rugby is that, although it is now legally acceptable to gain financially from playing, fewer than 20 per cent of players[43] in the Welsh first division can make their entire livelihood from participation. In the early professional era of the late 1990s there was no player at Pontypridd whose playing generated his entire income. Even Jonathan Davies, who joined Cardiff in 1995–96 after a number of years as a star in rugby league, had a job, at least on paper. Among other deals he was employed by the WRU as a development officer. This job entailed spreading the word of the game's benefits and coaching youngsters at various levels of proficiency. These jobs were reserved for players who were in the Welsh national squad.[44]

Even as a full-time professional a player is a contracted employee whose successful employment is based on his physical skill. He is therefore answerable to his club for the level of physical fitness he must maintain, as well as to the Union if he is a contracted member of the national squad. Many of the star players, such as Neil Jenkins, also have lucrative contracts with sportswear manufacturers. Athletic footwear is one of the primary tools used by all rugby players. Often more than any other tool in training and match performance it is open to individual taste. Adidas now has Jenkins under contract to wear its boots and leisure clothing. What is interesting about this is that the WRU signed a contract with Reebok footwear company for at least the three years from 1996 that stated all the players on the national squad were to wear Reebok footwear and kit for the Welsh matches and training sessions. This means that Jenkins cannot wear his 'favourite' kicking boots when he may need them the most. At first glance this may not seem important but the Adidas boots he uses have a corrugated toe which allows him to refine the direction of his kicks. The Reebok boots do not have this feature and therefore Jenkins has to adjust his kicking action to make allowances, something that the Welsh team perhaps should not want changed since it is so effective. This is just a small problem that is a result of the teething of commercialism in the game of rugby. If the Union had a better understanding of the sportswear marketplace and that some footwear is better than others they may have signed their contract for kit only. All of this results in the fact that Jenkins has to wear footwear that he is not pleased with while playing for Wales.

Conclusion

Many questions have yet to be answered regarding whether a game run by men raised on an amateur tradition can be successfully transformed, by them, into a professional sport in a short period of time. This transition should not be difficult in practice, however, since many of the members of the WRU are successful businessmen. It could be argued that in order to maintain hegemony over the clubs they are not putting these skills to their best use. The Unions and the clubs both feel that they have the answers regarding the future direction of rugby. Because their directions collide, the game off the pitch is presently in turmoil. Who the eventual winner will be (club or Union) is difficult to tell;[45] however, developments in Wales have a huge impact since rugby has for over a century had 'a symbolic unifying role'.[46] Payment for on-pitch performance has done nothing to unify Wales. The feud between 'club and country' will continue for some time. As the Union restructures the game in order to profit, clubs feel that they deserve a share. Some, like Cardiff, have based their future on financial success; others, like Pontypridd, are taking a more conservative approach and are clearly in a period of transition. Time will tell whether the distinctive habitus of Pontypridd is of benefit in clearing the obstacles involved in this transformation of tradition.

NOTES

1. D. Smith and G. Williams, *Fields of Praise: Official History of the Welsh Rugby Union 1881–1981* (Cardiff, 1981), p. 458.
2. P.D. Howe, 'Commercialising the Body, Professionalising the Game: the Development of Sports Medicine at Pontypridd Rugby Football Club', unpublished PhD thesis, University College, London, 1997.
3. Because payment for performance was against the rules of the union game for so long, the modern expectations of the players, clubs and unions have recently strayed from sustainable reality. As a result a financial crisis has hit many clubs. In the Welsh game both Bridgend and Neath have needed the help of the WRU. See G. Clutton, 'Bridgend May Lose Cash Lifeline', *Western Mail*, 22 April 1998 and 'Alarm Bells Ring as Neath Succumb to the Pressure', *Western Mail*, 18 July 1998. For more on the English context see B. Gallagher, 'Rugby Isn't Working', *Daily Telegraph*, Sport on Saturday, 1 August 1998.
4. To date, two books with illuminating titles *Rugby War* and *Rugby Disunion* have been published, discussing issues that are related to the professionalization of the game. P. Fitzsimons, *The Rugby War* (London, 1996) and D. Wyatt, *Rugby Disunion: the Making of Three World Cups* (London, 1995).
5. I am referring to the manner in which this concept has been used by Bourdieu. For a good overview of the value of this concept in the social analysis of sport see G. Jarvie and J. Maguire, *Sport and Leisure in Social Thought* (London, 1994), Ch.8.
6. The argument between those who advocate amateurism over professionalism has long been rooted in the principle of equality. An amateur has a job and therefore is left with little time for sport as a pastime. This has had two effects on the game of Rugby Union: as long as the game is played by individuals who are in the same circumstance with regard to the work/training time ratio, teams and competitions of near-equality will generate 'fair' matches which are exciting and entertaining. This principle is at the root of the establishment of leagues and divisions that typifies British sport today. In this structure ideally teams of near-equal resources and abilities play together.
7. Players are of fundamental importance here. The transformation of the habitus of the players at this time had a profound effect on what was to follow. Players in the upper divisions had begun to adopt a more progressive attitude to the fitness training needed to succeed in the game. This attitude could be seen as professional since the time commitment devoted to achieve an enhanced performance mirrored that of professional athletes in other sports.
8. P. Rees, 'It's Cardiff PLC', *Wales on Sunday*, 31 March 1996.
9. The rules have altered greatly over the last century, for the current rules see *Laws of the Game of Rugby Football* published annually by the Welsh Rugby Union.
10. For a detailed history of the Welsh Rugby Union see Smith and Williams, *Fields of Praise*.
11. This situation is currently rather dynamic since at the start of the 1998–99 season Cardiff and Swansea were thrown out of the WRU for not signing a ten-year loyalty agreement. Their season consisted of playing 'friendly' matches with the top English clubs after a proposed British league fell through. See G. Clutton, 'English Clubs Rally round Welsh Rebels', *Western Mail*, 25 August 1998.
12. The merit table was a loosely structured league in which all the larger clubs throughout Wales were involved. Individual clubs were still in charge of their own fixture lists and the results of these matches were recorded so that the club with the best record won the league. It was unofficial because not all the teams played each other in home and away matches. Because of the discontinuity from one club

to the next in terms of fixtures, even at the top flight of the merit table, this development may be seen as an embryonic form of the commercialized game, see E. Dunning and K. Sheard, *Barbarians, Gentlemen and Players: a Sociological Study of the Development of Rugby Football* (Oxford, 1979) also see Smith and Williams, *Fields of Praise*.

13. The South Wales Challenge Cup was played for between 1878 and 1897 but was discontinued. See Smith and Williams, *Fields of Praise*, pp. 485–6. The suspension of such competitions for more than 70 years coincided with the WRU's leaving the international rugby arena in a dispute over amateurism (or lack of it) in the game. For a good account of this see G. Williams, *1905 and All That* (Llandysul, 1991), Ch.7.

14. Participation in the national squad has for some time taken this philosophy for granted. It is the depth of the commitment to club rugby even in lower divisions, which is unique to the present.

15. Howe, 'Commercialising the Body', p. 139.

16. The English game is in disarray as well with many clubs, with amateur traditions, struggling for survival in the new professional age. See Gallagher, 'Rugby Isn't Working'.

17. P. Rees, 'Clubs Demand Peace in TV Cash Row', *Wales on Sunday*, 20 April 1997.

18. Ibid.

19. G. Roberts, 'Bridgend Plead for Help to Clear £1m Debt', *Western Mail*, 30 July 1998.

20. Pontypridd signed Neil Jenkins, the Wales and British Lion outside-half to a five-year £500,000 contract. As a result of this they asked the union to help them guarantee some of the contracts of their other leading players. G. Clutton 'WRU Ready to Take over Top Ponty Players', *Western Mail*, 3 June 1998.

21. Since it was established in 1881 the Union has been charged with upholding the amateur values on which the game was founded. Therefore its control of finances did originally have a value, but today in the open era, this role is in question.

22. See G. Whannel, *Fields in Vision: Television Sport and Cultural Transformation* (London, 1992).

23. This sort of drama has increased the value of television rights for games hosted by England to such an extent that terrestrial television could no longer afford them. International matches, as well as some high-profile English league fixtures are shown on Sky TV; B. Williams, 'If You Haven't Got One of These You Won't See This', *Wales on Sunday*, 11 January 1998.

24. One of the ways that television has influenced the game has been through the implementation of a 'sin-bin'. This is designed to stop players from killing the ball (reducing the flow of play) thus allowing for a more free-flowing spectacle which is more attractive as a product to be sold to television networks as well as for supporters at the ground. See A. Howell, 'Sin-bin Move for Fast-track Revival', *Western Mail*, 14 July 1998.

25. See the Welsh Rugby Union 1995–96 rule book for further detail.

26. Sport's being restructured in this way is a clear indicator that it is the medium that is the message. See M. McLuhan, *Understanding Media* (New York, 1964).

27. For the 1996–97 season the bonus-point system was altered again to make it more difficult to obtain bonus points on top of the two points available for a win.

28. Rees, 'Clubs'.

29. It is of interest to note that on my arrival in Pontypridd I was unable to appreciate rugby without a fluid running style. However, during my stay I gained an understanding and respect for the rucking and mauling involved in the game. It

was not until I had gained this awareness that I considered myself to have been a supporter of the game.

30. Howe, 'Commercialising the Body', Ch.4.
31. Ibid., Ch.3.
32. This gambling with the body may be seen as a manifestation of a culture of risk, which is fundamental to the habitus of the club. See P.D. Howe, 'Risk Culture as a Product of Pain and Injury' (forthcoming).
33. The association of smoking and poor health is well documented.
34. P. Rees, 'The Great Strip Teaser', *Wales on Sunday*, 1 January 1995.
35. The pressure referred to here is that involved in the transformation from a co-operative club to a business enterprise.
36. At the beginning of the 1998–99 season only Neil Jenkins was making his entire living from rugby.
37. The players on a team are one of a club's major assets. The power relationship between management, players and the medical team is dynamic and shifts markedly with the perceived value of a given match. See P.D. Howe, 'Pain and Injury in Professional Rugby Union: a New Focus on an Old Evil', paper presented at the North American Society for the Sociology of Sport Conference, Las Vegas, November 1998.
38. Howe, 'Commercialising the Body', Ch.3.
39. Ibid.
40. The observations may be qualified by my acceptance into every sphere at Pontypridd RFC, while my understanding of the other clubs was based on the physical structure of the clubhouse as well as limited observation. It is worthy of note, however, that several players commented on the positive nature of the 'club-life' at Pontypridd that was at odds with their experiences while playing for larger clubs.
41. Pontypridd RFC Match Programme, 2 September 1995.
42. By this I mean any companies who wish to provide playing kit, including the logo of the main sponsor, dietary supplements and all the other items that may be directly used by the players.
43. This estimate was made at the end of the 1996–97 season. It is quite clear that it is the desire of more players to be full-time professionals. It is perhaps this and the greed of the clubs (to keep their talent or attract it from elsewhere) that has forced several leading clubs in Wales into financial ruin.
44. This has its obvious benefits for the publicity of the sport; however, what happens if these players get injured or are no longer good enough to be in the national side? If their contracts are based on their on-field performance perhaps mistakes will be made in selecting the side since the coach will tend to pick fellow employees of the Union and perhaps ignore other high-quality players.
45. This struggle may be seen as emblematic of the struggle that Wales had in establishing the right for a voice in the British nation which has recently culminated in the founding of a Welsh assembly.
46. Williams, *1905 and All That*, p. 171.

10

Recapturing the Moment? Global Rugby, Economics and the Politics of Nation in Post-Apartheid South Africa

Douglas Booth

When we won the Rugby World Cup in 1995, never once in the history of [our] country, never for a single moment before, were the people so solidly united. Never! That was a remarkable, remarkable moment.... When [the Springboks] arrive [in Edinburgh] in November [1997], I can tell you there is going to be jubilation at home every time they lose, make no mistake about that. We have lost the moment. It is sad.

Steve Tshwete, South Africa's Minister for Sport[1]

Major international [sporting] events are now a standard part of 'boosterist' policies and development economics in countries with the infrastructure to compete on a global scale ... many politicians, capitalists and sports administrators have been drawn towards a cycle of events-driven development as one way to enhance the prestige and wealth of the new South Africa. Rugby will certainly play its part....

David Black and John Nauright[2]

The biggest event in South African rugby in 1998 was not the Springboks' victory in the Tri-Nations Cup. In fact, it did not take place on the field; it was Louis Luyt's resignation as president of the South African Rugby Football Union (SARFU). Luyt's abdication in May, after six stormy years of reign, followed a political crisis that included renewed threats to isolate South African rugby. For the ruling African National Congress (ANC), Luyt's resignation was critical to recapturing the nationalist euphoria associated with South Africa's victory in the 1995 Rugby World Cup (RWC). Within months of the victory, Luyt's 'white oligarchy' faced fresh allegations of racism, nepotism, maladministration and financial irregularities. Yet even Luyt's critics credit him with 'bringing business to rugby' and 'with building the organisational structure which made the RWC such a success'.[3] Moreover, as Black and Nauright suggest in the quotation above, the 'business' of rugby is now a part of South Africa's economic development programme. The latter raises important questions about the effects of global commercial forces on the 'nationalist logic' of South African rugby. In short, will the emerging business of global rugby alter historic nationalist objectives? This chapter examines the political and economic forces at work on post-apartheid rugby.

Rugby and the Afrikaner Nation

'No nation possesses an ethnic base naturally', writes Etienne Balibar. Rather, all states face problems of cohesion and must draw together disparate political, religious, ethnic and racial interests in a process Balibar calls 'nationalisation'. States 'nationalise' their social formations in the sense that they 'represent [them] in the past or in the future as if they formed a natural community, possessing of itself an identity of origins, culture and interests which transcends individuals and social conditions'.[4]

How do states nationalize their populations? History shows that they variously invent traditions, describe conquests within or beyond historical frontiers, celebrate diversity (by which they encourage their populations to mutually recognize each other within a common boundary), and impose uniform administrative practices. Sport too plays a role. Lincoln Allison regards sport as 'one of the most potent of human activities in its capacity to give meaning to life, to create and interconnect senses of achievement and identity'. 'Above all', he adds, 'sport has a complex and important interaction with nationality and the phenomenon of nationalism'.[5] This occurs in at least three ways. First, sport provides 'a form of symbolic action which states the case for the nation itself'.[6] Victories incarnate positive images of national virtues, strengths and way of life. Similarly, hosts of international sporting pageants display national wealth, technical expertise and organizational competence. Secondly, sporting events provide 'shared memories'. Occasionally these may act as 'turning points for national history' and help to forge ideas about 'common destiny'.[7] And thirdly, the symbols and anthems of representative teams are signifiers that separate and distinguish nations from each other. South African rugby illustrates each of these points.

British immigrants introduced rugby to (black and white) South Africans in the nineteenth century but Afrikaners appropriated the game as their own.[8] Rugby symbolized the 'convictions, aspirations and dreams' of Afrikaners: 'attached to their Voortrekker past, proud of their civilizing mission in a savage land, perceiving themselves as elected by God to reign on earth, conscious of their vocation as warriors – not soldiers but freemen under arms – inspired by faith and an uncompromising moral ethic to defend the cause of their people and their God, the Afrikaner people ... conquered the game'.[9]

Even before apartheid the different racial groups in South Africa[10] rarely played sport together. Whatever sporting contact took place was 'essentially informal and irregular'.[11] Early Springbok rugby teams refused, for example, to play against black nations; they even insisted that foreign opponents should exclude individual black players. New Zealand's All Black selectors excluded the Maori champion George Nepia from the 1928 tour of the Union in keeping with South Africa's racial traditions.[12] Apartheid reinforced racial segregation and took it to new levels. Lapchick argues that apartheid sport shared a fundamental racial tenet with Nazi sport. Just as the Nazis believed that only Aryans could represent the German nation, so only whites could represent South Africa.[13] This was especially true in rugby, as Prime Minister John Vorster made clear when he told Parliament in 1971 that:

> the Springbok rugby team is not representative of the whole of South Africa. It has never been that. It has never claimed to be representative of the whole of South Africa. It is representative of the whites of South Africa.[14]

Black South Africans affirmed their exclusion from Vorster's white nation by vociferously supporting South Africa's opponents. The Australian Wallaby Barry Macdonald recalled 'phenomenal support' from black spectators during the 1969 tour of South Africa: 'they would always barrack for the Wallabies, and were very excited when we won – they made us feel that we were playing for them.' His team mate James Roxburgh remembered that 'the blacks ... roared with excitement' after a try put the Wallabies in front near the end of one match.[15] Black sports people chose their own colours and symbols. Black rugby players in the Eastern Cape wore an elephant, although, interestingly, the emblem of the non-racial South African Rugby Union (SARU) incorporated two Springbok heads flanking a protea flower.[16]

Under growing pressure from international isolation, the apartheid regime progressively modified its sports policy.[17] In 1971, in keeping with its new policy of multinationalism (a grand political scheme that divided South Africa into ten black 'nations'), the government allowed black states to compete against white South Africa in so-called 'open' international events. Four years later it allowed sports to select multiracial 'invitation teams', although the Minister for Sport, Piet Koornhof, stressed that invitation sides did not represent South Africa. The French national rugby team toured the Republic in 1975 and played an Invitation XV that included two Africans and two Coloureds.[18] In 1976 Koornhof approved 'intergroup competition' at club level: sports associations and municipal councils could, 'in consultation with the minister, arrange leagues or matches enabling teams from different racial groups to compete [against each other]'.[19] Shortly after the government approved multiracial representative teams – chosen by way of racially-mixed trials. Despite the convoluted selection process, blacks in mixed representative teams could at last wear the sacred Springbok emblem.[20] Twenty-five blacks participated in the first mixed trials for the Springbok team in 1977, although none gained selection.[21] It was another three years before Errol Tobias became the first black Springbok.[22] Tobias played half a dozen games for the Springboks.

Logically, integrated representative sport defined South Africa as a multiracial nation. In reality integrated sport failed to nationalize black peoples. At best it gave a handful of exceptionally talented black athletes temporary respite, be it for ten seconds, 15 rounds or 80 minutes, from apartheid. While those who wore the Springbok greatly valued it, the emblem remained purely a symbol of sporting excellence; black Springboks suffered no illusions about their inclusion in the nation. Tobias, for example, says that it was not until the Republic's first fully-fledged democratic election in April 1994 that he felt like a real South African.[23]

Rugby and the National Transition

In 1990 State President F.W. de Klerk announced the end of apartheid: the deracialization, democratization and nationalization of South Africa began. Subsequent events, however, including the collapse of multiparty negotiations at the Convention for a Democratic South Africa, massacres in Boipatong and Bisho,[24] endless killings on the East Rand and in Natal, several suspensions of official political negotiations, and the assassination of the ANC and Communist Party leader Chris Hani[25] illustrated the enormity of the task. Nor was sport immune from the turbulence of transition.

In the 1970s and the 1980s the anti-apartheid movement and the international sporting community imposed a boycott on South Africa. In 1991 they demanded that South Africa meet four conditions before returning to international competition: a single controlling association in each code, the removal of apartheid rules and practices, the activation of development programmes in the townships to redress inequalities caused by apartheid, and new flags, anthems, colours and emblems.

The demand for a single controlling association in each code required negotiations, or unity talks, between officials from the non-racial movement and the apartheid establishment.[26] Talks had in fact started during the preceding 12 months but progress varied. In some sports, notably rugby, the Springbok emblem was a major source of division. Mluleki George, president of the anti-apartheid National Sports Congress (NSC)[27] and a key figure in rugby unity talks who later became vice-president of SARFU, said that there 'was no way we will compromise' on apartheid symbols.[28] The rugby sports establishment and Afrikaner nationalists were equally determined. While the world knew nearly all South African representative teams (and soldiers) as Springboks (popularly shortened to Boks in English and Bokke in Afrikaans), rugby developed a special affinity with the name. Danie Craven, president of the establishment South African Rugby Board (SARB), declared the Springbok 'non-negotiable'.[29] Right-wing, Afrikaner nationalists warned that black Communists and white liberals wanted to remove the Springbok because it represented Christian values.[30] Daan Nolte, the Conservative Party's spokesperson on sport, accused non-racial leaders of forcing South African sports people to represent a foreign nation:

> they will ... represent Azania, and they will stand to attention while the ANC's national anthem, *Nkosi Sikelel' iAfrika* [God Bless Africa] is played. The flying Springbok will obviously be replaced with an emblem more fitting ... of [the] new South Africa – a sinking banana on a red flag.[31]

The English and the Afrikaans press rallied behind the Springbok. Several papers ran polls which they said 'proved overwhelming support' for the Springbok. A telephone poll conducted by the *Sunday Times* recorded more than 12,000 calls in favour of retention and just 304 against.[32] Not surprisingly, the black press painted a different picture. *City Press* ran a telephone poll in which 'more than 90 per cent of callers rejected the Springbok'.[33] The columnist Jon Qwelane summed up the general black sentiments: 'those who hanker after the Springbok are reliving past glories; but, sadly, those glories were gained ... at the expense of locking other South Africans out because of their race'.[34]

The non-racial SARU and the establishment SARB agreed to amalgamate as SARFU in 1991 and the Springboks returned to the world stage. But amalgamation did not resolve the emblem issue. In March 1992 the NSC took unilateral action and announced that the protea would replace the Springbok in all sports. Although an NSC affiliate, SARFU refused to accept the decision. Matters came to a head in August 1992 during a rugby test against New Zealand at Ellis Park (Johannesburg). Several white spectators taunted the ANC's spokesperson on sport and the current minister, Steve Tshwete, by extending the apartheid flag for his autograph. Before the kick-off Louis Luyt, then vice-president of SARFU, instructed the announcer to play the national anthem – *Die Stem van Suid Afrika* (The Voice of South Africa). It was a deliberate breach of a pledge not to promote apartheid symbols. The crowd sang as one. In the furore that followed, the Afrikaans Sunday newspaper *Rapport* waxed lyrical about Afrikaner defiance and the heroic supporters who had declared 'here is my song, here is my flag. Here I stand and I will sing it today'.[35]

Following the Ellis Park incident, and with no sign of rugby development in the townships, NSC and ANC officials conceded the obvious. 'In hindsight', the NSC-founder Arnold Stofile said, '[sanctions] were lifted too soon. We made the fundamental mistake of believing that whites are ready for change.'[36] 'We have been taken for a ride', George added, 'certain people were never interested in unity ... they were more interested in international competition.'[37] The NSC and the ANC discussed reimposing the boycott. Tshwete said that 'present conditions are not conducive to international tours'.[38] The NSC withdrew support for the 1992 Springbok rugby tour of Britain and France and the 1995 Rugby World Cup, and tacitly approved demonstrations by the British Anti-Apartheid Movement. But, as both organizations soon learned, they could not turn the boycott on and off like a tap.

The Springbok emblem remained the subject of intense debate. Most former non-racial officials wanted to obliterate the past; however, they were painfully aware of the constraints. Unlike the National Party government which unilaterally removed *God Save the Queen* and the Union Jack as the official anthem and flag of the Union in 1957, the anti-apartheid sports movement could not impose its own anthems, emblems, flags and colours. The real problem, of course, was that South Africa was not a nation and its peoples refused to attach themselves emotionally to one symbol.[39]

Later in 1992 SARFU unveiled what it called an interim emblem: a leaping Springbok, vertical rugby ball and four proteas. From a non-racial perspective it was a major concession: the Springbok retained its privileged position both in the emblem and the name. No one was about to call South Africa's national rugby team the Springbok-Proteas or the Protea-Springboks, and certainly not the Proteas.

The inauguration of Nelson Mandela as President on 10 May 1994 ostensibly marked the end of 342 years of white power and the beginning of black rule. It was an emotional and joyous occasion perhaps best remembered for the black spectators who cheered air force planes as they passed overhead and swarmed over armoured police vehicles. Blacks now claimed as their own these former reviled instruments of white authority. Indeed, a black president and black ministers 'proved' black ownership. By contrast, no black people claimed ownership of the South African rugby team. It remained firmly bogged in the past. When England toured South Africa a month after the inauguration, the captain François Pienaar declared that his team represented a new nation. But when England trounced South Africa in the first Test, the well-known anti-apartheid sporting activist 'Cheeky' Watson reported that most blacks were ecstatic. 'It's quite sad', he added, 'but people in the townships find it hard to identify with Pienaar and his teammates, who don't know the words of *Nkosi Sikelel' iAfrika*.'[40] (The government of national unity made *Nkosi Sikelel'* and *Die Stem* the dual national anthems.)

In mid-1994 SARFU and the NSC (now the National Sports Council and one of two umbrella bodies overseeing sport in the Republic) agreed to retain the interim emblem until after the RWC to capture the Springbok's marketing potential.[41] Some commentators said that the Springbok was synonymous with rugby, just as Coca-Cola signified cola drinks. But the analogy ignored the political content of the 'product'. Sharon Chetty's description of the crowd's behaviour during the Test between South Africa and Manu (Western) Samoa is a poignant reminder that on the eve of the World Cup the Springbok was a political symbol of white South Africa:

> ... holding aloft the old South African flag, the rugby diehards sought momentary refuge in the confines of Ellis Park. [When] *Nkosi Sikelel' iAfrika* started up you could count the numbers who bothered to even keep still. But when *Die Stem* was played they stood to attention and sang with gusto – their voices in unison. Barring the good-natured vendors ... the number of darkies at Ellis Park could be counted on one hand. [One] young Fascist ... commanded a vendor to 'go stand under the spotlight. Maybe then you will become white'. His friends laughed. Rugby it seems is the last white outpost ... .[42]

Logically, then, there seemed little prospect of the 1995 World Cup Springbok team nationalizing South Africa. One could hardly expect a lily-white team,[43] predominantly white spectators and a racially-divisive emblem to inculcate national feelings of belonging among blacks. However, the day before the tournament began Mandela embraced the team: 'I have never been so proud of our boys. I hope we will all be cheering them on to victory. They will be playing for the entire South Africa.'[44] It was an unanticipated gesture. Mandela was the official host and protocol required his participation, but he could have maintained a stiff and indifferent formality. In fact, he admitted on several occasions to supporting the Springboks' opponents during apartheid. Instead Mandela showed a genuine and infectious enthusiasm.[45]

Heribert Adam and Kogila Moodley argue that 'politics is about the manipulation of symbols as a precondition for the exercise of real power'.[46] Does this explain Mandela's support? Only partly. Three factors influenced Mandela: his broad philosophy of reconciliation which, at that juncture, coincided with a fresh drive by the ANC to win white votes in the upcoming municipal elections and a steadily reforming rugby administration.

SARFU supposedly united the establishment SARB and the anti-apartheid SARU. But the overwhelming majority of personnel clung to the racial attitudes and management styles and practices of the old order. SARFU's director of development, Ngconde Balfour, resigned within one year, accusing senior administrators of using development as a smokescreen for international tours.[47] A disastrous tour of Britain and France in 1992 affirmed the Springboks' reputation as insensitive, petulant, boorish and arrogant. By the end of it their public image lay in tatters.[48] Slowly, however, SARFU began to reform, especially after the appointment as CEO in early 1995 of the former *Business Day* and *Sunday Times* sports reporter and staunch critic of establishment rugby, Edward Griffiths. Under his tutelage the Springboks became politically correct: they played under the slogan 'one team, one country', they supported the government's *Masakhane* (building for each other) campaign, they were polite, accessible, offered themselves for photo opportunities, and attended regular press conferences. Griffiths even began rewriting the history of South African rugby. For example, he removed photographs of Springbok legends from public view at rugby headquarters. 'Museum stuff', he called them, adding that 'SARFU was born in 1991'.[49]

Did Mandela's endorsement transform ordinary black opinion? Not initially. The *Sowetan* summed up black sentiment:

One of the biggest sporting events, the RWC, starts in Cape Town today and yet the majority of South African people are not interested. It is extraordinary in fact that white South Africa has tried to keep the game of rugby 'white' for as long as possible. It is a political statement to many who will be seen carrying the old South African flag... It is likewise to say that we will only have national unity when the sports played reflect the country's racial mix.[50]

Twenty-four hours later the mood had swung. South Africa's victory over the reigning titleholders Australia in the opening match of the tournament engendered perhaps the first palpable sense of nationalism among South Africans.

Balibar argues that nationalism requires people to produce themselves as a community and that this process 'presupposes the constitution of a specific ideological form' which assumes 'an a priori condition of communication between individuals and between social groups' and involves 'ideal signifiers' which convey 'sense[s] of the sacred and the affects of love, respect, sacrifice and fear'. Ultimately, however, the effectiveness of a national ideology requires the presence of 'another community' whose differences the nation seeks to project and protect itself against.[51] In front of an estimated world-wide television audience of 300 million, South Africa 'defeated' the ideal Other – Australia, the reigning champion. In just 80 minutes South Africa accumulated a plethora of positive national images. But 'defeat of the other' and inculcation of national pride offer only a partial explanation of emergent South African nationalism: there was also a linguistic component.

The following day the *Sowetan* triumphantly hailed the victory on its front page under the headline '*Amabokoboko*' ('The Boks, the Boks').[52] It was a moment more decisive than even Mandela's support. Conceived by subeditor Sy Makaringe and endorsed by the editor Aggrey Klaaste, *Amabokoboko* Africanized the team and gave blacks a stake in the Springboks for the first time. *Amabokoboko* injected an African component into the Springbok and provided a critical linguistic mechanism to transform its meaning. Balibar alerts us to the possibilities of linguistically reconstructing identity:

the linguistic construction of identity is by definition *open*. No individual 'chooses' his or her mother tongue or can 'change' it at will. Nevertheless, it is always possible to appropriate several languages and to turn oneself into a different kind of bearer of discourse and of the transformation of language.[53]

On 25 June, in an unprecedented act by any head of state, Mandela strode on to the turf before the final against New Zealand wearing a South African team jersey. The predominantly white audience rose to its feet chanting 'Nel-son, Nel-son, Nel-son'. Eighty minutes plus extra time later South Africa was the world champion. Black and white South Africans joined in celebration: Nelson Mandela hugged the team captain François Pienaar who told the world that 'We were inspired by the president';[54] black supporters toyi-toyied through downtown Johannesburg's Carlton Centre singing the theme song *Shosholoza* and shouting '*Amabokoboko*'. *City Press* followed suit the next day with 'Viva *AmaBhokobhoko*! Viva South Africa' as its front-page banner headline.[55] The Post Office sensed the occasion and introduced a special postage stamp depicting the Springbok and the protea with the words 'World Champions 1995' and '*Mabokoboko*'. The Nobel laureate Archbishop Desmond Tutu appeared in a Springbok rugby jersey. 'I did not expect this', he explained:

> but I am proud to wear it when a few years ago, even a few months ago, it was an anathema. I try to say what I believe is true and this thing, that was a very divisive and ugly symbol, could in fact have been magically used by God to weld us together. No one of us could ever in their wildest dreams have been able to predict that rugby ... could have this magical effect.[56]

Mandela wrote to Pienaar expressing his 'admiration for the role you and your team are playing in nation building'. And at a banquet to honour the players he said that 'rugby, once a symbol of division and exclusion, had crossed the threshold into a new era of a united and reconciled nation'.[57] It was a moment of intense nationalism, a moment when South Africans formed a 'natural' community whose interests transcended individual differences and social conditions.

Of course, even in this moment there were exceptions. Jeffrey Stevens, a 'Coloured' player who represented the Republic in junior and sevens teams between 1995 and 1997, remembered only two of the 50 people present at his home to watch the 1995 RWC supporting the Springboks: 'everyone else was cheering the All Blacks'.[58] Yet, even hard-nosed black commentators and officials conceded the possibility of new identities emerging in a changing institutional environment. Aggrey Klaaste said that, while the Springbok emblem reminded him of a time 'when blacks were pointedly excluded from being part of ...

the camaraderie of [sport]', he conceded that 'strange things are happening to my sporting ways'. Klaaste attributed these changes to the fact that his young sons 'worship the ground [the white cricketer] Jonty Rhodes throws himself at with such seeming abandon' and the fact that they could cheer 'pale-faced' South African cricketers against the West Indies. Mac Maharaj, the Minister for Transport, recounted his children's screaming support for the 'Bokke' and their refusal to discuss the historical meaning of the word.[59]

Mandela also asked the NSC to look afresh at the Springbok emblem: 'there is a real possibility that if we review our decision and accept the Springbok for rugby as our symbol, we will unite our country as never before'.[60] At its general meeting in March 1996 the NSC approved the Springbok as a symbol of national unity in rugby.

Rugby and the Rainbow Nation

By definition national identity is temporary,[61] and Desmond Tutu's 'rainbow nation' was no exception. The euphoria accompanying South Africa's victory in the RWC soon receded as different groups began to reflect on their positions. Some right-wing Afrikaners disavowed the Springboks, labelling the players traitors and declaring their support for the opposition. 'I support any team that plays against the Springboks', proclaimed a spokesperson for the paramilitary *Afrikaner Weerstandsbeweging*, who added that he 'wouldn't pay five cents to go to their games. The players have no national pride whatsoever. It is the Mandela team. Mandela is an enemy of the Afrikaners.'[62] In the wake of the final of the RWC at least one newspaper correspondent blamed the destruction of Afrikaner nationalism on integrated sport:

> In 1970 Jaap Marais ... said that it would start with one or two Maoris in the All Black team and it would finish with Black majority rule. How right he was. Saturday was another nail in the coffin of the Afrikaner.[63]

Likewise, several black commentators challenged popular notions that sport was a foundation for nationalization. *City Press*'s parliamentary reporter Rafiq Rohan wrote that 'it's going to take a lot more than a smiling and gleeful president sporting a [Springbok] jersey and ... cap to get everyone in the country to accept the symbol and colours of the historic enemy, the cultural, social, and political enslaver, and to proclaim them with pride'.[64] The *Sowetan* columnist Victor Tsuai agreed: 'No amount of hype and spurious explanation will convince blacks that politically or otherwise, the Springbok is the right symbol in this day and age. The whites have had their opportunity to embrace everybody with their Springbok tentacles but have sadly left it too late.'[65]

While not wishing to play down the enormity of the task confronting even the most determined nationalizing organization, the fact is that SARFU made no effort to nurture the embryonic nationalistic sentiments engendered by the RWC victory. On the contrary, to paraphrase Salman Rushdie, SARFU seeped back into the past.[66] As David Black and John Nauright put it in their political history of South African rugby, 'the apparent uniting of the nation behind the nearly all-white Springboks, right up to the highest political levels, allowed rugby officials, players and supporters [–] who were naturally reluctant to alter their familiar and cherished institutional and mental frameworks [–] to believe that they did not need to – or at least that what they were doing already was enough.'[67] Of course, in reality, there was precious little substance in these nationalizing sentiments, just a name – *Amabokoboko* – and a victorious team. And as subsequent events would prove, the 'glue' was too brittle.

Nineteen-ninety-six and 1997 were bad years on the field for the Springboks. Both New Zealand and the British Lions defeated South Africa on its home turf. It was an historic first for the All Blacks and only the second time for the Lions. Late in 1996 the new coach Andre Markgraaff unceremoniously dumped François Pienaar for the upcoming Springbok tour of Argentina and Wales. While the coach pointed to the injury-plagued Pienaar's poor form, many saw in his brusque methods the bullying hand of Louis Luyt. There was no love lost between Pienaar and Luyt. After the RWC, Pienaar and other Transvaal rugby players went on strike demanding a greater share of the profits from Luyt's provincial Transvaal Rugby Football Union (TRFU). No sooner did the strike end than Pienaar and Luyt found themselves on opposing sides in the struggle between the World Rugby Corporation (WRC), ostensibly backed by Kerry Packer, and Rupert Murdoch's News Corporation for control of the global media rights to rugby which was in the process of turning professional. Luyt supported Murdoch and to his chagrin Pienaar not only signed with the WRC but he recruited key Springboks. In the end Luyt had to pay R21 million (US$5 million) to secure the 'loyalty' of Pienaar and other Springboks.[68] It was an exorbitant price for a man who bowed only to God.

Equally insensitive as the decision to drop Pienaar was the selection of Henry Tromp, an Afrikaner convicted of killing a black farm labourer. While Tromp had served his time and publicly expressed remorse, he none the less represented 'all the ills' of apartheid and, by 'virtue of the jersey he [wore], ... transferred those ills back on to the game ..., further underpinning the perception in many parts of the community that the game had never changed anyway'.[69] Further reinforcing those perceptions was a resurgence of apartheid flags at international matches and the well-publicized charges by the TRFU vice-president Brian van Rooyen that racism continued to thrive in rugby.[70] Worse followed. In February 1997 the South African Broadcasting Corporation played a taped conversation between Markgraaff and a former provincial player in which the coach blamed all his troubles on 'fucking kaffirs' – the latter being the worst expletive in the Afrikaner vocabulary. Markgraaff resigned in a storm of controversy, but his successor Morné du Plessis proved incapable of lifting the team – on or off the field. Little wonder, then, that Mandela declined to attend matches and that Trevor Manuel, the Minister for Finance, declared his support for visiting teams, of most concern being his stated support for the old enemy, the All Blacks.

Throughout 1996 and 1997 black sports officials expressed their dismay about lily-white Springbok teams and SARFU's failure to take rugby to black, now euphemistically referred to as 'disadvantaged', communities. But in the last quarter of 1997 frustration and anger swelled. In October, for example, Achmat Esau, a primary school teacher and rugby administrator in the Western Cape insisted that:

> basically nothing is being done for poor players ... no real money is being spent on developing the game. People like Edward Griffiths wanted development to take shape, but Luyt is always against this. I think I should be the first person to say to Luyt's face that he is a racist and damaging the image of rugby beyond repair.[71]

Mluleki George raised the spectre of international boycotts and Steve Tshwete threatened legislation if national and provincial selectors refused to chose more black players. In rugby, Tshwete complained, 'linesmen are white, referees are white, team is white, everything is white'.[72]

The threats went unheeded: at the start of the 1998 Super 12 series the selectors chose only four blacks in the Republic's top 100 players.[73] Luyt, however, had every reason to feel secure and failed to recognize the new mood. In the 1996 TRFU presidential elections Luyt easily defeated, and then proceeded to humiliate and denigrate, van Rooyen; in 1997 he comfortably survived challenges for the presidency of

SARFU from Keith Parkinson (Natal) and Mluleki George (Border and senior vice-president of SARFU). George's loss cost him his seat on SARFU's executive and the vice-presidency.

Responding to intense public pressure, Tshwete instructed officials in his department to investigate rugby. And on the basis of a damning departmental report, the cabinet approved a full judicial enquiry, headed by the advocate Jules Browde, into the state of rugby in South Africa.[74] SARFU successfully challenged the enquiry in court. But a confident Luyt overplayed his hand. In an effort to humiliate Mandela and Tshwete, SARFU forced them to give evidence in court and face gruelling cross examinations. In court Mandela maintained his dignity. Rugby, he said, was a national asset and that it was his duty to ensure its proper administration. Luyt's reputation, Mandela noted, was that of a 'pitiless dictator'.[75] Judge de Villiers not only disagreed but, in his full judgment, delivered several months later, lambasted Mandela, accusing him of using the witness box as a 'political podium'![76]

The reaction of the ANC government, and particularly of the Minister for Sport, to the court's decision against the legality of the commission of enquiry revealed dangerous levels of political immaturity. Forgetting his position as a government minister in a state whose constitution allows the judiciary to review executive decisions, Tshwete dismissed de Villiers's ruling and called for an international boycott of Springbok rugby.[77] The government, he said, would force SARFU to cancel forthcoming rugby tests against Australia, New Zealand, Wales, Ireland and England. Tshwete's outbursts sent shivers through southern hemisphere rugby circles. However, his confidence in 'the rugby people' of Australia and New Zealand, and his belief that they would 'take their lead from their governments and [that] their governments [would] take their lead from [the South African] government',[78] was grossly misplaced. the Australian journalist Philip Derriman correctly questioned Tswhete's assumptions: 'it is by no means certain that Canberra would wish to intervene in what is really a domestic row and, even if it did, it is by no means certain that the Australian Rugby Union would fall into line'.[79] The weight of history supported Derriman.

Equally puerile was the reaction of the traditional beneficiaries of apartheid, who began to bleat about their loss of democratic rights. Luyt called Mandela's commission of enquiry 'draconian', 'unconstitutional' and 'in violation of fundamental human rights'.[80] Z.B. du Toit, a senior political reporter with *Rapport*, offered a longer, but just as fatuous, version:

What did Louis Luyt do that he should resign as president of the South African Rugby Football Union? To date … [those who] … want an answer with thorough evidence to this question have struck a blank. The claim was still that rugby, as a whole, needed to be investigated. It was like accusing a person of being a thief on the basis of vague allegations. Nobody is really interested any more in the grounds for this charge – Luyt has merely been found guilty, and sentenced. And, in the process, he has been successfully demonised. [There is a] democratic principle that limits should be placed on the state's power in terms of its rights to interfere in the affairs of autonomous organisations in civilian society. [South Africa] is exhibiting the characteristics of a one-party state more and more, it is essential that institutions that are part of the civil society retain a great deal of autonomy. Not only the supreme authority of the law but also individuals' free and unfettered access to the courts have been endangered by the Luyt debacle.[81]

Du Toit's polemic conveniently ignored 40 years of apartheid repression and the apartheid state's consistent circumvention of judicial decisions. The apartheid state not only demonized black people, because of the colour of their skin, it detained and clandestinely murdered thousands of black opponents.[82] In the same vein, the apartheid state denied civil institutions, such as sport, any form of autonomy.[83]

The ANC and the NSC issued one simple demand to Luyt and his executive: resign. Luyt refused. Displaying characteristic arrogance and belligerence, he said that 'no man is my master and I bow to no man, only to God. My resolve has not changed'.[84] The crisis continued as the ANC and the NSC extended their deadline from 11 April to 8 May. The second deadline also passed when Luyt suddenly and unexpectedly resigned. Most commentators attributed his departure to the threat of an international boycott. However, the ANC and the NSC had finally outmanoeuvred Luyt. First, they subjected four black members to intense pressure and 'persuaded' them to resign from SARFU's executive.[85] Secondly, they made plans to disband SARFU and set up an alternative structure that would control the game in South Africa and preserve all existing financial contracts. The object was to totally isolate Luyt.[86]

Conclusion

Have the ANC and the NSC defeated Afrikaner and white nationalists in the struggle to control rugby? The answer is unclear. Luyt is no longer president of SARFU, although he remained as president of the Gauteng Rugby Football Union (formerly the TRFU) and chairman of Ellis Park (a limited company listed on the Johannesburg Stock Exchange) after 1998. In these positions he is an integral part of South African rugby – and a potential disruptive force. Certainly his brand of hostility survives in South African rugby crowds. Even after their team defeated Australia in August and won the 1998 Tri-Nations Cup, the Ellis Park crowd jeered Luyt's successor Silas Nkanunu, when he stepped on to the field to present the trophy.[87] New administrative structures, however, would appear to make a Luyt resurrection impossible. SARFU will shortly have a new constitution that increases the power of the CEO and relegates the president to an essentially honorary title. The CEO (the present incumbent is Luyt's son-in-law Rian Oberholzer, although the pair have 'fallen-out') will report to a smaller, NSC-dominated board that will determine policy.[88]

Fundamental structural changes within rugby, however, complicate the politics. Marketeers, sponsors and television moguls now share control of the game with nationalist ideologues. Rupert Murdoch's News Corporation, for example, is a funding lifeline that keeps southern hemisphere rugby alive via the Tri-Nations Cup and the Super 12 competition. The ANC has been quick to recognize the importance of these changes. As Black and Nauright point out, the South African government now sees international rugby as a means to encourage tourism and to foster wider economic development.[89]

Discussing this shift, Black and Nauright raise an interesting question: what effect will rugby's 'global connections and economic influences' have on the nationalizing of South Africa and, more specifically, on whites?[90] In their analysis of rugby league in 'the age of globalisation', David Rowe and Geoffrey Lawrence caution against overstating the impact of 'globalising forces', which, they argue, 'must be "grounded" somewhere': 'the media infrastructure may exist to carry a minor (in world terms) sport like rugby league to the screens of content-hungry pay TV providers, but the foundation on which this world-wide dissemination can take place ... must be local, regional and national culture'.[91]

South Africa, of course, faces the problem of an exceedingly fragile national culture. Indeed, in his four-hour 'enemies of change' speech at the ANC's fiftieth conference in December 1997, Nelson Mandela, the champion of reconciliation, warned that the rainbow nation was unravelling. The South African journalist Lizeka Mda agrees:

the prospect of integration holds no appeal for the majority of

South Africans whatsoever. Splashing some colour on to our landscape has not changed the way we view things: in black and white. We may live in the same suburbs, to some extent, but we may just as well be on different planets for all the integration there is. The two nations concept is reinforced every time there is a sports event. The national anthem, a cop-out that is really two songs – *Nkosi Sikelel' iAfrika* from the struggle camp, followed by *Die Stem* from the apartheid establishment – finishes with *Sechaba sa Heso* for the spectators at Soccer City, while it only begins with *Uit die Blou* at Loftus Versveld or Newlands.[92]

Yet, paradoxically, the forces of globalization offer the ANC a 'local rhetoric' to gloss over the lack of nationalization. It is a rhetoric which, in the words of Rowe and Lawrence, promises, *inter alia*, to 'advertise' event locations as 'international tourist destinations', 'support local junior sport', 'contribute to local economies', and include 'local teams and their cities/regions [in] competitions involving the "best of the best"'.[93] This rhetoric will not recapture the lost moment of 1995 but it will ameliorate some of the frustration.

NOTES

All newspapers cited are from South Africa unless indicated otherwise.

1. 'Moment of Unity Has Been Lost', *Mail and Guardian*, 31 October 1997.
2. *Rugby and the South African Nation* (Manchester, 1998), pp. 152–3.
3. Edward Griffiths, 'Heart of the Matter', *SA Sports Illustrated*, 14 April 1997, p. 17.
4. Etienne Balibar, 'The Nation Form: History and Ideology', in Balibar and Immanuel Wallerstein, *Race, Nation, Class: Ambiguous Identities* (London, 1991), p. 96.
5. Lincoln Allison, 'The Changing Context of Sporting Life', in Allison (ed.), *The Changing Politics of Sport* (Manchester, 1993), pp. 4–5.
6. Grant Jarvie, 'Sport, Nationalism and Cultural Identity', in Allison, *The Changing Politics of Sport*, p. 74.
7. Jarvie, 'Sport, Nationalism and Cultural Identity', p. 76.
8. Albert Grundlingh, 'Playing for Power? Rugby, Afrikaner Nationalism and Masculinity in South Africa, c.1900–c.1970', in John Nauright and Timothy J.L. Chandler (eds), *Making Men: Rugby and Masculine Identity* (London, 1996), pp. 181–204.
9. Robert Archer and Antoine Bouillon, *The South African Game: Sport and Racism* (London, 1982), p. 73.
10. Racial classification was a hallmark of apartheid and pre-apartheid South Africa. The principal racial groups were African, Coloured (people of mixed race), Indian and white. Members of the first three groups were collectively referred to as blacks. Many black organizations, including sporting groups, that rejected racial classification subscribed to a non-racial, or colour-blind, philosophy.

11. See for example, Archer and Bouillon, *The South African Game*, pp. 121–2; and T. Dunbar Moodie, *The Rise of Afrikanerdom* (Berkeley, 1975), p. 246.

12. Finlay Macdonald, *The Game of Our Lives* (Auckland, 1996), p. 78; 80–2.

13. Richard Lapchick, *The Politics of Race and International Sport* (Westport, CT, 1975), p. 3.

14. Republic of South Africa (RSA), *House of Assembly Debates*, 1971, cols. 5031–2.

15. 'Sport and Apartheid', *Current Affairs Bulletin*, Vol.46, No.12, 1970, pp. 188–9.

16. The South African Rugby Union subscribed to a non-racial philosophy (see n.10) while the South African Rugby Board was a racist, whites-only organization.

17. The first policy shift occurred in 1967. See RSA, *House of Assembly Debates*, cols. 3959–68.

18. South African Institute of Race Relations (SAIRR), *A Survey of Race Relations in South Africa, 1975* (Johannesburg, 1976), p. 279.

19. SAIRR, *A Survey of Race Relations in South Africa, 1976* (Johannesburg, 1977), p. 394.

20. Ibid., *1976*, pp. 394–5.

21. Ibid., *1977* (Johannesburg, 1978), p. 564.

22. Ibid., *1980* (Johannesburg, 1981), p. 595.

23. 'The Future of Sport in Post-apartheid South Africa', *Time*, 29 May 1995.

24. In the early hours of 17 June 1992 an Inkatha *impi* (battalion) from the KwaMadala hostel (Vanderbijlpark, Southern Transvaal), allegedly assisted by South African police, massacred 42 residents in an adjacent squatter settlement known as Boipatong. On 7 September 70,000 ANC supporters staged a protest march in Bisho, capital of the Ciskei homeland. Ciskei troops, under the command of a colonel seconded from the South African Defence Force, opened fire and killed 28 people.

25. In April 1993 Janusz Walus, a Polish emigré linked with the Conservative Party and the paramilitary *Afrikaner Weerstandsbeweging*, assassinated the popular and militant leader.

26. In recognition of the apartheid state's increasing tolerance of racial mixing, non-racial groups adopted the term 'establishment' to refer to state-sponsored structures and organizations. Hence establishment sport refers to the white-dominated network of clubs, national associations and umbrella federations intertwined with the apartheid state.

27. During the apartheid era the anti-apartheid sports movement consisted of the South African Non-Racial Olympic Committee (SAN-ROC), the South African Council on Sport (SACOS) and the National Sports Congress (NSC). SAN-ROC was formed in the early 1960s but state harassment forced its leaders into exile. SACOS was formed in 1973 and became the internal wing of the sports liberation movement. In 1989 a number of officials split from SACOS and formed the NSC which aligned itself to the ANC.

28. 'New sports symbols likely', *City Press*, 19 May 1995.

29. 'Craven Says Bok Colours "not negotiable"', *Sunday Star*, 20 October 1991.

30. 'CP Vows to Keep Springbok Emblem', *The Citizen*, 31 July 1994.

31. 'Sport, Sport, Sport!', *Die Patriot*, 5 July 1991.

32. 'End of Argument', *Sunday Times*, 22 September 1991.

33. 'Readers Say No to Flag', *City Press*, 1 December 1991. The paper gave no indication of the number of callers.

34. 'Springbok a Symbol of Divided Past', *Sunday Star*, 3 November 1991.

35. '*Trane oor vlag en volkslied*', *Rapport*, 16 August 1992. See also John Nauright, '"A Besieged Tribe"?: Nostalgia, White Cultural Identity and the Role of Rugby in a Changing South Africa', *International Review for the Sociology of Sport*,

Vol.31, No.1, 1996, pp. 69–84.

36. 'Score One for Bad Behaviour', *Newsweek*, 23 November 1992.
37. 'New Row Threatens Rugby Tours', *The Citizen*, 1 April 1992.
38. 'Putting the Freeze on Sport', *New Nation*, 26 June 1992. See also, 'ANC Wants Reimposition of Sports Moratorium', *The Citizen*, 25 June 1992.
39. Heribert Adam and Kogila Moodley, *The Negotiated Revolution* (Johannesburg: 1993), p. 27.
40. 'Some Time before Blacks Become Rugby Heroes', *The Star*, 13 June 1994. For the story of the Watson family see Kristin Williamson, *Brothers to Us* (Melbourne, 1997).
41. 'Springbok in the Firing Line', *Sunday Times*, 26 February 1995.
42. Sharon Chetty, 'Rugby ... the Last White Outpost', *Sowetan*, 20 April 1995; see also 'When Fans Turn Blind to Colour', *Sunday Times*, 23 April 1995.
43. Injured during the test against Western Samoa, the Coloured player Chester Williams returned to the Springbok side only midway through the tournament.
44. 'Mandela: I am Proud of Boks', *The Citizen*, 25 May 1995.
45. 'Mandela Adores Cricket', *Cape Times*, 19 October 1991; 'Mandela: I am proud of Boks', *The Citizen*, 25 May 1995.
46. Adam and Moodley, *The Negotiated Revolution*, p. 43.
47. 'SARFU Director Balfour Resigns', *Cape Times*, 4 September 1993.
48. 'Score One for Bad Behaviour', *Newsweek*, 23 November 1992; Tommy Bedford, 'New Body, Same Old Face', *Guardian Weekly*, 27 November 1992.
49. Recounted by Tim Noakes, University of Natal, Pietermaritzburg, public lecture, 25 October 1995.
50. Editorial, *Sowetan*, 25 May 1995.
51. Balibar, 'The Nation Form', pp. 93–5.
52. '*Amabokoboko*', *Sowetan*, 26 May 1995; editorial, *Sowetan*, 29 May 1995.
53. Balibar, 'The Nation Form', pp. 98–9. See also Barry Hindess, 'Actors and Social Relations', in Mark Wardell and Stephen Turner (eds), *Sociological Theory in Transition* (Boston, MA, Allen & Unwin, 1988), p. 118.
54. 'On Top of the World', *Sowetan*, 26 June 1995.
55. *City Press*, 25 June 1995.
56. 'Tutu Sports "Magic" Bok Symbol', *The Star*, 21 July 1995.
57. 'Pride of the Nation', *The Star*, 26 June 1995; 'Boks "Help Build Nation"', *Cape Times*, 17 August 1995.
58. Donald McRae, 'Second Phase Is Taking an Age', *Mail and Guardian*, 27 June 1997.
59. Aggrey Klaaste, 'Strange Things Are Happening to a Closet Racist', *Sowetan*, 9 January 1995; 'Debate over Springbok Emblem Ignited', *Business Day*, 27 June 1995.
60. 'Keep Bok Emblem: Mandela', *The Citizen*, 26 June 1995.
61. Jean-Paul Sartre, *Critique of Dialectical Reason* (London, 1976), pp. 259–60, 300, 474.
62. Fred Rundle in 'Mandela's Bok Pride', *Eastern Province Herald*, 24 June 1995.
63. S.H. Gregan (letter), *The Citizen*, 29 June 1995. Marais was the leader of the far-right *Herstigte Nasionale Party*.
64. 'After the Vivas Are Over', *City Press*, 2 July 1995.
65. Victor Tsuai, 'Springbok – Sad Relic of the Past', *Sowetan*, 29 June 1995. See also editorial, *New Nation*, 30 June 1995.
66. *Shame* (London, 1983), p. 24.
67. Black and Nauright, *Rugby and the South African Nation*, p. 151.
68. Peter FitzSimons, *The Rugby War* (Sydney, 1996).

69. Jon Swift, 'Selections that Won't Change Perceptions', *Mail and Guardian*, 16 August 1996.
70. Max du Preez, 'Question and Answer', SATV3, 25 February 1997.
71. 'Why Louis Can't Lose', *Mail and Guardian*, 31 October 1997.
72. Denis Barnett, AFP, Cape Town, 10 February 1998, C-afp@clari.net.
73. McNeil Hendriks, Deon Kayser, Breyton Paulse and Chester Williams.
74. Black and Nauright, *Rugby and the South African Nation*, pp. 148–9.
75. 'Mandela Makes History in Court', *Mail and Guardian*, 20 March 1998.
76. 'Which Trial Was the Judge at?', *Mail and Guardian*, 14 August 1998.
77. Linda Rulashe, 'Louis Luyt Won't Step Down from SARFU Presidency without a Fight', *City Press*, 10 May 1998.
78. Philip Derriman, 'Black and White Mauls', *Sydney Morning Herald*, 3 April 1998.
79. Ibid.
80. 'Luyt: a Lot Lighter, but not Budging', *Mail and Guardian*, 8 May 1998.
81. Z.B. du Toit, 'In This Witch-hunt, No One Gives a Damn if Luyt is Guilty or Not', *City Press*, 10 May 1998.
82. See, for example, Kader Asmal, Louise Asmal and Robert Suresh Roberts, *Reconciliation through Truth* (Cape Town, 2nd edn, 1997); Antjie Krog, *Country of My Skull* (Johannesburg, 1998).
83. Douglas Booth, *The Race Game: Sport and Politics in South Africa* (London, 1998), Ch.3.
84. 'Luyt: a Lot Lighter'.
85. Rulashe, 'Louis Luyt Won't Step Down'. The four resignations were Silas Nkanunu, Tobie Titus, Jackie Abrahams and Arthob Peterson. Later they joined a SARFU delegation that met Mandela and apologized for dragging him into court.
86. 'Luyt Loop!', *Rapport*, 10 May 1998. Luyt told *Rapport* that he had been 'sold out' by the SARFU executive.
87. Nkanunu was also one of the four black members whose resignation from SARFU prompted Luyt's departure.
88. 'Black President for Rugby', *Mail and Guardian*, 22 May 1998.
89. Black and Nauright, *Rugby and the South African Nation*, pp. 152–3.
90. Ibid., pp. 153–4.
91. 'Framing a Critical Sports Sociology in the Age of Globalisation', in David Rowe and Geoffrey Lawrence (eds), *Tourism, Leisure, Sport: Critical Perspectives* (Sydney, Hodder Education, 1998), p. 166.
92. 'Has the Rainbow Faded For Ever?', *Mail and Guardian*, 27 December 1997.
93. Rowe and Lawrence, 'Framing a Critical Sports Sociology', p. 166.

Conclusion: A Rugby World or Worlds of Rugby?

John Nauright and Timothy J.L. Chandler

In the conclusion to *Making Men* we suggested that there were a number of themes in analysing rugby that we had not addressed in that book and that required further investigation. Here we have endeavoured to take up our own challenge through an examination of rugby beyond the confines of the predominantly 'white old boys' of the British Isles and settler empire. In so doing we have attempted to uncover how rugby was adopted, adapted, incorporated and/or assimilated in other cultural contexts. We have attempted to assess the degree to which the traditional masculine ethos of the game penetrated other cultures and to ask to what degree its diffusion was the product of emulation and/or integration as much as penetration and/or accommodation. In the first section, which has as its focus the issue of race in the development of rugby in the British Empire, MacLean and Nauright show that, for both Maori in New Zealand and Coloureds in Cape Town, rugby did not remain a static, cultural form immune from local influences. In New Zealand, Maori cultural forms were incorporated within a wider rugby culture that remained white-dominated, yet one which did not neglect the Maori. In South Africa, however, segregation practised by white sportsmen meant that rugby in black communities was ignored by whites. Indeed, even in the 1980s and the 1990s many white South Africans were unaware of the vibrant and rich historical black rugby cultures in their own country. Many white South Africans know more about the Maori, at least as mediated through their rugby relationship with New Zealand, than about the black rugby cultures in their own country.

In the second section of the book we looked at the expansion of rugby in non-British settings, focusing attention specifically on four distinct case studies of the diffusion of the game, raising questions about the degree to which it was accommodated and integrated within the local cultural milieu and the extent to which it remained an 'authorized' rather than a 'received' version of the game. To what extent was the traditional masculine culture of the English public school associated with the game in these 'other' environments? In France and Italy rugby arrived as part of an elite, anglophile masculinity in the late nineteenth and the early twentieth century, as leading continental men such as Baron de Coubertin thought British games-playing contributed to a making of men that was lacking on the continent. In Italy the game was taken up as part of the Fascists' efforts to create a militarily-prepared populace. In the USA the game was an alternative to gridiron football and an emblem of resistance in student culture. In Japan the game was imbued with the *samurai* warrior ethos and became a means of educating young men in the class values of that ancient elite class. In all these cases the game was developed by university students who had either experienced it outside their own country and returned home with it or as visiting students from abroad who had brought the game with them. The contributors of these chapters have argued that it is not without significance that young men, crossing the threshold between adolescence and manhood, who were preparing to move out into the world and become independent were responsible for the development of the game. In struggling to display their independence and their manliness these students developed a 'separate sphere' where they could undergo their rite of passage. Thus one of the major themes that emerges from these chapters in particular, but from the adoption of rugby in educational institutions in general, has been the game's apparent strength as a pedagogical tool.

The Victorian English are not the only ones who have seen pedagogical value in rugby. As Bonini has demonstrated in the case of Fascist Italy, although initially condemned for being a foreign game, rugby became a central tool in the regime's efforts to develop strong, muscular men for military and national service. And as Light has demonstrated for many Japanese high schools, rugby has become one of their leading sports with the national championship receiving widespread media attention. Rugby in Japan has been fused with older Japanese traditions in efforts to teach boys desired forms of behaviour centred on codes of honour and sacrifice. Likewise in France, as Terret has shown, while rugby was seen primarily as a way of displaying the characteristics of a particular form of masculinity it was also adopted as a way of imbuing those characteristics. Beyond these four specific case studies it should also be noted that, while becoming a central part of local Coloured culture and male physicality in Cape Town, rugby changed significantly from its original form; but it was still strongly encouraged by school teachers who believed in its ability to turn boys into men. Thus while we can see that rugby's culture and playing styles are grounded in localized contexts, at the same time the game itself is often employed as a means of teaching a range of other values such as group cohesion, self-sacrifice, team spirit and trust in male groups.

The third section attempted to move beyond this male limitation by focusing upon gender and rugby outside the confines of the traditional, masculine cultures that have surrounded the game. In the same way that Light adopted an ethnographic approach in attempting to understand the integration of Western values of masculinity, fair play, and athleticism with Japanese notions of honour *seishin, konjo, enyo* and *gaman,* so Carle and Nauright have also employed ethnography to 'unpack' the meanings of rugby to a group of women in Australia. In so doing they have attempted a rearticulation of masculinity since, for over a century, rugby has been closely linked to concepts of masculinity. Many male educationalists have argued that rugby is one of the best tools for instilling physical virtues, with such notions being grounded in the belief that the nature of the game and its style teach such virtues as self-discipline, loyalty and self-sacrifice. Yet, as Carle and Nauright have shown, women also believe that it is these same qualities that attract them to rugby. This is especially the case when we examine how players feel about playing the game. They make a supreme effort to aid and protect their teammates. Rugby indeed generates intense friendships that emerge from each player's willingness to put her body on the line for the good of the team. Players are able to do this because they know that each team member will do the same for them and will come to their rescue when necessary. These same virtues were thought to make good soldiers who would then be prepared to make the ultimate sacrifice for their nation. Yet, ironically, for women at least, such notions have emerged at a time when war was being removed from any direct relationship to physical prowess as servicemen did not even have to go near their enemies in order to inflict damage on them. 'Running through him/her' on the rugby field is no longer the equivalent of 'running him/her through' on the battlefield.

As women's experiences suggest, we need to think carefully about making generic links between rugby and masculinity. It is only through the level of analysis developed from ethnographic study that we have been able to begin to disentangle the relationship between rugby and masculinity and suggest that we cannot proffer an easy causal relationship between the two. Despite the blurring of gendered boundaries in and around rugby, women who play rugby have faced, and in many cases continue to face, widespread condemnation although they appear to enjoy many of the same benefits and also suffer many of the same difficulties (and the same injuries) as men. Additionally, we should ask whether there is something about the structure, form and rules of rugby that helps to create these intense bonds between teammates which Carle and Nauright highlight. As Light notes for the Japanese case, a game is defined by more than its rules, and certainly all the cases reviewed here would suggest that the cultural context is a vital component in any analysis. Yet the structure of the game itself, a game in which support for a teammate in possession of the ball is paramount if success is to be achieved, and a game in which such support has to be of the sort that says literally 'I'm right behind you', does suggest that there may be something in its structure which is worthy of further analysis, particularly in comparison with other contact team sports.

In an effort to look more closely at the organizational and economic aspects of present-day rugby in the fourth and final section, we focused our attention on the impact of commodifying processes on both the nature and the structure of rugby. Recently we have seen shifts in the commodification of leading English soccer clubs such as Manchester United, Leeds United, Newcastle United and Chelsea. All have developed to such a degree that supporters can virtually purchase all their needs from their club. These needs range from clothing to travel and even home mortgages, with larger purchases entitling supporters to discounted match tickets. In rugby league the infusion of capital from television contracts with the Murdoch organization have also seen the emergence of far more sophisticated club shops and the market segmentation of audiences as entertainment is provided. This has involved target-marketing aimed at specific groups ranging from children to sections of youth and younger adult supporters, as well as at the more traditional fan (although as many fanzines point out, the latter has been increasingly overlooked in the commercializing process). Indeed, to the new owners of these globalized sports it is the consumption of the club and its products, whether at the ground, in the shop or via television, that is paramount. In rugby union this process has accelerated rapidly since 1995 with leading clubs in England being bought by owners of other sporting and leisure enterprises as they seek market diversification. A number of such clubs have changed from being membership-based to being limited liability companies. These clubs now run as private enterprises where members have lost their democratic voice within the club and its operation.

How all this affects a 'white old boys' world order' that emerged from specific cultural practices and forms of which rugby union has been a part remains to be seen. Yet it is clear that the commodification of rugby union has led to a recasting of the power relations, both in a cultural and an economic sense, whereby rugby has been reinfused with new forms of masculinity packaged to attract an expansion of the game as its dominant discourses are marketed, bought and sold by those seeking to be a part of 'the game they play in heaven'.... Yet 'belonging' in rugby union cannot merely be bought, it must come from the experience that gives players the social and cultural capital to be 'of rugby'. Indeed, rugby operates internationally as a kind of 'sporting freemasonry' that will not be easily broken down by turning it at top levels into another sporting commodity. Yet, as we conclude in *Making Men*, it is not enough to wallow in a sea of nostalgia in rushing to condemn the forces reshaping the game, but rather, as Howe suggests, we must understand the complex interrelationships between the game and the forces surrounding it if we are to have any chance of shaping it in the future.

If the beginning of a new year offers opportunities for resolutions and the beginning of a new century offers the opportunity for pundits to make predictions for the lifetime of the current generation, then a new millennium ought to produce a bonanza of ideas about the future. In fact the pundits have found it hard to make predictions for the last year of the twentieth century let alone look around the corner to the next millennium. The future of rugby, they say, is far too uncertain to make long-term predictions. Some of the pundits at the end of the twentieth century are unwilling to go further than to say that the 1999 Rugby World Cup will be a financial and sporting success. They then 'cover' themselves by noting that ticket prices are too high and are excluding the genuine fan,[1] (although arguably the genuine rugby fan is better able to afford high ticket prices than the fan of many other sports) and that, because there will be 20 teams taking part in the final stages, there are likely to be some terrible mismatches and the awful possibility of a tragedy because of a broken neck from a collapsed scrum brought about by an imbalance in technique and strength.[2] Others have looked at the professionalization of the game and see rugby attracting many of the problems associated with other high-level professional sports. The pressures to win and to play injured will make drug use a high-profile issue, as it has already become in Australian rugby league. Other problems associated with the rapid development of a transfer market for players and coaches and the loss of opportunities for 'home-grown' players are also seen as being highly problematic elements of rugby's perceived future. The further influx of southern hemisphere stars into northern hemisphere clubs is expected to 'make the money-go-round spin even faster'.[3]

The IRB is currently working on a proposal to seek the (re-) acceptance of rugby as an Olympic sport for the Games in Athens in 2004. Many believe that we are unlikely to see rugby as a full Olympic sport until the games of 2008. (Crystal ball-gazers are predicting that Italy will play Argentina for the gold medal!) What is clear from a review of these and many other predictions is that rugby at the international and the national level is currently a sport very much in transition and that its future is far from clear. Thus the formation of new British, European and American leagues are all current possibilities. The need to embrace the values (and likewise the salaries) of the entertainment industry in order to survive as a professional sport, as posited by some of the pundits,[4] is likely to mean that the game will become available only to those in the upper income brackets. It may thus maintain something of its white old boy image, ethos and many of the upper-middle-class values for which it has long been noted, particularly in the British Isles and the settler societies of the Commonwealth. It may no longer be a sport that promotes class consciousness, but it may indeed continue to engender a consciousness of class.[5]

It is clear that the game of rugby union is markedly different today than when it first began to be played in the English public schools in the nineteenth century. Yet, despite the changes wrought by professionalism, the taking of rugby to new places and the playing of rugby by women in numerous places throughout the world, rugby has retained many elements within the game and its surrounding culture that would have been readily recognizable in the past. Having said this, it is also clear that in different geographical and cultural contexts playing and watching styles have altered the game and its culture. As we have endeavoured to show, rugby, played by colonized men, men from non-British cultures and women, while still clearly rugby, is no monolithic form. Still, there is something about the game that leads its adherents to call it reverently 'the game they play in heaven'. But is rugby really different from any other sport? Does it really have unique qualities as we began to suggest above?

Although differences within rugby in its several contexts are significant, we posit that there are some generalizations that need to be made about the form of rugby and the loyalty it generates. We have seen in several chapters the intense emotionality tied to the playing of rugby, its role as a teacher and definer of masculinities and the ways that rugby resonates strongly in communities that have been marginalized historically, either by region, class, race or gender. In the south of France, the smaller Italian cities, Coloured Cape Town and for

Maori and Pacific Island New Zealanders, and for women internationally, rugby has gained an intense loyalty and following. It has done so precisely because it is viewed as a site of resistance, even of the carnivalesque. Rugby in these contexts may be seen as a cultural performance, one that often parodies the rugby of the white old boys' world order. Yet, ultimately, all who play it have been incorporated within a global, rugby-playing fraternity (with some women as honorary 'blokes') which we may refer to as a 'global white (dominated) old boys' world order' led by Will Carling's '57 Old Farts' and their like. Yet even as this 'order' is in the process of becoming truly global, it is under threat from new interests in the game that come from increased commercial sponsorships linked to greater media coverage and interest, new owners of professional clubs and, indeed, players who are paid directly for their services for the first time in the game's history. The last aspect inevitably threatens the fraternal bonds that the rugby team and club generate as a global labour market for talent emerges at the top level. At club level the habitus in which rugby is played is challenged by these new forces, although the end result of this process will not be known for some time. It remains to be seen whether conviviality and sociability, such important reasons for participation in many sports, are maintained as central facets of rugby club culture. An analysis of these developments will no doubt be crucial in our understanding of the impact of the rapid professionalization and commercialization of rugby in the early twenty-first century. We hope that in *Making Men* and in this present work we have gone some way towards a construction of the historical and cultural underpinnings of modern rugby and the changes that have taken place as it has globalized and diversified. These processes are on-going and, as such, much more research on the history and contemporary issues of rugby union and rugby cultures is needed.

NOTES

1. Prices for a ticket to the final were planned, initially, to cost £150 and for the semi-finals £100.
2. Paul Ackford, 'The World at Our Feet', *Sunday Telegraph* (London), 27 December 1998.
3. Robert Armstrong, 'Boom or Bust in the Fast Lane', *The Guardian* (London) , 1 January 1999.
4. See Armstrong, 'Boom or Bust'.
5. See David Cannadine, *Class in Britain* (London, 1998), Introduction.

Select Bibliography

BOOKS

Adam, Heribert, and Kogila Moodley, *The Negotiated Revolution* (Johannesburg: 1993).

Alban-Lebecq, Pierre, *Paschal Grousset et la Ligue nationale d'éducation physique* (Paris, 1997).

Anzoletti, Armando Boscolo, *Il Rugby* (Milan, 1951).

Archer, Robert, and Antoine Bouillon, *The South African Game: Sport and Racism* (London, 1982).

Arnaud, Pierre, and Alfred Wahl, *Sports et relations internationales dans l'entre-deux-guerres* (Metz, 1994).

Arnaud, Pierre, and Jean Camy (eds), *La naissance du mouvement sportif associatif en France* (Toulouse, 1986).

Arnaud, Pierre, and Thierry Terret, *Histoire du sport féminin* (Paris, 2 vols, 1996).

Augustin, Jean-Pierre, and Alain Garrigou, *Le rugby démêlé* (Bordeaux, 1985).

Bale, John, and Joe Maguire (eds), *The Global Sports Arena: Athletic Talent Migration in an Interdependent World* (London, 1994).

Belich, James, *The New Zealand Wars and the Victorian Interpretation of Racial Conflict* (Auckland, 1986).

Bianda, Renato, Guiseppe Leone, Gianni Rossi and Adolfo Urso, *Atleti in Camicia Nera. Lo Sport nell'Italia di Mussolini* (Rome, 1983).

Black, David, and John Nauright, *Rugby and the South African Nation: Sport, Cultures, Politics and Power in the Old and New South Africas* (Manchester, 1998).

Blum, René (ed.), *Encyclopédie des sports* (Paris, 1924).

Bodis, Jean-Pierre, *Histoire mondiale du rugby* (Toulouse, 1987).

Booth, Douglas, *The Race Game: Sport and Politics in South Africa* (London, 1998).

Boutilier, M.A., and L. SanGiovanni, *The Sporting Woman* (Champaign, IL, 1983).

Collins, Tony, *Rugby's Great Split: Class, Culture and the Origins of*

Rugby League Football (London, 1998).

Colman, M., *Super League: the Inside Story* (Sydney, 1996).

Colosetti, Gianni, and Nicola Bizzarro, *Rugby razza Piave. Fatti, resultati ed immagini di 25 anni di rugby a San Donà di Piave* (1984).

Connerton, Paul, *How Societies Remember* (Cambridge, 1989).

Coubertin, Pierre de, *L'éducation anglaise en France* (Paris, 1889).

Coubertin, Pierre de, *L'éducation en Angleterre* (Paris, 1888).

Darbon, Sébastien, *Du rugby dans une ville de foot* (Paris, 1997).

Darbon, Sébastien, *Rugby, mode de vie. Ethnographie d'un club. Saint-Vincent-de-Tyrosse* (Paris, 1995).

Dauger, Jean, *Histoires de rugby* (Paris, 1965).

Davisse, Annick, and Catherine Louveau, *Sport, école, société: la part des femmes* (Paris, 1991).

Dumont, Jacques, Gilles Pollet and M. Berjat, *Naissance du sport moderne* (Lyon, 1987).

Dunning, E., and K. Sheard, *Barbarians, Gentlemen and Players: a Sociological Study of the Development of Rugby Football* (Oxford, 1979).

Edwards, H., *The Sociology of Sport* (Homewood, IL, 1973).

Fabbri, Andrea, and Marco Fogli, in Albero Nocenti (ed.), *Il rugby femminile in Italia* (Ferrara, 1992).

Fadda, Pierlugi, and Luciano Ravagnani, *Rugby: storia dalle origini ad oggi* (Milan, 1992).

Featherstone, M., S. Lash and R. Robertson (eds), *Global Modernities* (London, 1995).

Fitzsimons, Peter, *The Rugby War* (London, 1996).

Garcia, Henry, *La fabuleuse histoire du rugby* (Paris, 1992).

Ghirelli, Antonio *Stori del calcio in Italia* (Milan, 1974).

Goldin, Ian, *Making Race: the Politics and Economics of Coloured Identity in South Africa* (London, 1987).

Greenwood, J., *Think Rugby: a Guide to Purposeful Team Play* (London, 1986).

Grosz, Elizabeth, *Volatile Bodies: Towards a Corporeal Feminism* (Sydney, 1994).

Grundlingh, Albert, Andre Odendaal and Burridge Spies, *Beyond the Tryline: Rugby and South African Society* (Johannesburg, 1995)

Hall, M. Ann, *Feminism and Sporting Bodies: Essays on Theory and Practice* (Champaign, IL, 1996).

Hargreaves, Jennifer, *Sporting Females* (London, 1994).

Herman, E.S., and R.W. McChesney, *The Global Media: the New Missionaries of Global Capitalism* (London, 1997).

Holt, Richard, *Sport and Society in Modern France* (London, 1981).
Holt, Richard, *Sport and the British* (Oxford, 1989).
Houlihan, B., *Sport and International Politics* (London, 1994).
Hutchings, Graham, *A Score to Settle: a Celebration of All Black–Springbok Rugby, 1921–1996* (Wellington, 1997).
Ikeguchi, Y., *Kindai no Ragubi Hyaku Nen Kan* [A Hundred Years of Modern Rugby] (Tokyo, 1981).
Jarrat, P., *The Wallabies versus the World* (Sydney, 1987).
Jarvie, G., and J. Maguire, *Sport and Leisure in Social Thought* (London, 1994).
King, Michael, *Maori: a Photographic and Social History* (Auckland, revised edn, 1996).
Lapchick, Richard, *The Politics of Race and International Sport* (Westport, CT, 1975).
Laprévote, Gilles, *Les Ecoles Normales Primaires en France, 1879–1979* (Lyon, 1897).
Lebra, T., *Japanese Social Organization* (Honolulu, 1976).
MacClancy, Jeremy (ed.), *Sport, Identity and Ethnicity* (Oxford, 1996)
Maltby, M., *The Origins and Early Development of Professional Football* (New York, 1997).
Mangan, J.A. (ed.), *The Cultural Bond: Sport, Empire and Society* (London, 1992).
McCarthy, Winston, *Haka!: the All Black Story* (London, 1968).
McCarthy, Winston, and Bob Howitt, *Haka: the Maori Rugby Story* (Auckland, 1983).
McKay, Jim, *Managing Gender: Affirmative Action and Organizational Power in Australian, Canadian and New Zealand Sport* (Albany, 1997).
Messner, M. and D. Sabo (eds), *Sport, Men and the Gender Order* (Champaign, IL, 1990).
Michot, F., *Le Football Rugby* (Paris, 1922).
Morse, B., *California Football History* (Berkeley, CA, 1937).
Mrozek, D., *Sport and American Mentality 1880–1910* (Knoxville, TN, 1983).
Nauright, John, *Sport, Cultures and Identities in South Africa* (London, 1997).
Nauright, John, and Timothy J.L. Chandler (eds), *Making Men: Rugby and Masculine Identity* (London, 1996; revised reprint, 1999).
Nelson, Mariah Burton, *The Stronger Women Get, the More Men Love Football: Sexism and the American Culture of Sports* (New York, 1994).
Nocenti, A. (ed.), *Il rugby femminile in Italia* (Ferrara, 1992).

Oriard, M., *Reading Football: How the Popular Press Created an American Spectacle* (Chapel Hill, NC, 1993).

Ormezzano, Gian Paolo, *Storia del calcio* (Milan, 1990).

Pastre, G., *Histoire générale du rugby* (Toulouse, 5 vols, 1958–72).

Pearson, David, *A Dream Deferred: the Origins of Ethnic Conflict in New Zealand* (Wellington, 1990).

Pivato, Stefano, *L'era dello Sport* (Guinti, 1994).

Pociello, Christian (ed.), *Sport et société* (Paris, 1981).

Pociello, Christian, *Le rugby ou la guerre des styles* (Paris, 1983).

Pope, S.W., *Patriotic Games: Sporting Traditions in the American Imagination 1876-1926* (New York, 1997).

Rohlen, T., *Japanese High Schools* (Berkeley, 1983).

Ryan, Greg, *Forerunners of the All Blacks: the 1888–89 New Zealand Native Football Team in Britain, Australia and New Zealand* (Christchurch, 1993).

Sharp, Andrew, *Justice and the Maori: Maori Claims in New Zealand Political Argument in the 1980s* (Auckland, 2nd edn, 1997).

Sinclair, Keith, *A Destiny Apart: New Zealand's Search for National Identity* (Wellington, 1986).

Smith, Dai, and Gareth Williams, *Fields of Praise: Official History of the Welsh Rugby Union 1881–1981* (Cardiff, 1980).

Smith, Ronald, *Sports and Freedom* (London, 1988).

Somerville, David, *Encyclopedia of Rugby Union* (London, 1997)

Spoonley, Paul, Cluny Macpherson, David Pearson and Charles Sedgwick (eds), *Tauiwi: Racism and Ethnicity in New Zealand* (Palmerston North, 1984).

Stell, Marion, *Half the Race: a History of Australian Women in Sport* (Sydney, 1991).

Sugimoto, Y., *An Introduction to Japanese Society* (Cambridge, 1997).

Taylor, E.W., *Why the All Blacks Triumphed* (London, 1906).

Terret, Thierry (ed.), *Histoire des sports* (Paris, 1996).

Thibault, Jacques, *Sport et éducation physique: 1870–1970* (Paris, 1972) .

Whannel, G., *Fields in Vision: Television Sport and Cultural Transformation* (London, 1992).

Whiting, R., *You've Got to Have Wa* (New York, 1990).

Williams, G., *1905 and All That* (Llandysul, 1991).

Wyatt, D., *Rugby Disunion: the Making of Three World Cups* (London, 1995).

Zavos, Spiro, *Winters of Revenge: the Bitter Rivalry between the All Blacks and the Springboks* (Auckland, 1997).

BOOK EXTRACTS

Allison, Lincoln, 'The Changing Context of Sporting Life', in Allison (ed.), *The Changing Politics of Sport* (Manchester, 1993).

Augustin, Jean-Pierre, and Jean-Pierre Bodis. 'Le rugby français, ses champs d'action et son autonomie jusqu'en 1939', in Paul Voincvel, *Mon beau rugby* (Toulouse, 4th edn, 1948).

Birrell, Susan, and Nancy Theberge, ' Ideological Control of Women in Sport', in Margaret Costa and Susan Guthrie (eds), *Women and Sport: Interdisciplinary Perspectives* (New York, 1994).

Bodis, Jean-Pierre, 'Rugby et enseignement en France jusqu'au début de la seconde guerre mondiale', in Pierre Arnaud and Thierry Terret (eds), *Education et politique sportives* (Paris, 1995).

Brohm, Jean-Marie, 'Pierre de Coubertin et l'avènement du sport bourgeois', in Pierre Arnaud (ed.), *Les athlètes de la République* (Toulouse, 1987).

Dunning, Eric, 'Sport as a Male Preserve: Notes on the Social Acceptance of Masculine Identity and Its Transformations', in Susan Birrell and Cheryl Cole (eds), *Women, Sport, and Culture* (Champaign, 1994), pp. 163–79.

Fabrizio, Felice, 'Storia dello sport in Italia', in E. Guaraldi (ed.), *Dalle società ginanstiche all'associazionismo di massa* (Firenze, 1977), pp. 267–80.

Invernichi, Aldo, 'Rugby', in Eugenio Enrile (ed.), *Encyclopedia dello Sport* (Rome, 1997), pp. 977–1017.

Moeran, B., 'Individual, Group and *Seishin*: Japan's internal cultural debate', in T. Lebra and W. Lebra (eds), *Japanese Culture and Behaviour* (Honolulu, 1986).

Tasker, N., 'The World Cup: a Concept Born of Necessity', in N. Tasker (ed.), *Rugby World Cup 87: ABC Guide* (Crows Nest, NSW, 1987), p. 4.

Wheatley, Elizabeth, 'Subcultural Subversions: Comparing Discourses on Sexuality in Men's and Women's Rugby Songs', in Susan Birrell and Cheryl Cole (eds), *Women, Sport, and Culture* (Champaign, 1994), p. 207.

PERIODICAL ARTICLES

Abe, L., Y. Kiyohara and K. Nakajima, 'Sport and Physical Education under Fascistization in Japan', *Bulletin of Health and Sports Sciences,* Vol.13 (1990), pp. 25–46.

Bale, John, 'Women's Football in England: a Socio-Geographic

Perspective', *Physical Education Review*, Vol.3, No.2 (1980), p. 137.

Chandler, T.J.L., 'Games at Oxbridge and the Public Schools, 1800–1880: the Diffusion of an Innovation', *International Journal of the History of Sport*, Vol.8, No.2 (1991), pp. 171–204.

Donnelly, P., 'The Local and the Global: Globalization in the Sociology of Sport', *Journal of Sport and Social Issues*, Vol.20, No.3 (1996), pp. 239–57.

Donnelly, P., and K. Young, 'Reproduction and Transformation of Cultural Forms in Sport: a Contextual Analysis of Rugby', *International Review for the Sociology of Sport*, Vol.20, No.1 (1985).

Duncan, Margaret Carlisle, 'Sports Photographs and Sexual Difference: Images of Women and Men in the 1984 and 1988 Olympic Games', *Sociology of Sport Journal*, Vol.7, No.1 (1990), pp. 22–43.

Duncan, Margaret Carlisle, and Cynthia Hasbrook, 'Denial of Power in Televised Women's Sports', *Sociology of Sport Journal*, Vol.5, No.1 (1988), pp. 1–21.

Horton, Peter, 'Rugby Union Football and Its Role in the Socio-Cultural Development of Queensland, 1882–1891', *International Journal of the History of Sport*, Vol.9, No.1 (1992), pp. 119–31.

Lynch, M., and P. Lynch, 'World in Union or World in Super League', *International Rugby Review*, September/October 1995, p. 12.

Magdalinski, Tara, 'Organized Remembering: the Construction of Sporting Traditions in the German Democratic Republic, *European Review of Sports History*, Vol.1, 1998.

Maguire, J., 'Globalisation, Sport Development and the Media/Sport Production Complex', *Sport Science Review*, Vol.2, No.1 (1993), pp. 29-47.

Martin, M.,'Kickoff: Making Money for the Game', *Rugby World*, Issue 24 (December 1995), p. 28.

McKay, J., G. Lawrence, T. Miller and D. Rowe, 'Globalization and Australian Sport', *Sport Science Review*, Vol.2, No.1 (1993), p. 18.

Messner, M., 'Sport and Male Domination: the Female Athlete as Contested Ideological Terrain', *Sociology of Sport Journal*, Vol.5, No.3 (1988), pp. 197–211.

Messner, M., 'When Bodies Are Weapons: Masculinity and Violence in Sport', *International Review for the Sociology of Sport*, Vol.25, No.3 (1990), pp. 203–17.

Nauright, John, '"A Besieged Tribe"?: Nostalgia, White Cultural Identity and the Role of Rugby in a Changing South Africa',

International Review for the Sociology of Sport, Vol.31, No.1, 1996, pp. 69–84.

Nauright, John, 'Sport, Manhood and Empire: British Responses to the New Zealand Rugby Tour of 1905', *International Journal of the History of Sport*, Vol.8, No.2 (September 1991), pp.239–55.

O'Brien, Daniel, and Trevor Slack, 'Deinstitutionalizing the Amateur Ethic: an Empirical Examination of Change in a Rugby Union Football Club', *Sport Management Review* (forthcoming).

Park, Roberta, 'From Football to Rugby – and Back, 1906–1919: the University of California–Stanford University Response to the "Football Crisis of 1905"', *Journal of Sport History*, Vol.11, No.3 (1984), pp. 1–36.

Phillips, J.O.C., 'Rugby, War and the Mythology of the New Zealand Male', *New Zealand Journal of History*, Vol.18, No.2 (1984), pp. 83–103.

Pirinen, R., 'Catching up with Men?: Finnish Newspaper Coverage of Women's Entry into Traditionally Male Sports', *International Review for the Sociology of Sport*, Vol.32, No.3 (1997), pp. 239–49.

Rowe, D.,'The Global Love-Match: Sport and Television', *Media, Culture and Society*, Vol.18, No.4 (1996), p. 565.

Rowe, D., G. Lawrence, T. Miller and J. McKay, 'Global Sport? Core Concern and Peripheral Vision', *Media, Culture and Society*, Vol.16, No.4 (1994), p.673.

Ryan, Greg, 'Rugby Football and Society: the "New Zealand Native" Tour of 1888–89', *Historical News* (October 1992), pp. 12–14.

Stoddart, Brian, 'Sport, Cultural Imperialism and Colonial Response in the British Empire', *Comparative Studies in Society & History*, Vol.30, No.4 (1988), pp. 649–73.

Thompson, Shona, 'Challenging the Hegemony: New Zealand Women's Opposition to Rugby and the Reproduction of a Capitalist Patriarchy', *International Review for the Sociology of Sport*, Vol.23, No.3 (1988), p. 206.

Weber, Eugen, 'Gymnastics and Sports in Fin-de-siècle France: Opium of the Classes?', *American Historical Review*, Vol.76, No.1 (1971).

THESES

Carle, A., 'Crossing the Line: Women Playing a "Man's" Game. An Ethnographic Study of a Women's Rugby Union Team in Brisbane', BA Honours thesis, University of Queensland, 1998.

Howe, P.D., 'Commercialising the Body, Professionalising the Game:

the Development of Sports Medicine at Pontypridd Rugby Football Club', PhD thesis, University College, London, 1997.

Palmer, Farah, 'An Ethnographical Study of the Women's Rugby Subculture in New Zealand: Challenging and Contributing to Societal Norms of Femininity', BPhed Honours Thesis, University of Otago, 1994.

Wright, J., 'A Ruffian's Game for Gentlemen: Rugby Football in Sociocultural Contexts', doctoral dissertation, University of Delaware, 1993.

Notes on the Contributors

Gherardo Bonini is Archivist at the Historical Archives of European Communities in Florence, Italy. He has published a range of articles on archival matters and has written a number of contributions to the ABC-CLIO *Encyclopedia of World Sport* (1996) including those on motorcycling and motocross. He has also contributed articles on diving to forthcoming encyclopedias on women's sport and British sport and is the author of the International Cycling Federation's (UCI) website.

Douglas Booth is a senior lecturer in sport and leisure studies in the School of Physical Education at the University of Otago in Dunedin, New Zealand. His 1998 book *The Race Game: Sport and Politics in South Africa* won the book prize for the best book in sports history awarded by the North American Society for Sports History. He has published widely on the history and politics of sport in South Africa, Australia and New Zealand. He is the reviews editor of *Internatonal Sports Studies*.

Alison Carle completed a first class honours degree in Human Movement Studies at the University of Queensland where she undertook an ethnographic study on women's rugby. She is now studying at the University of Memphis in Tennessee. She has presented papers at a number of conferences and has published in *Football Studies*.

Timothy J.L. Chandler is an Associate Professor in the School of Exercise, Leisure and Sport at Kent State University in Kent, Ohio, USA, and Visiting Lecturer in the School of Physical Education, Sport and Leisure at De Montfort University, Bedford in the United Kingdom. He is co-editor (with John Nauright) of *Making Men:*

Rugby and Masculine Identity and author of a number of book chapters and articles on sport in the English public schools. His articles have appeared in the *International Journal of the History of Sport*, the *Canadian Journal of History of Sport* and *Youth and Society*. He is on the editorial boards of *Sports History Review*, *Football Studies* and the *Journal of Comparative Physical Education and Sport*.

P. David Howe is Lecturer in the anthropology of sport in the School of Sport at Cheltenham and Gloucester College of Higher Education. Trained as a medical anthropologist, he is currently writing a book based on his doctoral research. This research was undertaken in Pontypridd in Wales and examined the social implications of the professionalization of sports medicine in a specific community context.

Brett Hutchins is a doctoral student in the Department of Human Movement Studies at the University of Queensland. His thesis examines the meaning of Don Bradman as a cultural icon. He has also written a number of articles and book chapters on the historical, cultural and social dimensions of violence in the world of rugby league football.

Richard Light has recently completed a PhD at the University of Queensland. His thesis compares high school rugby in Japan and Australia. His work is published in several academic journals. Richard lived in Japan for many years where he taught school and coached rugby.

Malcolm MacLean is a doctoral student in the Department of Human Movement Studies at the University of Queensland. He has a background in the student and trade union movements and has worked in the History Department at the Victoria University of Wellington, New Zealand. He has published articles on ethnic relations and ethnicity, sporting contacts between South Africa and Aotearoa/New Zealand, the writing of cultural analyses and history, and labour law. He played schoolboy rugby in Aotearoa/New Zealand and South Africa but later found the distractions of student politics and the anti-apartheid movement more appealing.

John Nauright is a Senior Lecturer in the Department of Human Movement Studies at the University of Queensland. He has published widely on the history and sociology of sport and is the author of *Sport, Cultures and Identities in South Africa* (1997); co-author of *Rugby and the South African Nation* (1998) and *Socio-Cultural Foundations of Human Movement* (1996); editor of *Sport, Power and Society in New Zealand* (1995) and co-editor (with Tim Chandler) of *Making Men: Rugby and Masculine Identity*. He is the founding editor of *Football Studies*, the journal of the Football Studies Group; co-editor of *International Sports Studies*; and a member of the international editorial boards of the *International Journal of the History of Sport* and *Sport History Review*.

Murray G. Phillips is a Senior Lecturer in the socio-cultural aspects of sport in the Department of Physical Education, Exercise and Sport at the University of South Australia in Adelaide. He has written extensively on the rugby codes, World War I and sport, and gender and sport and has recently completed a monograph on the historical aspects of coaching in Australia. He is reviews editor of both *Sporting Traditions* and *Football Studies*.

Thierry Terret is a Professor at the University of Lyon 1 in France. He has published or contributed to many books including, most recently, *L'institution et le nageur* (1998) and *Le sport et ses espaces: 19ème-20ème siècles* (1998). He is currently the vice-president of the International Society of the History of Physical Education and Sport. When he is not playing rugby, he works regularly as a reviewer for a variety of national and international journals.

Index